HISTORIC SACRED PLACES
of PHILADELPHIA

HISTORIC SACRED PLACES
of PHILADELPHIA

ROGER W. MOSS

PHOTOGRAPHS BY TOM CRANE

A BARRA FOUNDATION BOOK

UNIVERSITY OF PENNSYLVANIA PRESS

PHILADELPHIA

For Dorothy Elizabeth Martin Moss (1914–2002)

10 9 8 7 6 5 4 3 2 1

Published by
University of Pennsylvania Press
Philadelphia, Pennsylvania 19104-4011

Library of Congress Cataloging-in-Publication Data
Moss, Roger W., 1940–
Historic sacred places of Philadelphia / Roger W. Moss ; photography by Tom Crane.
p. cm.
"A Barra Foundation book."
Includes bibliographical references and index.
ISBN 0-8122-3792-7 (cloth : alk. paper)
1. Sacred space—Philadelphia. 2. Philadelphia (Pa.)—Religion. I. Crane, Tom. II. Title
BL2527.P45 M67 2004
726.5'09748/11—dc22 2004052639

Designed by Adrianne Onderdonk Dudden

⊷➡ *Page i. Old First Reformed Church: Another survival from 1837 is the highly decorative ceiling ventilator in the sanctuary. See pages 78–81.*

⊷➡ *Frontispiece. Saint Timothy's Church: Looking east from the nave to the chancel and sanctuary, some of Burns's surviving decoration can still be seen on the ceiling. In 1892 Littell's wooden altar was replaced by one of marble, designed by G. W. and W. D. Hewitt. Three years later Mr. and Mrs. J. Vaughan Merrick donated the English mosaic reredos behind the altar; it blocks Littell's windows, which can still be seen on the exterior. The present rood beam replaced the original screen in 1914. See pages 288–291.*

⊷➡ *Endpapers. The auditorium of Mother Bethel Church. See pages 112–115.*

TO THE REVERED MEMORY OF WILLIAM HENRY FVRNESS STD
BORN XX APRIL AD MDCCCII DIED XXX JANVARY AD MDCCCXCVI
PASTOR OF THIS CHVRCH FROM AD MDCCCXXV TO AD
MDCCCLXXV AND PASTOR EMERITVS VNTIL HIS DEATH
IT IS NOT IN ANY FORMAL DOCTRINE BVT IN THE CHARACTER
IN THE PERSONAL LIFE IN THE SPIRIT OF JESVS THAT THE EN
LIGHTENING AND SAVING POWER OF CHRISTIANITY CONSISTS

First Unitarian Church: The William Henry Furness Memorial (1898) now hangs on the south wall of the sanctuary. It is carved marble embellished with applied mosaic. Originally there was a fireplace in this location. See pages 200–205.

Page vi. Old Pine Street Presbyterian Church: The churchyard contains approximately 3,000 interments. The original burial ground is east and south of the church, with two rows on the west. In the mid-nineteenth century the graves from First Presbyterian Church were relocated to the ground west of the church. Along the west wall of the church is the Hessian Trench, where the mercenaries who died in the church during the Revolution are buried in a common grave. See pages 66–69.

CONTENTS

*E*xcepting brief forays to Canada, I had never left the United States until a graduate fellowship made possible a summer abroad studying English country houses. Stepping off the interminable turboprop Icelandic Airlines flight to Glasgow— then the cheapest route across the Atlantic for countless students—I fully expected to be impressed by the likes of Chatsworth, Syon House, and Houghton Hall. But nothing had prepared me for British cathedrals and historic churches. Nor had I given them much thought. My experience with ecclesiastical architecture extended only to the starkly simple New England Congregational meetinghouses and modestly embellished Presbyterian preaching boxes of my youth—all decidedly low church Protestant.

My first close encounter with a Gothic cathedral nearly proved fatal. The architectural historian Alec Clifton-Taylor, then working on his *Cathedrals of England* (London, 1967), encouraged me to visit Norwich Cathedral, which boasts the tallest surviving Romanesque tower in England. This is topped by a graceful late fifteenth-century stone spire rising dramatically above the flat East Anglian countryside. Fortunately the architect in charge of the restoration happened to be on site and willing to conduct a private tour. After strolling around the nave and transepts, my guide offered to take me above the crossing to obtain a close view of the ribs and vaults. I quickly jumped at this rare opportunity and we set off climbing the narrow spiral stair built into the walls.

Eventually we came out above the crossing, and I could look down the attic and see the vaults of the nave from above. Craning to look upward, I noticed a wooden stair twisting around the interior wall of the tower, which eventually became a series of ladders rising up the steeple. "Would you like to see the view from the steeple?" asked my host. Foolishly I nodded in agreement, and we began to climb. All went well until the open stair and handrail became a series of narrow, wooden staged ladders. I began to think better of my decision at the second stage, especially as my leather-soled loafers slipped disconcertingly on the smooth, dry, wooden rungs. My palms moistened. By the third run of what seemed to be nearly vertical ladders, I froze. Looking down at the vaulting far below, I had visions of a small newspaper notice reading, "American Student Falls to Death in Norwich Cathedral. Causes Collapse of Norman Stonework. Preservationists Enraged." Gradually I talked myself back down. I'd encountered my first cathedral, and learned in the process that I suffer from vertigo.

A few days later I arrived in London during the World Cup finals without accommodations, little money, and no credit cards. I hadn't expected to need a hotel room. A friend had been invited to spend the long weekend at a country house in Kent—an invitation extended to me as well. Unfortunately, she broke a bone in her foot and the free trip to the country was off. Eventually I found an inexpensive room in a youth hostel, and with two days to kill set out with Nikolaus Pevsner's

Trinity Lutheran Church: The original church entrance was from Germantown Avenue through the graveyard to the pedimented entrance at the base of the tower. See pages 256–259.

Buildings of England (1957) on an intensive tour of cathedrals and historic churches: Westminster Abbey, Saint Paul's Cathedral, an assortment of Christopher Wren city churches, and, of course, James Gibbs's Saint Martin-in-the Fields. By the time I fell exhausted onto the night train back to Scotland and the flight home, I was an ecclesiologist-in-the-making, aesthetically infatuated by the architecture and decoration of historic sacred places. I also had developed a special fondness for church monuments and graveyards.

Two years later I found myself installed as executive director of the venerable Athenæum of Philadelphia, a special-collections library near Independence Hall that specializes in architecture. Within a month of arriving I was drawn into a controversy surrounding Holy Trinity Church, Rittenhouse Square (pp. 174–177). Designed in the mid-1850s by John Notman—architect of the Athenæum's own building—Holy Trinity anchors the northwest corner of the square at Nineteenth and Walnut Streets. Jack L. Wolgin, president of National Land and Investment Company, had offered a long-term lease for the highly desirable site; he proposed to demolish the church and erect in its place a twin-tower high-rise apartment building. The rector at the time cared little for the Victorian brownstone building; he saw it as an incubus constantly demanding expensive care and favored demolition and the use of the developer's funds for social needs of the parish. The congregation had steadily declined after World War II, and the decision to demolish would ultimately turn on a vote by the relatively small number of communicants.

Here is a classic situation: large, expensive, historic church structure on highly desirable urban real estate subject to development pressures, declining congregation, and clergy not qualified or inclined to care for the church as a work of art. In subsequent decades I would see this scenario repeated in Philadelphia and all across America, in urban areas where the middle class has abandoned the city core, leaving behind thousands of sacred places that once were the pride of their congregations. This is not a problem unique to the United States, of course—our cousins in the United Kingdom struggle constantly with redundant parish churches and great cathedrals that are financial black holes. In the United States, however, the problem may be more acute. Here we have no established church enjoying government support, nor do we have—as in the case in some older and wiser European nations— government grants for maintenance of aesthetically significant sacred places.

In addition, the wide diversity of sects and denominations in the United States splinters any effort of shared responsibility. It is not uncommon to have three or four different denominations represented by a like number of soaring Victorian churches within a few yards of one another—each represented by congregations struggling to hold together both the human community that is the church and the fabric of the building that houses the congregation. So sensitized are Americans to the separation of church and state that even the National Register of Historic

Places, "the official Federal list of districts, sites, buildings, structures, and objects significant in American history, architecture, archeology, engineering, and culture," specifically bars "properties owned by religious institutions or used for religious purposes" from being considered for registration unless they derive "*primary significance from architectural or artistic distinction or historical importance*" (see www.cr.nps.gov/nr; emphasis added).

This situation may be changing. In May 2003 the secretary of the interior announced a reversal of the Justice Department prohibition against active religious institutions receiving federal grants under the Save America's Treasures program. Clearly, however, the only defensible argument for state aid must ultimately rest on the rock of architectural or artistic distinction rather than pastoral reasons. Like it or not, the chance of financial aid from public coffers for maintenance or restoration of historic sacred places is unlikely. Even when private foundation funding is available for the care of historic buildings, sacred places must compete with the whole universe of other historic sites clamoring for a slender slice of the pie. Faced with so many competing demands, it is too often easier for funders to pass over all sacred places rather than sort out the most deserving.

Learning of the threat to Holy Trinity, Rittenhouse Square, I offered the Athenæum's reading room to the Society of Architectural Historians as a venue where the pros and cons of sale or lease and inevitable demolition could be debated. For speakers the preservationists drafted George B. Tatum, then H. Rodney Sharp Professor at the University of Delaware—a specialist in nineteenth-century architecture—and Jonathan Fairbanks, then at Winterthur Museum, later at the Boston Museum of Fine Arts, who had researched Notman's churches for his thesis. We also invited the entire congregation of Holy Trinity. I could not have anticipated the response. Two local television stations sent camera crews to cover the event (a first for the Athenæum), and, under the threat of their empty chairs being photographed, the Rev. Dr. Cuthbert Pratt, rector of Holy Trinity, and the Rt. Rev. Robert L. DeWitt, bishop of the Episcopal Diocese of Pennsylvania, agreed to participate.

While the church officials could have made a stronger case than they did, the preservationists were able to label the churchmen as vandals right from the beginning, a branding from which they never recovered. Shortly thereafter the congregation voted overwhelmingly to decline the developer's offer and to preserve the church, although the church house next door was sacrificed. I'd won my first preservation battle. That it was a church designed by John Notman could not have been more satisfying. Now, thirty-five years later, I'm proud Holy Trinity is one of the subjects featured in this book rather than an ugly statistic mentioned in passing.

Which brings me to this project which was conceived as a companion to *Historic Houses of Philadelphia* (University of Pennsylvania Press, 1998). The team that made *Historic Houses* possible worked so well together that shortly after the first book appeared we began to discuss *Historic Sacred Places*. My one precondition to undertaking the book was that master photographer Tom Crane be commissioned to take the photographs and that Adrianne Onderdonk Dudden be the book's designer. I have few illusions that it is my text alone which sells books. Tom Crane and Adrianne Dudden are so skilled they make me look good, and I'm honored to be working with them again. Cartographers Alice and Will Thiede are new additions to the team to provide the easily accessible maps.

Early in the project I had the essential assistance of Kenneth Henke, who first came to my attention as a Charles E. Peterson Intern at The Athenæum of Philadelphia. Ken is now on the staff of the Princeton Theological Seminary. He performed much of the preliminary work of contacting the responsible parties at each site and compiling the bibliography. I'm thankful for his attention to detail; he saved me many an embarrassing slip in matters of liturgy and terminology—both potential mine fields for anyone writing about sacred places. I'm grateful for Ken's efforts, but the errors that inevitably remain are my fault alone. As ever, I treasure the intellectual and emotional support of Gail Caskey Winkler, Ph.D., FASID, who took time from her own work critically to read the final draft of this book.

Fortunately my editor at the University of Pennsylvania Press, Jo Joslyn, agreed that we should move on the project as soon as possible. She approached Robert L. McNeil, Jr., then president of The Barra Foundation, Inc. Barra had made *Historic Houses* possible, and Mr. McNeil saw the advantages of following up on that success with a similar book covering the historic churches, synagogues, and meeting houses of Philadelphia. All of us involved with this project are grateful for the support and encouragement of The Barra Foundation trustees. Finally, Tom Crane and I appreciate the assistance of the rectors, pastors, rabbis, ministers, priests, custodians, and keepers of the sacred places discussed in the pages that follow. Without the aid of those who selflessly serve the congregations here represented, this book would not have been possible.

SELECTING THE HISTORIC SACRED PLACES
According to a recent survey by the University of Pennsylvania, there are 16,000 congregations in the city of Philadelphia. A substantial number of these are housed in structures of historic and aesthetic merit. Since this book is a companion to *Historic Houses of Philadelphia*, it was necessary to limit coverage to fifty historic sacred places from among the hundreds of possibilities. Inevitably this decision will disappoint many readers, especially the members of congregations whose beloved sacred places have been omitted.

Like Dr. Johnson—who drew a nice distinction between what is worth seeing and what is worth going to see—I have attempted to select sacred places in Philadelphia which a visitor may find worth *going* to see for architectural or other aesthetic reasons. Some readers may object to this point of view, arguing that sacred places were not meant to serve the cause of aesthetics, that the abundant beauties of these structures are a byproduct of a desire to glorify the Creator. Without disagreeing, my purpose is simply to call attention to these sacred places as repositories of our artistic and cultural patrimony that should be valued by churchman and nonbeliever alike.

The specific criteria for the inclusion of a sacred place in this book were

☞   The sacred place must be *in the City of Philadelphia*. Some architecturally significant and artistically embellished places from the suburbs are mentioned in the Introduction, but all fifty of the sites discussed individually in the pages that follow are within the city limits.

☞   The building must have been *erected before 1900*—although I've been slightly more flexible on that rule. Also, this is a book on historic architecture, not historic congregations; many of the latter are now housed in newer buildings and are thus omitted.

☞   The sacred place must be reasonably *accessible*. This is one of the most vexing problems facing those who wish to visit Philadelphia's churches, synagogues, and meeting houses. Declining congregations, restricted budgets, and concerns for vandalism and theft all contribute to the likelihood of finding the door barred against the unexpected visitor. I therefore have favored historic sacred places where it is possible with a little forethought to gain access—this means always telephoning first. I've also leaned toward geographically accessible sites. The closer the historic sacred place is to Center City, the more likely it is to have been included. This means I may have omitted sites in West, South, and North Philadelphia that might otherwise have been considered.

A final thought. I hope this book will ultimately encourage public awareness and visitation while emboldening congregations to provide greater public access. The most effective defense against vandalism, theft, and ultimate redundancy is a living community of worshipers who sustain their spiritual place that may incidentally be important to our artistic heritage. It is unlikely that cultural tourism will sustain more than a few of the places discussed and illustrated in this book. As congregations decline and operating costs escalate, it becomes increasingly difficult and expensive to manage these cultural resources. It is generally thought inappropriate to charge visitors for admission to sacred places as is done at historic houses—although this is becoming more common abroad. Even if visitors are not charged, there usually is a box for donations, and every cultural tourist should leave behind a cash contribution for the preservation and maintenance of the building that initially prompted the visit—say an amount equal to the cost of a seat in the local multiplex motion picture theater.

HISTORIC SACRED PLACES
of PHILADELPHIA

⤐ *Christ Church: The brickwork at Christ Church is of great virtuosity. Laid in Flemish bond with "blew headers" (bricks with glazed ends used to create a distinctive pattern), the belt course (the horizontal trim below the upper windows) uses custom-molded shapes superior to those found elsewhere in eighteenth century Philadelphia. The urns on the roof balustrade were imported from England in 1736; the wooden originals were replaced by cast-iron copies in 1908. See pages 40–45.*

*T*wenty-first-century Americans too often take for granted the freedom to worship (or not to worship) according to one's own prerogative. The first amendment to the Constitution of the United States, ratified on December 15, 1791, states without qualification, "Congress shall make no law respecting an establishment of religion, or prohibiting the free exercise thereof . . ." In the eighteenth century—an intolerant age of established, regulated, and subsidized religions—this unusual, if not dangerously radical, separation of church and state must have been viewed by some with suspicion. But in Pennsylvania, tolerance for religious diversity had been commonly practiced for decades. In William Penn's Charter of Liberties, Franchises and Privileges (1701), the proprietor declared:

> Because no People can be truly happy, though under the greatest Enjoyment of Civil Liberties, if abridged of the Freedom of their Consciences, as to their Religious Profession and Worship . . . , I do hereby grant and declare, That no Person or Persons, inhabiting in this province or Territories, who shall confess and acknowledge *One* almighty God, the Creator, Upholder and Ruler of the World; and profess him or themselves obliged to live quietly under the Civil Government, shall be in any Case molested or prejudiced, in his or their Person or Estate, because of his or their conscientious Persuasion or Practice, nor be compelled to frequent or maintain any religious Worship, Place or Ministry, contrary to his or their Mind, or to do or suffer any other Act or Thing, contrary to their religious Persuasion.[1]

Not that there weren't periods of overt intolerance, most notably directed toward Roman Catholics, whose sacred places too often became the target of the fearful and ignorant in the eighteenth and nineteenth centuries.

But on the whole, Pennsylvania enjoyed religious heterogeneity unknown elsewhere, and Penn's "holy experiment" bequeathed to modern America its antecedent for a pluralistic society. Even eighteenth-century visitors commented on this toleration for diversity. The Swedish naturalist Peter Kalm recorded during his visit in 1748, "every one who acknowledges God to be the Creator . . . and teaches or undertakes nothing against the state, or against the common peace, is at liberty to settle . . . , be his religious principles ever so strange." Even those who entertain "erroneous principles of the doctrine which he follows" will not be molested. "And he is so well secured by the laws . . . , and enjoys such liberties, that a citizen of *Philadelphia* may in a manner be said to live in his house like a king."[2] A century later, when the hateful memory—if not the acrid odor—of burning Catholic churches lingered in the air, Philadelphia attorney Thomas I. Wharton (1791–1856), boasted that among the socially prominent members of the Athenæum of Philadel-

St. Augustine's church steeple. See pages 86–91.

phia library no discrimination was tolerated. As a metaphor for pluralism he listed what could be found on the library's periodical reading room table:

> I have seen lying together, the Catholic Herald and the Jewish Advocate; the Banner of the Cross and the Evangelical Luminary; the Presbyterian Magazine and the Methodist Review; the Swedenborgian Chronicle and the Millennial Harbinger; the Unitarian Examiner and the Protestant Churchman; all apparently in perfectly good humour with themselves and their neighbors.[3]

How did we reach such diversity and liberality? The story is so familiar it need only be repeated in outline. The British Crown gave William Penn a proprietary grant in North America to discharge debts owed his father. To Penn and his heirs, Philadelphia constituted a vast real estate development intended to improve the family fortune while offering refuge to Quakers and other religious denominations attracted by the proprietor's liberal guarantee of freedom to worship. "Though I desire to extend religious freedom," Penn wrote in 1681, "yet I want some recompense for my trouble."[4] Announcements of the "holy experiment" found a receptive audience in the British Isles as well as in Holland and Germany. William Penn—raised in the established Church of England—had become a Quaker in 1667. To settle Pennsylvania he particularly appealed to his co-religionists, and most of the earliest settlers drawn to Pennsylvania were Quakers—nearly 2,000 arrived in 1682 alone. But people of other persuasions were attracted as well, including some of the most persecuted European religious minorities.[5]

THE SOCIETY OF FRIENDS   Shortly after arriving in Philadelphia, the Quakers erected a meeting house near the Delaware River—called the Bank Meeting—on the west side of Front Street north of Arch Street. (An earlier meeting house erected on Center Square proved impractical and was quickly abandoned.) Bank Meeting was replaced by a more substantial brick meeting erected at the southwest corner of Second and High (now Market) Streets called the Greater Meeting House, which served until the Arch Street Meeting was erected in 1804 (pages 46–49) (figure 1). It is the Greater Meeting House that figures in Benjamin Franklin's autobiographical account of his arrival in Philadelphia. Having landed at the foot of High Street, he purchased fresh rolls at a bakery and set out to explore his adopted city. "Thus refresh'd," he writes,

> I walk'd [up High] Street, which by this time had many clean dress'd People in it who were all walking the same Way; I join'd them, and thereby was led into the great Meeting House of the Quakers near the Market. I sat down among them, and after looking around a while and hearing nothing said, being very

drowsy thro' Labor and want of Rest the preceding Night, I fell fast asleep, and continu'd so till the Meeting broke up, when one was kind enough to rouse me. This was therefore the first House I was in or slept in in Philadelphia.[6]

Several meeting houses were erected in Philadelphia prior to the American Revolution, including one at Second and Pine Streets—known as the Hill Meeting—and the Fourth Street Meeting erected next to the Friends School in 1763 (figure 2). All these were deliberately "plain style" places of worship without ornament and free of explicit iconography, in contradistinction to "steeple houses"—a derisive term used by Friends to describe Anglican churches. The auditoriums were fitted out with simple wooden benches, many had galleries for use by the children, and there were separate doors for men and women. In smaller meetings a movable partition separated men's and women's meetings; this could be removed for worship. All the early meeting houses in the River Wards have been demolished, although many historic Quaker meeting houses survive throughout the five-county region.[7]

Figure 1. W. L. Breton watercolor of the Greater Friends Meeting House at the corner of Second and High Streets (left) and the old court house. The meeting house was demolished after the completion of Arch Street Meeting in 1804. The Athenæum of Philadelphia.

Figure 2. W. L. Breton watercolor of the Fourth Street Meeting and Friends School, southeast corner of Fourth and Chestnut Streets. The structure was erected in 1763 and demolished in the mid-nineteenth century. Typically, these meeting houses looked more like private homes than Anglican "steeple houses." The Athenæum of Philadelphia.

THE SWEDES AND WELSH The Quakers arriving in the late seventeenth century quickly outnumbered the Swedes who had attempted to establish a foothold in the Delaware Valley. The Swedish Lutheran settlements predate the arrival of William Penn's Quaker vanguard, although the surviving Swedish churches were erected by British-trained craftsmen after the founding of Philadelphia. Gloria Dei (Old Swedes') is the oldest church in Philadelphia and is discussed at some length in the pages that follow (pages 34–39).[8] Less well known is the appealing Saint James Church (figure 3), Kingsessing, erected in 1762 to relieve the overcrowding at Gloria Dei and to serve the farmers of Swedish descent who then occupied the west bank of the Schuylkill.[9] While relations with the Quakers were cordial, the Swedes ultimately were unable to maintain a separate religious and cultural identity. In 1844 the congregations of both Gloria Dei and Saint James united with the Episcopal Diocese of Pennsylvania.[10]

Welsh colonists—albeit in smaller numbers—were also attracted to Pennsylvania, where they settled at Merion, Radnor, and Haverford in what came to be called the "Welsh Tract," 40,000 acres eventually split among what is now Montgomery,

Delaware, and Chester Counties. Originally Quakers, some of the American Welsh joined the Church of England during the Keithian schism.[11]

At this point it is worth pausing to introduce this colorful colonial figure. The Scottish Presbyterian George Keith (1639–1716) converted to Quakerism in the 1660s and became a friend of William Penn and head of the institution now known as William Penn Charter School. Following the death of Quaker leader George Fox in 1691, whom Keith may have aspired to succeed, Keith attacked the Society of Friends, charging lax discipline and doctrinal heresy.[12] The London Yearly Meeting ultimately disowned Keith after he proposed introducing the sacraments to Quaker services. In 1700 Keith entered the Church of England, took orders, and became an aggressively anti-Quaker missionary priest for the Society for the Propagation of the Gospel. Keith helped bring some Welsh Quakers into the Anglican fold. In 1704 this intrepid group of frontier families petitioned the Society for the Propagation of the Gospel to send Welsh prayer books, a Bible, and a Welsh-speaking missionary from London. The Anglicans at Radnor first erected a log meeting house, which they replaced in 1715 with "a handsome stone church" of modest size, 27' x 40', laid out on an east-west axis. Radnor—and Saint David's Church (figure 4)—became a

Figure 3. Saint James Church of Kingsessing at 6838 Woodland Avenue was erected as a chapel of ease for the Swedish Lutheran Gloria Dei Church in 1762. It remains an active Episcopal congregation.

hotbed of rebellion during the American Revolution, and the congregation, led by Anthony Wayne, forced the loyalist rector from the pulpit. The church suffered severely at the hands of both armies during the Revolution. Several soldiers who died of wounds at the Battle of the Brandywine are buried in the churchyard, as is General Wayne, who died in 1796.

The growing wealth and prosperity of the Main Line in the late nineteenth century resulted in expansion and repairs to the church, but the congregation resisted the temptation to demolish the old structure in favor of a fashionable high Victorian confection.[13] Visitors still sense the tranquility that inspired the romantic poet Henry Wadsworth Longfellow to write "Old St. David's at Radnor," which begins:

Figure 4. Saint David's Church, Radnor. Seventeenth-century Welsh farmers settled in Delaware County and erected a simple log church, which they replaced in 1715 with a new stone structure named for the patron saint of Wales.

What an image of peace and rest
    Is this little church among its graves!
All is so quiet; the troubled breast,
The wounded spirit, the heart oppressed,
    Here may find the repose it craves.

It continues:

> Were I a pilgrim in search of peace,
>> Were I a pastor of Holy Church,
> More than a Bishop's diocese
> Should I prize this place of rest, and release
>> From farther longing and farther search.[14]

Another Keithian congregation to separate from the Society of Friends in the 1690s formed what is now Trinity Church, Oxford (figure 5). Like Saint David's Church, Radnor, they replaced an early log meeting house with a new brick church

Figure 5. Trinity Church at 6900 Oxford Avenue, Philadelphia, was erected in 1711 to house a Church of England congregation probably dating to 1698. It is one of the oldest congregations and church structures in Pennsylvania.

in 1711, which is laid in Flemish bond with decorative patterns. Both churches were served by Robert Weyman—a missionary from the Society for the Propagation of the Gospel—from 1719 until 1732. Built on an east-west axis, the modest church (25' x 36') was extended in the late eighteenth century, and in 1833 two wings were added. The tower appeared in 1839 and was extended by Frank Furness in 1875 to accommodate a new bell. In response to the Anglo-Catholic revival in the late nineteenth century, a recessed chancel was created. This is the oldest Episcopal church in Pennsylvania wherein services have been continuously held.[15]

THE CHURCH OF ENGLAND So far little has been said about the beginnings of the Church of England in Philadelphia. Penn desired to found a New World colony where Quakers and other dissenters from the established English church might gather to worship in safety. But Pennsylvania was indelibly a British colony; Anglicans could be neither excluded nor ignored. Penn's original grant from the Crown guaranteed the bishop of London the right to send "any Preacher or Preachers to reside within the Province without any denial or molestation whatsoever." As a consequence, Philadelphia Anglicans in 1695 purchased property on Second Street just above High Street—"for the publick worship of God . . . as . . . professed in the Church of England"—and erected the first Christ Church (pages 40–45).[16] This would be the only Anglican church in Philadelphia until, as the congregation expanded, a group of "Gentlemen from the south end" petitioned the Christ Church vestry to permit them to approach Thomas and Richard Penn for a lot of ground on Third Street between Pine and Lombard Streets on which to erect a "chapel of ease" that would become Saint Peter's Church (pages 60–65).[17]

While working at Saint Peter's, the Scottish-born master builder Robert Smith (1722–1777) received an invitation to design yet another Anglican church, this one not calculated to please the vestry of Christ Church. Strategically sited on Third Street below Walnut, between Christ Church and the soon to be completed Saint Peter's Church, the new parish could gather congregants from both sides. The inducement for the new parish was the evangelical preaching of William McClenachan, a former Presbyterian minister who joined the Church of England, was ordained an Anglican priest in London, and arrived in Philadelphia as a missionary, where his preaching at Christ Church in 1759 caused a furor. The rector of Christ Church attacked McClenachan's "railings and revilings in the Pulpit" and his "Extemporaneous Praying & Preaching." Under such criticism McClenachan withdrew from Christ Church to found his own parish, taking a substantial number of Christ Church members with him. Saint Paul's Church (figure 6) proved to be a leader in outreach ministries and founded the first Episcopal Sunday School in the United States in 1816. Both William Strickland and Thomas Ustick Walter are responsible for alterations and additions in the 1830s, but the parish began to decline

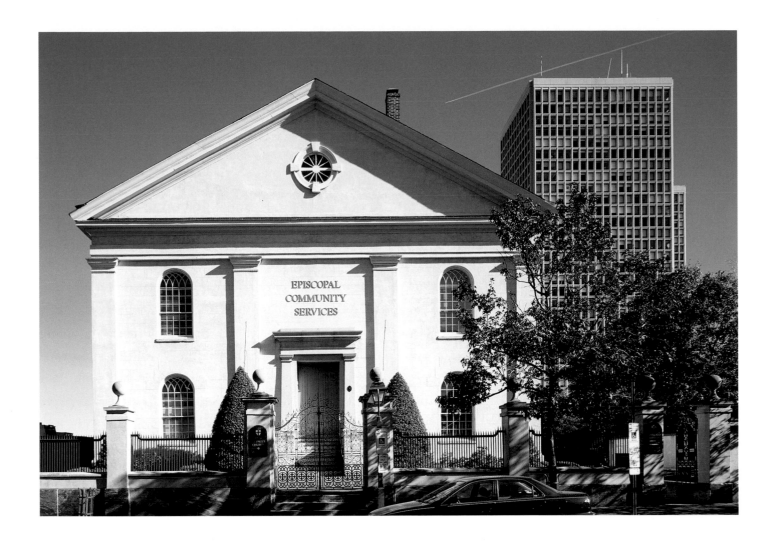

after the Civil War. In 1903 the church closed and the building became the head-quarters of Episcopal Community Services.[18]

While the Anglicans were establishing a foothold in Quaker Philadelphia, other non-Quaker migrants of British descent were arriving in ever larger numbers. Most represented challengers to the English established church. These dissenting denominations included the Presbyterians, Baptists, and Methodists, who tended toward an evangelical religion that was more personal and passionate than Anglican formality.[19] The colonial-era Scotch-Irish Presbyterians proved ultimately to be the most numerous of these dissenters.

THE SCOTCH-IRISH PRESBYTERIANS The first American Presbyterians appeared in New England prior to the founding of Pennsylvania, but by 1698 a Presbyterian presence existed in Philadelphia. In 1704 the first congregation erected a meeting house on the south side of High (Market) Street at White Horse Alley (Bank Street). This simple frame building—familiarly called Old Buttonwood after a nearby grove of trees—was expanded several times and finally replaced in

Figure 6. Saint Paul's Church on Third Street below Walnut Street was designed by Robert Smith in 1761 to house a new Anglican congregation founded the year before by the followers of William McClenachan. In the late nineteenth century the parish could no longer afford a rector, and the building was adaptively reused by Episcopal Community Services. In the 1980s the exterior underwent extensive restoration by architect Edward Parnum (1901–1993). The interior was sympathetically renovated by Dagit-Saylor Architects; it retains many of the decorative features of the church interior.

1794 by a neoclassical revival structure with a giant order portico (illustrated on page 196). In the meantime, the Irish-born Scottish missionary Francis Makemie (1658–1708) had arrived in 1683 and begun organizing congregations in virtually all settled areas of North America. By 1706 Makemie called together a group of Presbyterian ministers to meet in Philadelphia, where they organized the first American presbytery.

Especially after 1717, the rough and tumble Scotch-Irish tribe began to arrive in significant numbers. According to most estimates, more than 200,000 Scotch-Irish migrated to America between 1717 and 1775, largely for economic rather than religious reasons.[20] The Quakers encouraged these new arrivals—most of whom were impoverished farmers with little more to their name than a burning desire to exchange Ulster rack rents for cheap bottom land—to pass through Philadelphia to Chester County and points west. Many found their way to Lancaster, where they followed the Great Philadelphia Wagon Road south, ultimately peopling Appalachia, or journeyed to Pittsburgh to plunge down the Ohio River and subdue the riverine west, but a sizable number remained in the city to erect churches to their Calvinistic faith. So numerous had the Presbyterians become by 1788 that there were 220 congregations, organized into sixteen presbyteries and four synods. (The first synod had been formed in Philadelphia in 1716, just on the eve of the great Scotch-Irish migration, when the American Presbyterian Church had only 3,000 members and forty churches.)[21]

THE BAPTISTS Philadelphia would also gather the greatest number of American Baptists in the late seventeenth century, largely migrants from Ireland and Wales. Baptists had arrived in Philadelphia from Newport, Rhode Island, by 1684, and Welsh Baptists from the Pennepek Baptist Church—now Lower Dublin Baptist Church—began to drift into town after 1688. The first formal congregation came together for worship in 1698. At first the Baptists met in a storehouse with the Presbyterians, then in a brew house until 1707, when they occupied a simple Quaker meeting house near Christ Church abandoned by the followers of George Keith. That same year, several congregations formed the Philadelphia Baptist Association, the first such fellowship among American Baptists. A brick meeting house replaced the frame building in 1731, which was in turn enlarged in 1762 and again in 1808. The congregation remained there until 1856, when it moved to the northwest corner of Broad and Arch Streets (pages 184–187).

Another historic Baptist sacred place deserving of mention is the Baptist Temple at Broad and Berks Streets; it is omitted from more detailed discussion here because the church is presently standing empty with its future use by Temple University uncertain (figure 7). Historically it is significant as the birthplace of Temple University, and architecturally it may be the finest work by architect Thomas P.

Figure 7. The Baptist Temple on North Broad Street (Thomas P. Lonsdale, architect, 1889–1891) is the largest of the many sacred places erected on Broad Street in the late nineteenth and early twentieth centuries. In the late 1980s, Temple University announced plans to demolish the building, but backed away under pressure from Temple graduates and the preservation community. The future of the building remains in doubt.

Lonsdale (1855–1900).[22] The congregation responsible for commissioning this extraordinary rock-faced granite Richardsonian Romanesque structure was founded in 1871 as Grace Baptist Church. The church faltered until Russell H. Conwell was called to the pulpit. His preaching electrified the congregation, and soon a new church was needed to accommodate the thousands who wanted to hear Conwell speak. One of his lectures, "Acres of Diamonds," became so popular he delivered it 6,150 times throughout the country.[23] To design his new church, Conwell turned to Lonsdale, who had not yet established his reputation as an ecclesiastical architect; in fact, Grace Baptist Church may be his first major commission in independent practice. A native of Norristown, Lonsdale entered Girard College and following graduation apprenticed with James H. Windrim. He established an independent practice in 1885, limping along with residential commissions until approached in 1889 to design the new Baptist Temple, which opened in 1891. The great amphitheater—which Temple University may adaptively reuse as a performing arts space—was designed to seat 4,200 persons and is said to have excellent acoustics. Beginning in 1888, Conwell had also sponsored night classes to provide an education for those without access to traditional colleges. Out of that modest beginning grew the great university that still carries the Temple name.

THE METHODISTS   Methodism, "one of the most dynamic and consequential religious movements in modern times, a movement whose import would nowhere be more forceful and enduring than in America,"[24] also traces its American roots to Philadelphia. John Wesley (1703–1791), son of a nonconformist Lincolnshire Anglican minister, gradually became evangelical under the influence of Moravian pietism. Barred from Anglican churches because of his radical views, Wesley set out "field preaching" as an itinerant, traveling 200,000 miles in the British Isles and converting thousands who formed Methodist societies. Finally, in 1784, Wesley ordained ministers who could administer the sacraments in America. In fact, Methodists came lately to the American colonies; not until the 1760s did some migrants form societies or classes that worked within the framework of the Church of England without forming new churches. The first "class" of Philadelphia Methodists had been organized by Thomas Webb in 1767, a year after the first American society had been founded in New York. This colorful former British army officer had been converted by Wesley and licensed as a lay preacher. He proved to be a natural orator; John Adams called him "one of the most fluent men I have ever heard."[25] Saint George's Church (pages 82–85) was purchased in 1769 and Francis Asbury—destined to be known as "the father of American Methodism"—preached there in 1771. Today Saint George's is revered as "the world's oldest Methodist Church edifice in continuous service," or, as it is often called, "the Cradle of American Methodism."[26]

The Methodist Episcopal Church was organized and formally separated from the Church of England at a 1784 general conference in Baltimore. Asbury would become the first superintendent and—to the astonishment of Wesley—assumed the title of bishop. It would be Asbury who called St. George's "the Cathedral of Methodism," and Methodist meetings gradually began calling themselves churches (see pages 82–85). Philadelphia is also uniquely important to black Methodists. Richard Allen, a former slave who had purchased his freedom, received a license to preach from Saint George's, the first African American Methodist to be so licensed in America. He organized Bethel Church (pages 112–115) and in 1816 became the first bishop of the African Methodist Episcopal Church.[27]

THE GERMAN PIETISTS   Out of German pietism of the Reformation there emerged many radical sects[28] whose members believed that the institutional church had lost the purity of early Christians; that the Catholic church placed too much emphasis on the sacraments; that church and state should be separate; and that Christians should withdraw from worldly activities.[29] One of the largest of these German sects attracted to Pennsylvania were the Mennonites—named for the six-

Figure 8. The Mennonite meeting house at 6119 Germantown Avenue dates to 1770. It replaces an earlier log structure—the First Mennonite meeting in America—erected in 1708 on the same site. During the Battle of Germantown (October 1777) Americans taking shelter behind the church walls shot and killed British General James Agnew.

Figure 9. The Germantown Church of the Brethren, 6611 Germantown Avenue, erected in 1770, is the mother church (first congregation) of the American Brethren.

teenth-century Dutch priest Menno Simons (1492–1559). They were Anabaptists who broke with Martin Luther over the ritual of infant baptism, which they believed was scripturally groundless. Several families of Mennonites and Dutch Quakers migrated to Pennsylvania in 1683 and founded Germantown on a grant of 18,000 acres from William Penn. After worshiping for many years in private homes, the sect erected a log meeting house in 1708, replacing it with the present random-laid stone meeting house in 1770 (figure 8). Like Quaker meeting houses, the modest rectangular structure is simple to the point of austerity.[30]

Another Anabaptist sect attracted by Penn was the Church of the Brethren—commonly called "Dunkers" or "Dunkards" (from the German *tunken*, to immerse)—who arrived in Germantown beginning in 1719. Alexander Mack (1679–1735) founded the Church of the Brethren, who "covenanted and united

together as brethren and sisters into the covenant of the cross of Jesus Christ to form a church of Christian believers." The Dunkers also practiced rites based on biblical precedent: the holy kiss after communion, foot washing, the love feast (breaking bread in fellowship), plus the *trine* immersion—baptism thrice repeated in the name of the Trinity. In Germantown the most famous Dunker was Christopher Sauer, who established a printing press where he produced the first Bible in a European language printed in America. Like the Mennonites, the Brethren erected a log meeting house, which they also replaced in 1770 with a simple stone structure that continues to serve an active, largely African American congregation (figure 9).

Figure 10. Augustus Lutheran Church, 717 Main Street, Trappe, Pennsylvania, is often called "America's Shrine of Lutheranism." It remains virtually unaltered from the eighteenth century. Erected in 1743 and dedicated in 1745 under Henry Melchior Muhlenberg's supervision, it is generally considered the oldest Lutheran church in America.

THE LUTHERANS   While the Swedish Lutherans struggled to maintain their language and mode of worship, the German Lutherans from the Palatinate

Figure 11. Zion Lutheran Church at Fourth and Cherry Streets (Robert Smith, master builder, 1766; burned 1794; rebuilt 1796; demolished 1869) was the largest auditorium in colonial America, seating 3,000. When George Washington died, the official congressional memorial service was held here. The Athenæum of Philadelphia.

and other Rhenish provinces gradually filtered into Pennsylvania. The dominant figure of eighteenth-century Lutheranism is the missionary Henry Melchior Muhlenberg (1711–1787)—"Patriarch of the Lutheran Church in America"—who, in 1742, arrived in Philadelphia. Three years later he organized the first permanent American Lutheran synod which became the Ministerium of Pennsylvania, the oldest organization of Lutherans (beyond the congregation level) in America. The earliest surviving Lutheran church structure in Pennsylvania, the Augustus Lutheran Church in Trappe (figure 10), falls outside the scope of this book, but for its religious and architectural significance is well worth going to see.[31]

Prior to the arrival of Muhlenberg, Philadelphia Lutherans had been unable to unite all their factions to build a major church. By 1748, however, Saint Michael's Church on Fifth Street had been erected. Unfortunately it rapidly proved inadequate for the growing congregation; one of the greatest German migrations in American history had begun, and 12,000 Germans landed at Philadelphia in 1749 alone. Even more frustrating to the congregation, the church building was found to be structurally unsound. Peter Kalm commented during his tour of Philadelphia, "it had a little steeple, but that being put up by an ignorant architect, before the walls of the church were quite dry, they leaned forwards by its weight, and therefore they were forced to pull it down."[32] Robert Smith was called in to survey Saint Michael's to see whether it could be reinforced and expanded; he recommended the building be demolished and a new church erected. In 1766 the Lutherans decided to erect the "neue kirche" at the southeast corner of Fourth and Cherry Streets, designed by Smith, whom Muhlenberg called the "Master-Builder or Architector of our new Church"—an early use of the title "architect" in colonial America. Zion Lutheran Church (figure 11) not only would be one of the most handsome Middle Georgian buildings in Philadelphia—with its elegant Palladian window, modillion cornice, and numerous roof urns—but it was also the largest church in the city. During the British occupation of Philadelphia in 1777 the interior was gutted while being used as a hospital. After the Revolution the interior was restored, but the entire building was destroyed by fire in 1794.

THE JEWS   The narrative of Philadelphia's Jews begins with the defeat of the Moors in Spain and the expulsion of the cultured and prosperous Spanish and Portuguese Jews by their most Catholic majesties Ferdinand and Isabella in 1492. Some fled to Portuguese Brazil, others chose the Netherlands, but eventually most havens became unsafe. Finally, in 1654, a group of the Brazilian refugees found their way to New York and by 1657 to Newport, Rhode Island, where they were tolerated if not welcomed. The first Jewish congregation in America may have been Shearith Israel in New York City (1680), while the oldest surviving synagogue building is Touro in Newport (Peter Harrison, architect, 1763). When the first Jews settled in Philadelphia is uncertain, but Nathan Levy arrived with his family and children perhaps in 1737. The next year one of his children died, and Levy—not wishing to bury his child in unsanctified soil—purchased "a small piece of ground" as a permanent family burial plot. In 1740 a larger plot of land was acquired and set aside as a cemetery for the entire Jewish community (figure 12). By this time the Levy family had been joined by the David Franks family and others who began to meet to worship in private homes and rented rooms. Congregation Mikveh Israel—worshiping in the Sephardic, Spanish-Portuguese tradition—dates its founding to the 1740s. By the end of the colonial period, Philadelphia had the largest Jewish population in America.[33] In 1782 the congregation erected a simple, one-story synagogue on Cherry Street west of Third Street. This building was replaced by a second synagogue with an elegant late Federal domed interior—illuminated by a lantern—and women's galleries; it could seat approximately two hundred persons.

As architect the congregation selected William Strickland (1788–1854), whose facile mastery of diverse styles, particularly his skill in the neoclassical idiom, would make him one of Philadelphia's favorite designers of churches from 1817 until he moved to Nashville, Tennessee, in 1845. By 1822 Strickland had designed several high profile projects such as the Second Bank of the United States and the Chestnut Street Theater. His Gothic Saint Stephen's Church (pages 130–135) was also under construction. For Mikveh Israel, Strickland provided the first Egyptian Revival building in Philadelphia and one of the earliest in America (figure 13). The cornerstones were laid on September 26, 1822, and the building was dedicated January 21, 1825.[34]

As Congregation Mikveh Israel— and the residential neighborhood at Third and Cherry—declined, a third building at Seventh Street above Arch Street, designed by John McArthur, Jr. (1823–1890), was erected in 1860, then a fourth building by the New York architects Lewis F. Pilcher and W. G. Tachau (1909) at Broad and York Streets.[35] With the decline of North Broad Street, the congregation

Figure 14. Beth Sholom Synagogue on Old York Road in Elkins Park, Pennsylvania, is one of Frank Lloyd Wright's last buildings and his only major project in this region. He is reported to have exclaimed of the design, "At last a great symbol! Rabbi Mortimer J. Cohen gave me the idea of a synagogue as a 'traveling Mt. Sinai'—a mountain of light."

elected to sell their building to Dropsie University and return to their Philadelphia roots near Independence Hall. The congregation commissioned a new building at 55 North Fifth Street in 1975. The current building—designed by the firm H2L2 (Harbeson, Hough, Livingston, and Larson)—includes the National Museum of American Jewish History, which presents educational programs to "preserve, explore and celebrate the history of Jews in America."[36]

What follows includes discussions of three architecturally significant synagogues, Society Hill (pages 74–77), Kesher Israel (pages 70–73), and Rodeph Shalom (pages 234–237); however, another synagogue falling outside the parameters of this book should to be mentioned because of its architectural importance. Beth Sholom Synagogue at Old York Road and Foxcroft Road, Elkins Park, Pennsylvania, is one of the most famous houses of worship designed by the American master Frank Lloyd Wright (1867–1959)—and the only major Wright building in the Philadelphia area (figure 14). In 1953 Rabbi Mortimer J. Cohen began corresponding with Wright about how a modern building could be designed to reflect the ideals of Judaism and evolve from elements of the Jewish faith. Wright was the son of a Presbyterian minister and a practicing Unitarian, yet he proved to be surprisingly knowledgeable on the Jewish religion. Out of this fruitful correspondence between Cohen and Wright came a hexagonal synagogue to seat 1,000 members of the Conservative congregation. (Wright provides an image of cupped hands held together—when worshipers enter the synagogue they are in the hands of God.) This would prove to be one of his last projects; the building was dedicated in 1959, shortly after Wright's death.[37]

THE ROMAN CATHOLICS   The arrival of Roman Catholics in Philadelphia proved to be the most controversial event in Philadelphia's religious history and the greatest test of William Penn's "holy experiment." Saint Joseph's was the first Catholic congregation in the City of Philadelphia (pages 50–53) dating to 1733. As mentioned above, Penn's 1701 Charter of Liberties guaranteed religious freedom to all who confessed "One Almighty God," but British law prohibited the public celebration of the Catholic Mass. Shortly after the modest Catholic chapel had been erected, Lieutenant Governor Patrick Gordon asked the Pennsylvania Provincial Council to look into the matter because

> he was under no small Concern to hear that a House lately built in Walnut Street . . . had been sett apart for the Exercise of the Roman Catholick Religion, and it is commonly called the Romish Chappell, where several Persons . . . resort on Sundays, to hear Mass openly celebrated by a Popish priest; that he conceives the tolerating of the Publick Exercise of that Religion to be contrary to the Laws of England.[38]

The Provincial Council met a few days later to consider their decision. After listening to a reading of the Charter of 1701 "concerning Liberty," the council upheld the charter by taking no action against the "Romish Chappell."

Gradually the number of Philadelphia Catholics increased; there were four hundred English, Irish, German, and French Catholics in the city and its liberties by 1757. To accommodate this growing population, the 1730s Saint Joseph's chapel was first replaced by a larger structure; in 1763 a new church (Saint Mary's) was erected nearby on Fourth Street above Locust Street (pages 54–59). Soon they would be joined by Holy Trinity in 1788 (pages 116–119) and Saint Augustine's in 1796 (pages 86–91). It is the latter church that succumbed to the deadly riots of May 1844, when an anti-Irish mob, incited to violence by working-class fears of foreign-born and largely Catholic immigrants, torched the church and nearly succeeded in doing the same at Saint Philip Neri in South Philadelphia (pages 98–101). These anti-Catholic riots were among the darkest days in Philadelphia's religious history, although the riots ultimately resulted in a reaffirmation of Catholic rights to equal protection of the law.

THE ORTHODOX CHURCHES   In the late nineteenth and early twentieth centuries, Greek, Romanian, Russian, and Ukrainian Orthodox congregations began appearing in Philadelphia for the first time in measurable numbers, bringing their rich cultural heritage to the city.[39] Often these late immigrant groups were without the resources to erect new sacred places in which to celebrate their Eastern faith. Just as late nineteenth-century Jewish immigrant congregations adopted former Protestant Christian churches being abandoned by their congregations (see pages 70–77), many Orthodox congregations moved into sacred places erected originally by Protestants who had moved to escape changing neighborhood demographics. Discussed in the pages that follow, for example, are the Greek Orthodox Cathedral of Saint George (pages 120–123) and the Russian Orthodox Saint Nicholas Church (92–95). The Catholic Ukrainians of the Byzantine Rite of Philadelphia followed a similar pattern by purchasing a former Methodist church on Franklin Street in 1910 and turning it into a cathedral. In 1963, with an expanding Ukrainian Catholic population of worshipers within the Archdiocese of Philadelphia, the time had come to erect a new cathedral. The resulting structure falls outside the parameters of this book, but it has become such a strong architectural feature of the city that it deserves to be mentioned. The Ukrainian Cathedral of the Immaculate Conception at 833 North Franklin Street is a contemporary interpretation of Byzantine architecture, designed by the Ukrainian architect Julian K. Jastremsky (1910–1999).[40] Its large central dome—covered with gold-fused Venetian glass tile—strikes a brilliant note in its otherwise unremarkable surroundings (figure 15).

THE SWEDENBORGIANS   Mentioning sacred places outside this book's parameters—erected in Philadelphia prior to 1900—treads dangerously close to setting a precedent and opening the gates to a host of critics who will already be agitated by the omission of their favorite sacred place. However, the Swedenborgian Bryn Athyn Cathedral (1913–1929), approximately fifteen miles north of Philadelphia, is well worth going to see (figure 16). It is certainly one of the twentieth century's architectural treasures in the region. Only one Swedenborgian church is included among the fifty sacred places discussed in detail in this book, and it has been adaptively reused as commercial offices (pages 188–193). The Swedenborgian denomination teaches the Bible as illuminated by the eighteenth-century Swedish scientist, philosopher and mystic Emanuel Swedenborg (1688–1772).[41] A general

Figure 15. The Ukrainian Cathedral of the Immaculate Conception at 833 North Franklin Street boasts a golden dome rising above the surrounding neighborhood. It was designed by the Ukrainian architect Julian K. Jastremsky (1910–1999).

Figure 16. Bryn Athyn Cathedral in Bryn Athyn, Pennsylvania, is famed for its use of traditional craft skills and for its "optical refinements" in the use of curved lines. The cathedral is open for tours.

convention of Swedenborgian congregations was held in Philadelphia in 1817; a separate body broke off in 1890 and in 1897 took the name General Church of the New Jerusalem, with headquarters at Bryn Athyn, Pennsylvania.[42] Work began in 1913 on a cathedral for the New Church, designed by the neo-Gothic specialists Ralph A. Cram (1863–1942) and Frank Ferguson (1861–1926), a gift of John Pitcairn (1841–1916), founder of Pittsburgh Plate Glass Company. In 1916 the architects were dismissed and amateur architect Raymond Pitcairn (1885–1966), son of John Pitcairn, took full control. The cathedral has been in use since 1919, although work continues on the complex; the council hall was completed in 1926 and the choir hall in 1928.[43]

AFTERWORD   This brief introduction to the historic sacred places of Philadelphia began with a quotation from William Penn's Charter of Liberties (1701). Fifty years after Penn's proclamation, a great bell was cast to hang in the tower of the Pennsylvania State House, a building now hallowed as Independence Hall. The inscription cast into that bell carries a biblical quotation from Leviticus (25: 10):

> And ye shall hallow the fiftieth year, and proclaim liberty throughout
> all the land unto all the inhabitants thereof; it shall be a jubilee unto you . . .

Most visitors to Independence Hall, the Liberty Bell, and the Constitution Center have some idea of the political forces at work in eighteenth-century Pennsylvania, although they may conflate "proclaim liberty throughout all the land" with the clarion call of the American Revolution. This is unfortunate, for it plays down Philadelphia's far-reaching role in establishing the fundamental freedom to worship and live in a pluralistic society.

To this day, Philadelphia remains a center of Quaker influence. The first presbytery was founded here, launching the American Presbyterian Church. Since the establishment of the Philadelphia Association in 1707, Philadelphia has been a force for Baptists—and the American Baptist Convention is still here. The Protestant Episcopal Church was constituted in Philadelphia, and Bishop White helped shape the American church as a body separate from the Church of England. In the eighteenth century Philadelphia's Roman Catholics defended their freedom to worship, and in a nineteenth-century trial by fire they confirmed the right to equal protection of the law that emboldened the great migrations of Eastern European Catholics and Jews in the nineteenth and twentieth centuries, helping Philadelphia transform itself into an industrial powerhouse. What became the Keystone State was central to the American Lutherans as well; the first Ministerium was established here. Pennsylvania welcomed the German Reformed churches and the Moravians, Mennonites, Amish, Schwenkfelders, Dunkers—all would flourish here. And from the Methodists who sent down deep roots in Philadelphia would also bloom the African Methodist Episcopal Church, which has become such a potent force in the daily lives of African Americans throughout the nation and abroad. These denominations, and others as well, owe an irredeemable debt to William Penn's liberality.

NOTES TO INTRODUCTION

1. Henry Steele Commager, ed., *Documents of American History* (New York: Appleton-Century-Crofts, 1958), 40–42.

2. Peter Kalm, *Travels into North America*, trans. John Reinhold Forster (Barre, Mass.: Imprint Society, 1972), 38. Kalm describes each of the major denominations and sects in both Philadelphia and Germantown, probably the earliest such compilation.

3. Roger W. Moss, *Philadelphia Victorian: The Building of the Athenæum* (Philadelphia: The Athenæum of Philadelphia, 1998), 4, 144 n. 10. Of the forty-three founders of the library in 1814 whose religions are known, fourteen were Episcopalians, thirteen were Quakers, six were Presbyterians, five were Jews, three were Methodists, one was a Roman Catholic, and one was a Lutheran. J. Thomas Scharf and Thompson Westcott, in their encyclopedic *History of Philadelphia, 1609–1884* (Philadelphia: L.H. Everts, 1884), celebrate the city's religious diversity by devoting 218 pages to cataloguing the religious denominations of Philadelphia, beginning with the Swedes in the seventeenth century and ending with assorted spiritualists. While Scharf and Westcott do not provide sources that can be confirmed, their discussion remains a useful starting point for research on the congregations represented in the late nineteenth-century city. The most recent study of Philadelphia congregations, conducted by the Philadelphia Census of Congregations at the University of Pennsylvania, estimates there are 2,120 houses of worship in Philadelphia. "Philadelphia's Map of the Faithful," *Philadelphia Inquirer*, March 30, 2003, B5. The full report is available at www.ssw.upenn.edu/orsw/orsw.htm.

4. "Instructions of William Penn to the Commissioners for settling the colony, 30 7th Mo. 1681," *The Papers of William Penn, 1680–1684*, ed. Mary Maples Dunn and Richard S. Dunn (Philadelphia: University of Pennsylvania Press, 1982–1985), 2: 121. On the settlement of Philadelphia see Hannah B. Roach, "The Planting of Philadelphia: A Seventeenth-Century Real Estate Development," *Pennsylvania Magazine of History and Biography* 92 (January 1968): 3–476; (April 1968): 143–94. See also Gary B. Nash, "City Planning and Political Tension in the Seventeenth Century: The Case of Philadelphia," *Proceedings of the American Philosophical Society* 112 (February 15, 1968): 54–73. The best general history of Philadelphia is Russell F. Weigley, ed., *Philadelphia: A 300-Year History* (New York: W.W. Norton, 1982). For a broader scope, see Randall M. Miller and William Pencak, eds., *Pennsylvania: A History of the Commonwealth* (University Park: Pennsylvania State University Press, 2002).

5. Histories of individual denominations and sects are cited with the sources following each entry. For general histories of religion in America, see Robert T. Handy, *A History of the Churches in the United States and Canada* (New York: Oxford University Press, 1977); Sydney E. Ahlstrom, *A Religious History of the American People* (New Haven, Conn.: Yale University Press, 1972); and Edwin Scott Gaustad, *A Religious History of America*, new rev. ed. (New York: Harper-Collins, 1990). For brief summaries of the sacred places recorded by the Historic American Buildings Survey, see Richard J. Webster, *Philadelphia Preserved: Catalog of the Historic American Buildings Survey* (Philadelphia: Temple University Press, 1976). All the buildings discussed in this book, as well as the life and careers of the architects and builders responsible for designing and erecting them, are included in the Philadelphia Architects and Buildings web site managed by The Athenæum of Philadelphia at www.philadelphiabuildings.org. Before the creation of this web site, biographical sketches of most Philadelphia architects appeared in Sandra L. Tatman and Roger W. Moss, *Biographical Dictionary of Philadelphia Architects* (Boston: G.K. Hall, 1985). In the individual site essays, credit is given as Tatman and Moss, although all the essays are also available over the Internet via the PAB web site. In addition to biographies and histories of the buildings, the web site links to the official list of historically registered buildings in Philadelphia, the Commonwealth list of registered buildings, and the structures recorded by the Historic American Buildings Survey, a program of the National Park Service, Department of the Interior.

6. Benjamin Franklin, *The Autobiography of Benjamin Franklin*, ed. Leonard W. Labaree (New Haven, Conn.: Yale University Press, 1964), 77.

7. Edwin B. Bronner, "Quaker Landmarks in Early Philadelphia," in *Historic Philadelphia, from the Founding Until the Early Nineteenth Century: Papers Dealing with Its People and Buildings*, Transactions of the American Philosophical Society 43, Part 1 (Philadelphia: American Philosophical Society, 1953), 210–16. For a discussion of Quaker meeting houses within the range of Philadelphia Yearly Meeting, see Jennifer Beer, Charles Walker, and Chel Avery, eds., *Silent Witness: Quaker Meetinghouses in the Delaware Valley, 1695 to the Present* (Philadelphia: Philadelphia Yearly Meeting, 2002). This useful publication includes a locator map of the meeting houses, excellent photographs, and measured drawings. One early meeting house not mentioned elsewhere is the Free Quaker Meeting House, which still stands in Independence National Historical Park at Fifth and Arch Streets. It was erected in 1783 by Quakers expelled by the Friends for participating in the American Revolution. The building is not currently open to the public. Webster, *Philadelphia Preserved*, 74–75. Charles E. Peterson, *The Free Quaker Meeting House* (Washington, D.C.: Ross and Perry, 2002). Harold W. Rose points out that of the 345 surviving colonial sacred places, 73 (21 percent) are Quaker meeting houses; *The Colonial Houses of Worship in America* (New York: Hastings House, 1963), 70. General histories attempting to survey the architecture of the entire country rarely are successful. See, for example, Peter W. Williams, *Houses of God: Region, Religion, and Architecture in the United States* (Urbana: University of Illinois Press, 1997), who bases most of his coverage of early Pennsylvania sacred places on the work of Harold W. Rose and John Thomson Faris, *Old Churches and Meeting Houses in and Around Philadelphia* (Philadelphia: J.B. Lippincott, 1926).

8. For a brief overview, see Webster, *Philadelphia Preserved*, 173–74.

9. John Milner Associates, "An Historical and Architectural Analysis of St. James Church of Kingsessing," unpublished report prepared for the Historic Religious Properties Preservation Program, Philadelphia, 1987. Copy on file at The Athenæum of Philadelphia. The nineteenth-century historians Scharf and Westcott discuss the Swedish churches at some length. Scharf and Westcott, *History of Philadelphia*, 2: 1229–41.

10. The Swedish Lutheran Church maintained bishops, and the episcopacy of the Swedish church made a bond with the Church of England easier. Consequently, when social and political realities encouraged the merger of the American Swedish churches with another denomination, they looked to the Episcopalians rather than the German Lutherans.

11. See Frederick B. Tolles, "The Culture of Early Pennsylvania," *Pennsylvania Magazine of History and Biography* 81, 2 (April 1957): 127–30.

12. Ahlstrom, *Religious History of the American People*, 210, 221–22.

13. J. Wesley Twelves, *A History of the Diocese of Pennsylvania* (Philadelphia: Episcopal Diocese of Pennsylvania, 1969), 108–9. Church history and locator map available at www.stdavids church.org.

14. *The Poetical Works of Henry Wadsworth Longfellow* (Boston: Houghton Mifflin, 1884), 398.

15. Herbert R. Sparks et al., *An Account of the History of Trinity Church, Oxford, Philadelphia, 1698 to 1973* (Philadelphia, c.1973); Historic American Buildings Survey, Trinity Church, Oxford, Philadelphia County, Pennsylvania, available at http://lcweb2.loc.gov; Webster, *Philadelphia Preserved*, 339; George E. Thomas, Michael J. Lewis, and Jeffrey A. Cohen, *Frank Furness: The Complete Works* (New York: Princeton Architectural Press, 1991), 193.

16. Deborah Mathias Gough, *Christ Church Philadelphia: The Nation's Church in a Changing City* (Philadelphia: University of Pennsylvania Press, 1995); Webster, *Philadelphia Preserved*, 66–67.

17. Frederick L. Richards, Jr., National Historic Landmark Nomination, Saint Peter's Church, Philadelphia, Pennsylvania, 1994; Webster, *Philadelphia Preserved*, 28.

18. Twelves, *History of the Diocese*, 10–11; Charles E. Peterson, Constance M. Grieff, and

Maria M. Thompson, *Robert Smith: Architect, Builder, Patriot, 1722–1777* (Philadelphia: The Athenæum of Philadelphia, 2000), 68–70; Norris Stanley Barratt, *Outline of the History of Old St. Paul's Church* (Philadelphia: Colonial Society of Pennsylvania, 1917); Webster, *Philadelphia Preserved*, 96.

19. Gaustad, *Religious History*, 46.

20. For a readable survey of the Scotch-Irish, see James G. Leyburn, *The Scotch-Irish: A Social History* (Chapel Hill: University of North Carolina Press, 1962). See also the classic study *Presbyterians in Colonial Pennsylvania* by Guy Soulliard Klett (Philadelphia: University of Pennsylvania Press, 1937). Benjamin Franklin estimated the number of Scotch-Irish in Pennsylvania at 350,000 in 1776; Ahlstrom, *Religious History*, 276.

21. Presbyterians favored a hierarchy of judicatories (church courts) arranged in ascending order into *sessions* (which governed each congregation), *presbyteries*, *synods*, and *general assembly*. William P. White and William H. Scott, *The Presbyterian Church in Philadelphia* (Philadelphia: Allen, Lane, and Scott, 1895). Ahlstrom, *Religious History*, 265–79.

22. Tatman and Moss, 484–87.

23. Robert Shackleton, "Conwell's Life and Achievements," in Russell H. Conwell, *Acres of Diamonds* (New York: Harper and Brothers, 1915).

24. Ahlstrom, *Religious History*, 324–29.

25. Fred P. Corson, "St. George Church: The Cradle of American Methodism," in *Historic Philadelphia, from the Founding Until the Early Nineteenth Century: Papers Dealing with Its People and Buildings*, Transactions of the American Philosophical Society 43, Part 1 (Philadelphia: American Philosophical Society, 1953), 230.

26. Kenneth Cain Kinghorn, *The Heritage of American Methodism* (Nashville, Tenn.: Abingdon Press, 1999), 32.

27. Rose, *Colonial Houses of Worship*, 82–85. See Joe William Trotter and Eric Ledell Smith, eds., *African Americans in Pennsylvania* (University Park: Pennsylvania State University Press, 1997) and Carol V. R. George, *Segregated Sabbaths: Richard Allen and the Emergence of Independent Black Churches, 1760–1840* (New York: Oxford University Press, 1973).

28. Throughout this book the term "sect" is not used negatively. As pointed out by Ahlstrom (*Religious History*, 230), "the word derives from *sequi* (to follow) not from *secare* (to cut); it thus emphasizes a group's response to a leader and not the group's existence as a tiny fraction or section of the whole."

29. Ahlstrom, *Religious History*, 230–50.

30. Webster, *Philadelphia Preserved*, 272–73.

31. John Peterson, "Historic Lutheran Sites in the Philadelphia Area," *Lutheran Quarterly* 10, 4 (Winter 1996): 467–77 (includes a useful map locating all the sites in the region). See also William O. Fegely, *Augustus Lutheran Church, Trappe, Pennsylvania: The Shrine of Lutheranism* (Trappe, Pa.: W.O. Fegely, 1939). A tour of Lutheran landmarks is available at www.thelutheran.org.

32. Kalm, *Travels into North America*, 27.

33. The word "synagogue" is from the Greek *sinago*, to gather. On Philadelphia Jews and synagogues, see Harry D. Boonin, *The Jewish Quarter of Philadelphia, 1881–1930* (Philadelphia: Jewish Walking Tours of Philadelphia, 1999); Murray Friedman, ed., *Jewish Life in Philadelphia, 1830–1940* (Philadelphia: Institute for the Study of Human Issues, 1983); Esther H. Klein, *Guidebook to Jewish Philadelphia* (Philadelphia: Jewish Times Institute, 1965); Rachel Wischnitzer, *Synagogue Architecture in the United States* (Philadelphia: Jewish Publication Society of America, 1955); and Edwin Wolf II and Maxwell Whiteman, *The History of the Jews of Philadelphia from Colonial Times to the Age of Jackson* (Philadelphia: Jewish Publication Society, 1957).

34. Tatman and Moss, 767–71; Wischnitzer, *Synagogue Architecture*, 28–33. Most of what is known of the Strickland Mikveh Israel Synagogue is based on a report by Alfred Bendiner, architect and artist, undertaken with a 1953 grant from the American Philosophical Society. *Year*

Book of the American Philosophical Society (Philadelphia: American Philosophical Society, 1959), 529–33. Bendiner's report includes reconstructed plans, elevations, and section drawings of the long-demolished building. See also Richard Meier, *Recent American Synagogue Architecture* (New York: Jewish Museum, 1963). Thomas Ustick Walter, who studied with Strickland, would later use the Egyptian Revival style for a synagogue designed for Congregation Beth Israel in 1849.

35. A biographical sketch of Pilcher and the firm of Pilcher and Tachau can be found on the PAB web site: www.philadelphiabuildings.org and in hard copy in Henry F. Withey and Elsie R. Withey, *Biographical Dictionary of American Architects* (Los Angeles: New Age, 1956), 473.

36. A. S. W. Rosenbach, *Dedication of the New Synagogue of the Congregation Mikve Israel at Broad and York Streets on September 14, 1909* (Philadelphia, 1909); Tatman and Moss, 510–12.

37. Simeon J. Maslin et al., *One God, Sixteen Houses: An Illustrated Introduction to the Churches and Synagogues of the Old York Road Corridor* (Elkins Park, Pa.: Keneseth Israel Press, 1990). See also Mortimer J. Cohen, *Beth Sholom Synagogue: A Description and Interpretation* (Elkins Park, Pa.: Beth Sholom Synagogue, 1957).

38. *Minutes of the Provincial Council of Pennsylvania* (Philadelphia, 1852), 3: 546, 547, 563–64.

39. Ahlstrom, *Religious History*, 985–97; Gaustad, *Religious History*, 251–54; Handy, *History of the Churches*, 334–55, 406–7.

40. Obituary for Julian K. Jastremsky, AIA, appears in *Ukrainian Weekly*, August 1, 1999.

41. For a discussion of Swedenborg, see pages 188–193 and www.newearth.org/~bac. Also Sig Synnestvedt, *The Essential Swedenborg* (New York: Swedenborg Foundation, 1977).

42. There are three major bodies of Swedenborgians: the General Conference in England, the General Convention in the United States, and the General Church of the New Jerusalem based at Bryn Athyn.

43. *A Handbook of Information Concerning the Cathedral-Church of Bryn Athyn* (Bryn Athyn, Pa.: General Church Book Center, 1967): E. Bruce Glenn, *Bryn Athyn Cathedral: The Building of a Church* (Bryn Athyn, Pa.: Church of the New Jerusalem, 1971).

THE RIVER WARDS
SOUTHWARK TO NORTHERN LIBERTIES

⌐⊶ *The West Room of the Arch Street Meeting is virtually unchanged from its construction in 1810–1811. Originally only the doors and columns were painted and the walls were whitewashed. Typical of most Friends meeting houses, the interior woodwork was otherwise unfinished. This treatment may illustrate Quaker simplicity or a practical means of avoiding the cost of repetitive painting. To the left is the facing bench (elders' gallery) with its curved sounding board above. The balcony that extends around three sides of the room was intended as a "youth's gallery"; a partition down the middle of the north balcony separated boys from girls.* See pages 46–49.

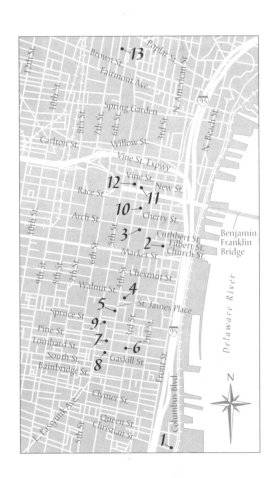

GLORIA DEI (OLD SWEDES') CHURCH

*Columbus Boulevard and
Christian Street
Philadelphia, PA 19147*

*Joseph Yard and John Harrison,
master builders, 1698–1700*

*Telephone for visitor information:
215.389.1513*

www.gloriadei-oldswedes.org

Venerable Gloria Dei Church reminds us that Swedes settled the Delaware River Valley half a century before the founding of Philadelphia. When William Penn arrived he found them well entrenched near the site of his proposed capital city. "They kindly received me," Penn wrote. "I must needs to commend their respect to authority, and kind behavior to the English." At the same time the Swedes commented favorably on the toleration of Penn's agents. "The English have received us extremely well," one Lutheran minister reported, "and some of them even come to our meetings. We live scattered among the English and Quakers, yet our language is preserved as pure as anywhere in Sweden. There are about twelve hundred persons that speak it." Yet the Swedes' culture and virtually all their architecture gradually submerged in the tidal wave of late seventeenth- and early eighteenth-century British immigration. So it is one of history's ironic twists that the best-documented seventeenth-century building in Philadelphia and the earliest surviving church in Pennsylvania should be Swedish. Lest visitors expect an example of Scandinavian architecture, it must immediately be said that the building itself is the product of

⇒ The center pulpit (replacing the original octagonal pulpit with sounding board that stood on the north wall) dates from 1846, as do the stained glass and the encaustic tile floor. The stained glass is among the earliest surviving examples in Philadelphia in its original location.

⇒⇒ Diminutive Gloria Dei (Old Swedes', erected 1698–1700) is the oldest church in Pennsylvania in continuous use. The porch and sacristy on the south and north walls were added to buttress the sanctuary walls in 1704; the steeple dates to before 1800. Among those buried in the churchyard is Alexander Wilson (1766–1813), author of American Ornithology, *who is said to have selected Old Swedes' as his final resting place so birds would sing over his grave in perpetuity.*

English-born and trained craftsmen who came to create William Penn's "greene Country Towne" on the Delaware.

In the 1690s Delaware Valley Swedes petitioned Charles XI of Sweden for priests and books so they might preserve their Lutheran religion and native language in face of English domination. In 1698 Eric Bjork and Andreas Rudman landed in America in response to that call; Rudman assumed the congregation at Wicaco in what would become the Southwark area of Philadelphia and Bjork that at Crane Hook (Christina), now modern Wilmington, Delaware. Both men found their charges inadequately housed in makeshift wooden structures, and they promptly set about providing new brick church buildings. Bjork's Christina congregation began first by contracting with the Philadelphia "mason and bricklayer" Joseph Yard and the master carpenter John Harrison ("a sober, industrious and capable man") and his sons. This same team began work on the Wicaco church in 1698. Both buildings are simple rectangular structures approximately 30' x 60', with

☞ In the floor directly before the pulpit is a marble tablet with incised cherubs and an inscription that reads: "THIS MARBLE COVERS THE REMAINS OF THE REVEREND ANDREW RUDMAN: BEING SENT HITHER FROM SWEDEN. HE FIRST FOUNDED & BUILT THIS CHURCH, WAS A CONSTANT, FAITHFUL PREACHER IN TH' ENGLISH, SWEDES & DUTCH CHURCHES ELEVEN YEARS IN THIS COUNTREY: WHERE HE ADVANC'D THE PIETY, BY SOUND DOCTRINE & GOOD EXAMPLE. HE DIED SEP^R 17, 1708. AGED 40 YEARS." *Nearby are simpler tablets marking the graves of the Rev. Mr. John Dylander, Swedish missionary and minister who died in 1741 at the age of thirty-two, and the Rev. Mr. Olof Parlin, who died in 1757. The Latin inscription on the latter tablet begins (in translation): "Stop, traveler, who art thyself mortal, and drop a tear upon this receptacle of corruption. Here lies quietly and in peace, after a happy death, a man conspicuous in erudition."*

To meet the demand of a growing congregation in the 1840s, balconies were added to three sides of the sanctuary. At the same time the high-backed colonial pews were reduced, wainscoting added around the walls, and double-hung sash installed in place of the seventeenth-century leaded casement windows. Hanging from the ceiling are a Swedish brass chandelier, a carved wood angel Gabriel said to be a replica of one in Gothenburg—and models representing the Kalmar Nyckel and Fogel Grip, pinnaces that brought a group of Swedes to America in 1643. Directly under the organ (not shown in this view) are carved wood cherubs and an open Bible that are believed to have been brought to Gloria Dei from an earlier church erected on Tinicum Island in 1646.

walls of local brick laid in Flemish bond over stone foundations. Both reflect Anglican Protestant church form with windows in the east end under which the altars are placed with pulpits along the north wall. The original pulpit at Gloria Dei (replaced in 1846) was octagonal with a sounding board—similar to the one that survives at Crane Hook in Wilmington, both probably the work of John Harrison (d. 1708), who had been apprenticed as a carpenter in London and would establish a prominent family of Philadelphia master builders.

While Joseph Yard (fl. 1690s, d. 1716) is recognized as a major figure (he later worked at Christ Church), his walls at Gloria Dei soon began to bulge and had to be reinforced in 1704 by the addition of a small sacristy to the north and entrance porch to the south. It is generally believed that the west tower was planned but not completed at first and that the steeple is later still. (However, both tower and steeple show in the 1800 Birch view.) Following the death of the last Swedish priest, the congregation became part of the Episcopal Diocese of Pennsylvania (1845). The first Episcopal priest, Jehu Curtis Clay, proved to be so charismatic that the congregation rapidly expanded, prompting a major renovation of the interior, including the introduction of balconies, which occasioned the relocation of the pulpit from the north side to directly in front of the east window.

Throughout the nineteenth and early twentieth centuries wharfs, warehouses, and other commercial structures were erected between Gloria Dei and the Delaware River. Train tracks were laid in Delaware Avenue to service these establishments and there were often long rows of box cars sitting a few yards from the apse. In the post-World War II era, however, when the National Park Service was developing Independence National Historical Park, Gloria Dei received renewed attention. Nearby structures were acquired and demolished, protective walls erected, and the surroundings landscaped. Now entering its fourth century, this much beloved church once again enjoys a resurgent neighborhood as the gritty, commercial waterfront is redeveloped for residential and recreational use.

The marble baptismal font, long thought to have been brought from Europe, is actually a local product carved in 1731. It rests in a nineteenth-century base that may have been part of the 1846 renovations. The central wall tablet in the background is in memory of the Rev. Mr. Jehu Curtis Clay (1792–1863), the first Episcopal clergyman of Gloria Dei.

CHRIST CHURCH

Second Street between Market and Arch Streets, Philadelphia, PA 19106

Various builders, from 1727; Robert Smith, steeple, 1751–1754

Telephone for visitor information: 215.922.1695

www.christchurchphila.org

Christ Church is the oldest Anglican congregation in Philadelphia. Its present church edifice dates from the eighteenth century and is the closest approximation to a London parish church in the city. Not surprisingly, it is one of the most popular tourist attractions in the historic district. Once visitors have toured Independence Hall and the Liberty Bell, Christ Church is often their next historic site. This is as it should be. Christ Church is one of the handsomest and most evocative sacred places in the nation.

Visitors to Philadelphia are generally aware of William Penn's desire to establish a colony in the New World where Quakers and other dissenters from the established Church of England might gather to practice their religion in safety. It is not generally known that Penn's original grant from the crown guaranteed the bishop of London the right to send "any Preacher or Preachers to reside within the Province without any denial or molestation whatsoever." As a consequence, Anglicans in 1695

☞ *The Christ Church "wine glass" pulpit is an extraordinary survival. It dates from 1769 and is the work of John Folwell, based on designs from Batty Langley's* City and Country Builder's and Workman's Treasury of Designs *(London, 1740). Fitted with a sounding board now lost (see example at Saint Peter's), the pulpit originally stood directly in front of the Palladian window in the east wall. The cathedra (bishop's chair) in the background of this photograph is by Philadelphia cabinetmaker Ephraim Haines and dates from the early nineteenth century. Notice the carved bishop's miter on the crest rail.*

☞☞ *Christ Church reflects three major building campaigns in the eighteenth century. The western half of the church dates from 1727, the eastern half with its Palladian window overlooking Second Street from 1735, and the steeple from 1751–1754. The resulting composition—clearly influenced by London churches designed by Christopher Wren and, especially, James Gibbs's St. Martin-in-the-Fields—is one of the finest Georgian buildings in America.*

The interior of Christ Church is less embellished today than it would have been in the eighteenth and nineteenth centuries. Successive decorative campaigns intended to update the old church have been reversed, including the removal of stained-glass windows. When a late Victorian stone altar was removed from under the Palladian window, it was replaced by a Federal-era communion table made by Philadelphia cabinetmaker Jonathan Gostelowe in 1788. The original box pews—similar to those at Saint Peter's (page 63)—were replaced with open-ended slip pews in the 1830s during alterations by Thomas Ustick Walter.

purchased a lot of land on Second Street just above High (Market) Street "for the publick worship of God . . . as . . . professed in the Church of England." Anglicans may have been a minority sect in seventeenth-century Philadelphia, but they planned to be near the center of political and economic power.

The first Christ Church, a frame building probably erected by a parishioner, the master builder John Harrison, who designed Old Swedes' (pages 34–39), was only a short distance from the court house on High Street. By 1727 immigration forced consideration of a new church "to Accomodate divers New Settlers and other well wishers to the Church who are forced either to stay at home or frequent dissenting Congregations for want of Seats." The 1690s church had been erected flush with the

The octagonal walnut baptismal font is believed to have been sent to Christ Church from All Hallows Church, Barking-by-the-Tower, London, in 1697. It is also said to have been used during the baptism of William Penn in 1644.

To the Memory of
Mrs MARY ANDREWS late of this City,
Who died March 29, 1761 Aged 78,
And was a confiderable Benefactrefs to this
CHURCH.
Erected by her Executors, William Peters and
Benjamin Price Efq^{rs} in purfuance of her Will.

Christ Church is embellished with many handsome memorials. One of the most interesting commemorates a 1761 bequest to the church from Mary Andrews to provide bread for the poor at Christmas, a new pulpit, and a suitable memorial in the church. Carved of wood and painted to simulate marble, her tablet is attributed to the same John Folwell who designed the pulpit, again working from designs by Batty Langley.

east end of the lot. Rather than replace this structure immediately, the new church went up in two installments. The first was erected to the west of the existing church. Then the original structure was demolished and the second half of the new church erected on the east beginning in 1735. By 1740 the east end was sufficiently completed to allow the pulpit to be installed in the new building. Unfortunately the architect of this new church remains unknown. Dr. John Kearsley, who headed the building committee, is often credited, but there is no evidence that he actually served as architect—this is one of those ancient Philadelphia myths repeated over and over in secondary works that, like the roots of a wisteria vine, resists being eradicated. Another theory suggests that the unknown designer came from London, or sent his design from there. This, too, is uncorroborated. Perhaps a future discovery will allow the author of this sophisticated composition to be given proper credit.

The soaring 200-foot steeple would not be realized until 1753–1754, when the young Scottish master builder Robert Smith—who would later be responsible for Saint Peter's Church (pages 60–65) and Old Pine Street Presbyterian Church (pages 66–69)—designed and erected what would be the tallest structure in Philadelphia until John McArthur's Tenth Presbyterian Church (pages 178–183). By the mid-eighteenth century, the Anglicans of Christ Church had established themselves as the wealthiest and most fashionable congregation in the city. Here the governor of Pennsylvania and Benjamin Franklin worshiped. As the Revolution approached, and when Philadelphia became the capital city of the new nation, pews might be occupied by George Washington, John Adams, and more than a dozen other signers of the Declaration of Independence. But the independence movement would have grave consequences for the Church of England. The break with England cast adrift thousands of Americans who desired to remain within the Anglican communion. The solution was to found the Protestant Episcopal Church of the United States with Christ Church pastor Dr. William White, who had served as chaplain of the Continental Congress, as the first bishop of Pennsylvania. (White and Samuel Provoost of New York were consecrated by the archbishops of Canterbury and York in 1787.) Two years later a general convention resolved differences between Episcopalians from different regions of the United States, revised and adopted the Book of Common Prayer, and declared the formation of the Protestant Episcopal Church.

ARCH STREET MEETING

320 Arch Street
Philadelphia, PA 19106-2114

Owen Biddle, master builder, 1804

Telephone for visitor information:
215.627.2667

www.archstreetfriends.org

Geographically it is but a few steps from the Anglican grandeur of Christ Church to the Quaker simplicity of the Arch Street Meeting of the Religious Society of Friends. Aesthetically the architectural and decorative distance eloquently testify to the fierce religious differences that raged in colonial Philadelphia. At Arch Street Meeting you look in vain for pulpit, religious symbols, stained-glass windows, or shrines; nor will you find evidence of an ecclesiastical hierarchy, prayer book setting forth the creed, or organ to encourage voices raised in song—any or all of these might detract from the quiet contemplation of the spirit of God that Quakers believe resides in the individual. In the words of the poet Marianne Moore, "the deepest feeling always shows itself in silence." As explained by the Friends, "the group gathers, seeking inwardly

Elevation of the Arch Street Meeting, c. 1803, by Philadelphia "House Carpenter and teacher of architectural drawing" Owen Biddle (1774–1806). His drawing of the proposed meeting house is one of the earliest documented uses of perspective by a native-born builder. The Athenæum of Philadelphia, gift of George Vaux, 1983.

The three "houses" and burial ground that together constitute the Arch Street Meeting occupy nearly the entire city block from Third to Fourth Streets. For a century prior to their construction, the site had been used as a burial ground by Friends. The handsome brick wall laid in Flemish bond with recessed panels of glazed headers was constructed in 1801–1802 "to prevent [the burial ground] being frequently and very improperly intruded upon by rude Boys and others." The following year bodies were moved from the middle of the enclosure and construction began on the east and middle houses; the west house followed in 1810–1811, which completed the intended composition.

The unfinished poplar-wood pews in the West Room are believed to date from 1810–1811. Although they are shown in this photograph without seat cushions, such comforts were commonly provided in the eighteenth and nineteenth centuries. Also note the original yellow pine floor, which has never been treated with varnish or shellac. This is a typical Philadelphia practice; such floors were swept and scrubbed as needed, gradually taking on a pleasingly uniform coloration. See page 32.

to feel the presence of the living Christ—'The Light that lighteth every man.' To any one of those in attendance may come a message or a prayer to be shared with the Meeting through spoken words."

As the dominant religious sect in colonial Philadelphia, the Quakers erected several meeting houses (pages 4–5). In the years following the American Revolution, however, it became increasingly apparent that there was no single building adequate to house both the Men's Yearly Meeting and the Women's Yearly Meeting (which met separately for their business sessions) and serve the needs of the Yearly Meeting as well. Consequently a committee was appointed to consider all these needs and to erect a new meeting house with large wings. The site selected was already a place sacred to Philadelphia Quakers. It had been granted "To the use & behoof of the People called Quakers in Philadelphia . . . for a Burying place" by William Penn in 1701, having been in such use for that purpose since 1693.

To design what would become the largest meeting house in America, the Yearly Meeting called on Owen Biddle (1774–1806), "House Carpenter and teacher of architectural drawing," who is primarily remembered as the author of *The Young Carpenter's Assistant*, one of the earliest books on architecture written and published in the United States. Of Biddle's lamentably brief but promising career, too little is known. His father was a member of Philadelphia Monthly Meeting and the lad had served apprenticeship as a house carpenter, becoming in 1800 a member of the Philadelphia guild of master builders known as the Carpenters' Company. Following his design of the Arch Street Meeting—a highly visible commission for such a youthful master carpenter—Biddle worked on the Schuylkill Permanent Bridge and served as master builder for amateur architect John Dorsey's Pennsylvania Academy of the Fine Arts (1805–1806; burned, 1845). Arch Street Meeting is Biddle's principal monument; it survives virtually unchanged after two centuries.

While Biddle's design is for a single brick structure laid in Flemish bond on an east-west axis, it actually was to consist of three "houses." The east wing and center building were constructed in 1803–1805 and immediately put to use by the Women's Yearly Meeting and by the Philadelphia Monthly Meeting. When the west wing was completed in 1811 the Women's Yearly Meeting moved there and the Men's Yearly Meeting relocated from the Greater Meeting House at the corner of Market and Second Street, which was sold and demolished. The resulting building is straightforward and unadorned. The pedimented center building carries an 1804 date stone (above the central porch). Otherwise there are no decorative elements, in keeping with meeting house traditions.

Visitors to Arch Street Meeting are welcomed on a regular schedule and tours can be arranged with one of the knowledgeable volunteer guides. The meeting house continues to be used for the Monthly Meetings of Friends of Philadelphia and the annual sessions of Philadelphia Yearly Meeting. Changing exhibitions are mounted in the east wing, and there are dioramas on the life and work of William Penn and his Philadelphia "holy experiment."

OLD SAINT JOSEPH'S CHURCH

321 Willings Alley
Philadelphia, PA 19106

John Darragh, master builder,
1838–1839

Telephone for visitor information:
215.923.1733

www.oldstjoseph.org

Saint Joseph's was the first Roman Catholic congregation in the city of Philadelphia. It dates to the arrival of a Jesuit missionary priest, Father Joseph Greaton, who acquired land near Fourth and Walnut Streets in 1733 and erected thereon a simple chapel attached to his residence. Here he could celebrate Mass for a congregation of forty souls.

William Penn's 1701 Charter of Liberties guaranteed religious freedom to all who confessed "One Almighty God," but British law prohibited the public celebration of Catholic Mass. Shortly after Father Greaton erected his chapel, Lieutenant Governor Patrick Gordon asked the Pennsylvania Provincial Council to look into the matter because

> he was under no small Concern to hear that a House lately built in Walnut Street . . . had been sett apart for the Exercise of the Roman Catholick Religion, and it is commonly called the Romish Chappell, where several Persons . . . resort on Sundays, to hear Mass openly celebrated by a Popish priest; that he conceives the tolerating of the Publick Exercise of that Religion to be contrary to the Laws of England.

The Provincial Council met a few days later to consider their decision. After listening to a reading of the Charter "concerning Liberty," the Council upheld the Charter, leaving it to the Governor to "represent the matter to our Superiors at home [England], for their Advice and Directions in it" if he felt the necessity. There is no record that the governor ever "represented the matter."

Gradually the number of Philadelphia Catholics increased; there were four

⟡⟶ The clergy house faces the courtyard and dates from 1789–1790. A major addition in 1850 included this handsome entrance provided for the newly founded Saint Joseph's College. (St. Joseph's College moved from the Willings Alley building in the 1880s and is now located on City Line Avenue, becoming Saint Joseph's University in 1978.)

⟡⟶⟡⟶ The entrance to Old Saint Joseph's Church on Willings Alley is through this arch hung with heavy iron gates, leading into a courtyard with a decidedly European feel. To the right is the clergy house.

On the sanctuary ceiling is a large painting, Exaltation of St. Joseph into Heaven, *by Filippo Costaggini (1886), who succeeded Constantino Brumidi at the Capitol of the United States and embellished Saint Augustine's Church (pages 86–91).*

hundred English, Irish, German, and French Catholics in the city and its liberties in 1757. To accommodate this growing population, the 1730s Saint Joseph's chapel was first replaced by a larger structure, and then, in 1763, a new church (Saint Mary's) was erected nearby on Fourth Street above Locust Street (pages 54–59). Saint Mary's was intended to be the principal Catholic church, while Saint Joseph's would serve as a "chapel of ease" for the priests who lived in a clergy house erected at Saint Joseph's in 1789–1790. Once Saint Joseph's and Saint Mary's became separate parishes, both congregations expanded. This forced Saint Joseph's for a third time to build. The cornerstone of the present church was laid on June 4, 1838, and the completed structure was consecrated on February 11, 1839.

Designed by master builder John Darragh (fl. 1828–1836), the new Saint Joseph's Church was embellished and altered throughout the nineteenth century, most notably in the 1880s, when the galleries were cut back, Victorian pews and wainscoting were installed, and the walls and ceiling were decorated by artist Filippo Costaggini. As changes in taste swept over Philadelphia in the mid-twentieth century, Saint Joseph's was colonialized: the walls painted white, the wainscoting and Victorian pews removed, and box pews installed. Vatican II also had its effect. Several statues and decorative candelabra were lost when liturgical changes required reconfiguration of the altar. Fortunately, through all these changes the painting of the Crucifixion over the altar by Sylvano Martinez dating from the 1840s has survived. In the 1980s the congregation launched an extensive and ongoing program of sensitive conservation and restoration. Original colors have been reintroduced, and a modern lighting system simulating the nineteenth-century gas lamps has been installed. Most recently the stained-glass window over the Crucifixion painting (*Angels Adoring the Eucharist*) has been conserved.

The present appearance of the church interior reflects several modifications after its construction in 1838. The original galleries were cut back in 1886 to the sinuous line shown here. At the same time, pointed Gothic windows were replaced with round-headed windows filled with stained glass. The altar rail, brass gates, and mosaic tile floor date to renovations by the architects Ballinger and Perrot in 1904.

OLD SAINT MARY'S CHURCH

252 South Fourth Street
Philadelphia, PA 19106

Builder unknown, 1763

Telephone for visitor information:
215.923.7930

www.stmaryholytrinity.org

Saint Mary's, the second Roman Catholic church in Philadelphia, stands on ground acquired in 1754 by Saint Joseph's for use as a Catholic cemetery. The easternmost section of that lot—which extended westward from Fourth Street through the block to Fifth Street—was conveyed in 1763 for the construction of a new church. The intention was to replace the modest Saint Joseph's chapel with a larger and more accessible church. Prudence still dictated that Catholics maintain a low profile for their places of worship. Saint Mary's was consequently modest, without tower or

Access to Old Saint Mary's Church in the eighteenth century was from Fifth Street through the graveyard established in 1754 for the burial of Philadelphia's Catholics. Here rest John Barry, father of the American Navy, Michel Bouvier, cabinetmaker, Thomas Fitzsimons, signer of the Constitution, publisher Mathew Carey, and artist John Neagle.

✝ *The high Victorian interior of Saint Mary's Church is documented by this lithograph from the 1880s. American Catholic Historical Society Collection.*

PRAY FOR THE SOULS
OF
THOMAS H. GREEN
MARY K. GREEN, MARGARET R. GREEN,
PATRICK GREEN, MARGARET R. BUNN,
CATHARINE GREEN, LENA GREEN, LEWIS.

steeple. Moreau de St. Méry thought it looked like "an ordinary house with a large door in front and another on the side."

As for the interior of this Middle Georgian style church, we must rely on the comments of visitors, since no views are known. John Adams recorded in his diary that "the scenery and the music are so calculated to take in mankind, that I wonder the Reformation ever succeeded!" Strong words from the puritanical New Englander. After attending services at Saint Mary's in 1774, he reported to Abigail at home in Braintree:

> This afternoon, led by curiosity and good company, I strolled away to mother church, or rather grandmother Church; I mean the romish chapel. . . . The dress of the priest was rich with lace. His pulpit was velvet and gold. The altar-piece was very rich; little images and crucifixes about, wax candles lighted up. But how shall I describe the picture of our Saviour, in a frame of marble over the altar, at full length upon the cross, in the agonies, and the blood dripping and streaming from His wounds? The music consisting of an organ and a choir of singers, went all the afternoon except sermon time, and the assembly chanted most sweetly and exquisitely.

The eighteenth-century entrance to the church was from Fifth Street via a long path lined with graves of the departed faithful. Upon entering the large rectangular room, the worshiper encountered two aisles separating eighty-one pews into three groups facing the sanctuary at the east end of the church, with pulpit and sacristy to the south and special pews on the north side reserved for ambassadors and other dignitaries.

George Washington—as well as John Adams—recorded having attended services at Saint Mary's during meetings of the Continental Congress (1774). Following the accidental drowning of French general Philippe Du Coudray in 1777, Congress attended his funeral there, just before abandoning the city to the British. Unlike other churches that suffered dearly at the hands of the occupiers, Saint Mary's appears to have escaped such deprivations, perhaps because the British army successfully recruited a regiment of Philadelphia Catholic loyalist volunteers—who then evacuated with the British in 1778.

Despite American ambivalence over Catholic loyalty to the Revolution, there was no denying the importance of our European Catholic allies. In 1779, at the suggestion of the French minister plenipotentiary, the first Catholic celebration of Independence Day was held at Saint Mary's and the following year the funeral for the Spanish merchant Juan de Miralles of Spain was attended by the diplomatic corps,

⇥ *A small memorial chapel on the east wall of Old Saint Mary's is defined by a carved marble railing, brass gate, and dark stained wood canopy—all in the Gothic style. The enclosure is sacred to the memory of the Green family interred in the crypt. The altar base is inscribed, "PRAY FOR THE SOULS OF THOMAS H. GREEN, MARY K. GREEN, MARGARET R. GREEN, PATRICK GREEN, MARGARET R. RUNN, CATHARINE GREEN, LENA GREEN LEWIS." Resting on the altar is a life-size marble Pietà (the Virgin Mary mourning over the body of Christ) by French sculptor Alfred Boucher (1850–1934), who was elected a Chevalier de la Légion d'Honneur in 1887 and won the Grand Prize at the 1900 Exposition Universelle. Boucher was a contemporary of Auguste Rodin, and his work appears in many French museums. It is unrecorded how he obtained the Green memorial commission, but according to church records the Pietà was set in place and blessed on April 19, 1891.*

Congress, and several general officers. Finally, a Mass of thanksgiving was celebrated at Saint Mary's on November 7, 1781, following the Franco-American victory over British General Cornwallis at Yorktown. The audience included most of Congress, the Supreme Executive Council, and the Pennsylvania Assembly. It is safe to say that during Philadelphia's brief decades of cultural and political preeminence in the late eighteenth and early nineteenth centuries, Saint Mary's was one of the largest and most influential Catholic churches in the United States.

By 1808 the See of Philadelphia had been carved out of the first American diocese at Baltimore. Father Michael Egan, a Franciscan priest serving at Saint Mary's, became bishop-elect. Since Saint Mary's would become the first Philadelphia cathedral (1810–1838), expansion resulted. These changes were significant. A new façade was applied to the Fourth Street end of the original church, and eventually the interior was reversed, placing the sanctuary and high altar at the west end of the church as it is today. During the 1880s the interior took on the same Victorian richness found at Old Saint Joseph's and Saint Augustine's (see page 55).

Gradually the forces that marked the decline of all sacred places near the Delaware River took their toll on Old Saint Mary's. As population centers moved west, the newly constructed Saint John the Evangelist (pages 136–139) became the pro-cathedral, to be replaced in turn by the permanent Cathedral of Saints Peter and Paul (pages 152–157). Efforts to modernize the interior of Old Saint Mary's in the post-Vatican II era resulted in the destruction of many nineteenth-century embellishments. Nonetheless, the importance of Saint Mary's Church in the early years of our nation's formation should not be overlooked.

⌐➾ *The memorial plaque to Commodore John Barry on the Fourth Street façade of Old Saint Mary's was unveiled on June 14, 1913, by Franklin D. Roosevelt, then assistant secretary of the navy.*

SAINT PETER'S CHURCH

313 Pine Street
Philadelphia, PA 19106

Robert Smith, master builder,
1758–1761; William Strickland,
architect, tower and spire, 1842

Telephone for visitor information:
215.925.5968

www.stpetersphila.org

Visitors to Philadelphia's historic Society Hill are often startled to find adjoining pre-Revolutionary churches set amid large, evocative, tree-shaded church yards filled with memorials inscribed with names famous in early American history. That both Old Pine Street Presbyterian Church (pages 66–69) and Saint Peter's Episcopal Church were designed and erected by Philadelphia's leading colonial master builder makes them all the more interesting.

In the mid-eighteenth century, Christ Church on Second Street above High (Market) Street remained Philadelphia's lone Anglican church. The Quaker grip on the political and economic life of the city had loosened in the face of Anglican and

⌖ The chancel, raised above the marble floor and set off by an altar rail, is on axis with the central aisle and the east wall Palladian window, which is covered by the organ case. In the chancel is a Georgian communion table, a cathedra (bishop's chair), and a baptismal font. The cathedra is thought to be the earliest example in the United States, presented by John Swanwick in 1787; the font is also believed to have been presented by Swanwick in 1796.

⌖⌖ In 1842 Philadelphia architect William Strickland added the tall tower and steeple to the west end of Robert Smith's Middle Georgian style St. Peter's Church (1758–1761). The tower holds a chime of eight bells cast in London and given by Benjamin Chew Wilcocks. The evocative churchyard, surrounded by a high brick wall erected in 1784, extends along Pine Street from Third to Fourth Streets. Here rest artist Charles Willson Peale, banker Nicholas Biddle, and Commodore Stephen Decatur, together with seven Indian chiefs and a vice president of the United States, George Mifflin Dallas.

Presbyterian immigration. William Penn's heirs had returned to the Anglican fold, and non-Quaker leaders such as Pennsylvania Chief Justice Benjamin Chew and Philadelphia Mayor Samuel Powel had risen to prominence. In addition, Third Street south of Walnut was becoming the most fashionable address in the city. (On the eve of the Revolution, the Willings, Powels, and Governor John Penn lived side by side on Third Street and would later be joined by Benjamin Chew and the even wealthier merchant banker William Bingham—all of whom would attend Saint Peter's church.) This increase in population and southern drift by parishioners caused the Rev. Dr. Jenney of Christ Church to complain, "many Persons are obliged to stay at home and neglect divine Service, or go into dissenting Meetings" for lack of available pews. (The idea of losing congregants to the Presbyterians or Methodists was not to be countenanced!) Consequently, a group of "Gentlemen from the south end" petitioned the Christ Church vestry to permit them to approach the proprietaries for a lot of ground on Third Street between Pine and Lombard Streets on which to erect a "chapel of ease." Thomas and Richard Penn gave land at Third and Pine, and in subsequent years additional lots were purchased to provide a commodious graveyard.

To erect the new church the vestry turned to master builder Robert Smith (1722–1777), well known to them from his design and construction of the Christ Church steeple. Born in Lugton near Dalkeith, Scotland, Smith had arrived in Philadelphia circa 1748 already versed in the art and mystery of architecture and ready to seize opportunity in the burgeoning city. He rapidly became the leading master builder/architect in pre-Revolutionary America. These were prosperous years, especially after the defeat of France in the French and Indian War. Smith and his colleagues of the Carpenters' Company would embellish Philadelphia with notable villas and country houses—Bush Hill, Belmont, Mount Pleasant, Port Royal, and Cliveden—as well as civic structures and a remarkable number of outstanding Georgian churches. Saint Peter's was Smith's first opportunity in Philadelphia to design and erect an entire church.

Saint Peter's today survives largely as it appeared during Smith's lifetime. The building contract specified a rectangular structure 60' x 90', built of brick with "Rustick Work on each Corner of the said Building" (quoins). On the east end there was to be "One large Venetian Window neatly finished" and on the west end a "Cupola Erected and Compleatly finished . . . Ten feet Diameter and at least thirty two feet high." This cupola would be removed in 1842, when William Strickland designed the present tower and spire to contain a chime of eight bells that had been donated to the church. Smith's contract also called for "five large Urns properly placed & fixed at the Corners & tops of one Pedement at the Ends of the sd Building." These elegant Middle Georgian embellishments found in Philadelphia at Christ

From the pulpit on the west wall looking toward the chancel on the east wall, the central focus is the organ case that originally stood in the north gallery. In 1789 it was moved to its present location, which overwhelms the chancel and covers the Palladian window. The carved wood figures were commissioned in 1812 from the American sculptor William Rush (1756–1833) to adorn the organ case at nearby St. Paul's Church (page 11). The figures— representing "Praise," "Exhortation," and "Cherubim Encircled by a Glory"—were given to Saint Peter's in 1831 when alterations at Saint Paul's forced their removal.

Church, the Pennsylvania State House, Zion Lutheran Church, Cliveden, and the Duché House were never installed at Saint Peter's, probably to reduce costs.

The interior is a simple three-aisle plan with a wide central aisle and two lesser side aisles on an east-west axis. There are galleries on the north and south walls running parallel with the aisles. Originally the east (chancel) end had been dominated by the Palladian window in the manner of Christ Church. In the late eighteenth century, however, the organ was relocated from the north gallery and placed over the chancel, blocking the Palladian window. Church historians maintain this awkward arrangement resulted from complaints from pew holders seated near the organ, but there may be a more practical explanation: moving the organ permitted a modest expansion of marketable pews. The carved embellishments of the organ case are by America's first sculptor, William Rush; they were installed in 1831. The chancel is a platform raised one step above the marble floor set off by a turned baluster communion rail.

At the west end is Smith's ("wine glass") reading desk and pulpit, built in 1763–1764 and probably based on an English pattern book by Batty Langley which Smith is known to have owned. This is an extraordinary intact survival. Originally the window lights were clear glass, but gradually, over the second half of the nineteenth century, they were replaced by stained-glass memorials. Most of the stained-glass windows were removed as part of the renovations relating to the Bicentennial of American Independence.

An architectural treasure of Saint Peter's is the combination reading desk and pulpit (1763–1764) designed by Robert Smith and based on Batty Langley's City and Country Builder's and Workman's Treasury of Designs *(London, 1740), which Smith is known to have owned in 1751. Its unusual placement on the west wall, directly opposite the chancel on the east wall, requires the congregation to turn during services. Several explanations for this arrangement have been advanced; the true reason is lost to history.*

OLD PINE STREET PRESBYTERIAN CHURCH

*(Third, Scots, and Mariners
Presbyterian Church)*

*412 Pine Street
Philadelphia, PA 19106*

*Robert Smith, architect, 1768;
John Fraser, architect, 1857*

*Telephone for visitor information:
215.925.8051*

www.oldpine.org

Old Pine is the only Presbyterian church in Philadelphia still housed in its pre-Revolutionary building. It has survived the ebb and flow of Society Hill for nearly 250 years, according to one plain-spoken minister, because the church "refused to adopt the easy and popular solution of moving . . . to a new neighborhood every time it required courage and backbone to hold the fort." Like congregations of all faiths determined to preserve their historic buildings, Old Pine has survived by periodically reinventing itself.

Just as increases in the Anglican congregation of Christ Church on Second Street above High (Market) Street had prompted the erection of Saint Peter's (pages 60–65), so First Presbyterian Church—then housed on High Street—recognized its "Congregation is daily increasing," making it difficult to "Accommodate the members of our Society with Pews in our Church." They consequently applied to the proprietors Thomas and Richard Penn for a lot of ground on Society Hill "in the South part of the Town, on which we might build a new Church." The lot they received at Fourth and Pine Streets put them across from the churchyard of Saint Peter's, the new Anglican "chapel of ease."

As architect the Presbyterians selected Scottish-born Robert Smith (1722–1777), one of the leading builders of Philadelphia. He had already erected the Second Presbyterian Church at Third and Arch Streets (1749/50, demolished), and he had embellished Society Hill with Saint Peter's Church at Third and Pine and Saint Paul's Church on South Third Street (pages 10–11). Not surprisingly, the new "Presbyterian meeting house" that opened for services in May 1768 was similar to the Second Presbyterian Church: a 60' x 80' brick "preaching box" aligned north

The earliest known image of Old Pine Street Presbyterian Church shows it essentially as designed by the colonial master builder Robert Smith, but after alterations to the east elevation that provided two pedimented doors in place of a single entrance. John Welwood Scott, An Historical Sketch of Pine Street, or Third Presbyterian Church *(1837). Presbyterian Historical Society.*

and south (as opposed to the typical east and west Anglo-Catholic orientation) with entrances on both ends below Palladian windows. The tympana of the pedimented gables were ventilated with bull's-eye windows. A secondary entrance was provided on the ground level of the east elevation, flanked on either side by pairs of windows. At the upper level there were five symmetrically spaced, round-headed windows. The west elevation remained blank, save for a single window behind the pulpit. Whether the specified galleries were constructed in the 1760s is unknown; if so, they did not survive the Revolution and had to be reconstructed after the war, when the

John Fraser's Greek Revival portico dating from 1857 extended the Pine Street façade of the colonial church to the sidewalk. The roof was also raised and the brick walls stuccoed.

The sanctuary dates from John Fraser's Greek Revival expansion of 1857. This space was redecorated in the 1980s in an effort to recapture some of the rich coloration of the Victorian redecoration in the 1860s and 1880s. See page 298.

east elevation door was replaced by two pedimented doors shown in the earliest known view of the building dating from 1837.

In 1771 George Duffield became pastor of Old Pine. A fervent advocate of Independence, Duffield made his ardent patriotism known from the pulpit, and when open warfare erupted, he joined the American cause together with a large number of his parishioners. He was appointed Chaplain of the Pennsylvania Militia and served throughout the war. Duffield's views remind us that the colonial Scotch-Irish had little love for the English. Joseph Galloway, the Philadelphia Tory, remarked that the Revolution was led by "Congregationalists, Presbyterians and Smugglers," while one Hessian denounced the war as "nothing more or less than an Irish-Scotch Presbyterian rebellion."

It is perhaps not surprising that the occupying British expressed anti-Presbyterian views by seizing Old Pine during their occupation of the city during the winter of 1777–1778. Old Pine first became a hospital for British and Hessian troops wounded in the Battles of the Brandywine and Germantown. (Hessians who died of their wounds or disease were buried in an unmarked common grave in the churchyard; see page vi). To keep patients warm, the pews and pulpit—and, possibly, the galleries—were burned for firewood. When all the available interior woodwork had been consumed, the building shell was turned into a stable.

Renovated and redecorated after the Revolution, the interior of Old Pine was horizontally bisected to create two levels in 1837. A new sanctuary (assembly room) was created on the upper level and the south wall was extended to permit the pulpit to be moved from the west wall. Two decades later, in 1857, the church hired the Scottish émigré architect John Fraser (1825–1906) to cloak Smith's Middle Georgian colonial building in fashionable Greek Revival dress, which included stuccoing the brickwork, raising the roof, and adding a portico of Corinthian columns to the north façade, which extended the church out to the sidewalk on Pine Street. During the Victorian period the interior was stenciled and decoratively painted in 1868 and again in 1886, when many of the stained-glass windows were also installed.

Victorian decorations—no matter how grand—could not halt the inexorable westward shuffle of Presbyterians, Episcopalians, Lutherans, Methodists, Baptists, Jews, and Catholics—all abandoning their historic sacred places. By the 1950s membership at Old Pine had fallen to fewer than sixty souls who were unable to maintain the church building or the surrounding churchyard. However, the establishment of Independence National Historical Park and massive postwar urban renewal sparked a residential renaissance in Society Hill. Old Pine found itself strategically located to benefit from the return of Philadelphians to the urban core. The Friends of Old Pine was organized in 1951 to restore the church and expand its usefulness to the community. In 1953 Old Pine (Third Presbyterian) merged with the Hollond-Scots Presbyterian Church, thereby becoming the "Third and Scots Presbyterian Church," with a membership of 130; in 1959 it merged with the Mariners' Presbyterian Church becoming the "Third, Scots, & Mariners Presbyterian Church." These mergers provided funds for the acquisition of adjoining real estate, on which was constructed the Presbyterian Historical Society and a community center (1977), which made Old Pine a focus of Presbyterianism. The church also reached out to the community by providing preschool day care, hosting meetings of civic groups, and sponsoring chamber music concerts.

KESHER ISRAEL SYNAGOGUE

(formerly First Independent Church of Christ; First Universalist Church)

412–418 Lombard Street
Philadelphia, PA 19147

Master builder unknown, 1793–1795; J. Franklin Stuckert, major addition, 1895; Martin Jay Rosenblum and Associates, restoration architect

Telephone for visitor information: 215.922.7736

Kesher Israel Synagogue began as a modest brick meeting house erected in 1793 for the first Independent Church of Christ, a sect commonly called the Universalists. The terrible yellow fever epidemic that year—in which an estimated 10 percent of Philadelphians died—delayed progress on the building. Laid in Flemish bond, the original church extended 80 feet along Lombard Street and 50 feet in depth. It probably differed little from the late colonial meeting houses erected for nonconforming congregations all across the city. There were originally five arched openings along the flank elevation where now there are four windows filled with stained glass. A passageway led from Lombard Street to a graveyard in the rear. According to a later pastor, "when the house was first occupied for worship, the walls were without plastering and the only seats, plain benches. I was told that the first pulpit was a rough platform made by a mast maker and a shoemaker." It was to this simple church that Joseph Priestley (1733–1804) came in 1796, when he was not permitted to preach the Unitarian creed elsewhere and a Unitarian Church in America had not yet been founded (see pages 200–205). Priestley's lectures inspired a small group of largely English-born merchants to organize as the "Society of Unitarian Christians," the first church in the United States to take that name.

In the mid-nineteenth century there were several building campaigns to embellish and expand the church, although the author of a newspaper account in 1872 remarked, "grandeur has not been attempted in [the church's] appearance, but it is a very neat and church-like building. With its heavy stone cross over the entrance door, it might reasonably be mistaken for a Catholic Chapel."

In the 1880s the First Universalist Church gave up the struggle to maintain an independent church and disbanded, selling the building to a Russian Jewish congregation that became Kesher Israel Synagogue in 1890. As a precondition of the sale, the bodies were removed from the burial ground and reinterred at Fernwood Cemetery; the "heavy stone cross" was taken down and used to mark the new grave site.

Shortly after acquiring the building, Kesher Israel engaged the architectural services of John Franklin Stuckert (c. 1850–1931), who had studied at the Franklin Institute Drawing School and began his practice in 1871. Over the course of a long career he appears to have specialized in smaller projects for churches and synagogues. His son F. Russell Stuckert (fl. 1890–1930) joined him about the time of the Kesher Israel job, and they both may have worked on the synagogue. Stuckert created a new Roman brick pavilion on the east end of the building, with a vestibule and stair hall. This pavilion is topped by a minaret with a Star of David.

Stuckert's renovations to the main sanctuary consisted of conversion of the tabernacle frame to an *aron kodesh* (the holy ark holding the Torah scrolls) by insert-

Kesher Israel Synagogue began as a simple meeting house erected for the First Independent Church of Christ in 1793. Acquired in 1890 by a congregation of Russian Jews, it was extensively expanded by architect J. Franklin Stuckert in 1895.

ing a compartment between the pilasters. In the center of the auditorium a *bimah* (an elevated platform—traditionally in the center of the synagogue—where the Torah is read) with a railing was erected, and around the east end a curving women's gallery was added. In the 1950s the sanctuary received murals painted by Morris Balk depicting the Exile in Babylon, the Return to Judah, and the Second Temple.

After a period of decline in the 1970s and 1980s, Kesher Israel has enjoyed a renaissance. An extensive campaign of restoration and conservation was completed in 1998.

☞   *The large tabernacle frame on the west wall dates from renovations in the 1830s. It now incorporates the* aron kodesh *or ark to hold Torah scrolls. Murals by Morris Balk dating from the 1950s flank the ark. This view of the sanctuary looks down from the women's gallery added by Stuckert onto the elevated* bimah *where the Torah is read.*

(formerly Spruce Street Baptist Church)

*418 Spruce Street
Philadelphia, PA 19106*

Thomas Ustick Walter, architect, 1829, façade 1851; James O. Kruhly, architect, south extension, 1985

Telephone for visitor information: 215.922.6590

Thomas Ustick Walter (1804–1887) is one of the most important American architects of the nineteenth century. Born in Philadelphia, the son of a bricklayer, he worked in the office of William Strickland, attended lectures by John Haviland, and learned watercolor techniques from the landscape artist William Mason—what Walter called a "liberal but not collegiate" education. He also served an apprenticeship with his father and by 1831 had begun actively to practice architecture. He first gained local attention with his Gothic style Moyamensing Prison (1831–1835) and then national recognition for his monumental neoclassical Girard College (1833–1848). Hundreds of commissions both at home and abroad followed, leading to his successful competition entry for the wings and dome of the Capitol of the United

☞ *Reproduced here is Walter's original 1851 drawing for a new façade for his own Spruce Street Baptist Church, which now houses the Society Hill Synagogue. Philadelphia Contributionship for Insuring Houses from Loss by Fire.*

States in Washington, where he was engaged throughout the 1850s and early 1860s. In 1865 he returned to Philadelphia and late in life worked for John McArthur, Jr., on City Hall.

The Walters were Baptists. While young Thomas worked with his father as a bricklayer in 1829, a schism in the First Baptist Church caused the conservative members—including the Walters—to establish a new congregation, ultimately to be known as the Spruce Street Baptist Church of Philadelphia. Walter provided drawings for the new meeting house with an appropriately unadorned "preaching

The tripartite elevation of the Society Hill Synagogue was designed by Thomas Ustick Walter in 1851 for the original Spruce Street Baptist congregation. The building became a synagogue in 1911. The Yiddish inscription above the massive entrance doors reads: "the Great Roumanian Shul."

box" auditorium, baptistry, and simple pulpit. Walter did not supervise the construction and one day after attending services there he confided to his diary, "I hate the pulpit in Spruce St. worse and worse. Mr. O'Neill [the carpenter] thought he knew more than anybody else and reduced the size of the columns; [I'd] almost as soon have my legs reduced. How dreadful to have a Carpenter, or Bricklayer obtruding his opinion." Walter's frustration prompted him to design a new pulpit and, on the drawing preserved at the Athenæum, he noted, "Had this pulpit made, and finished complete and presented it to the Spruce St. Bap. Church, May 1836." Several years later, in 1851, just before departing for Washington, Walter designed a grand façade for his church with twin towers. It rises from a rusticated ground floor with small entrances at the base of each tower and a large central entrance elevated to the auditorium level reached by two runs of stairs. The upper walls are stuccoed and scored to resemble cut stone (ashlar). Today the building appears truncated because the tops of Walter's towers have been removed.

By the early twentieth century, Society Hill had become an immigrant Jewish neighborhood and members of the Baptist congregation began edging west. The building was finally abandoned in 1908 in favor of a new location at Fiftieth and Spruce Streets, and in 1911 the Congregation Beth Hamedresh Hagodal acquired the property. This demographic shift is important in late nineteenth- and early twentieth-century Philadelphia history, and it influenced many sacred places in the River Wards. Until 1880 most Philadelphia Jews were of German or western European origin, few of whom lived in Society Hill. However, pogroms in Russia after the assassination of Alexander II in 1881 encouraged young Russian Jews and other eastern European nationalities to pack up their families and flee to America. Unlike the descendants of Philadelphia's colonial era Jews and the more recent Germans, these new immigrants settled around the eastern end of South Street, gradually creating a "Jewish quarter" that ultimately spread westward as far as Eighth Street, north to Spruce Street, and south to Christian Street. This became the Philadelphia de facto ghetto. As a consequence, the number of synagogues created in what is now known as Society Hill rapidly increased. With the exception of the Society Hill Synagogue and Kesher Israel (pages 70–73), most of these date from the turn of the twentieth century. Of these later synagogues—which once numbered nearly two dozen—B'nai Abraham Synagogue on Lombard Street (1910) is a rare survival. It houses the first Orthodox congregation in the neighborhood, founded in 1882 for Russian Jews.

The first Jewish congregation to own and occupy the former Spruce Street Baptist Church soon failed and was replaced in 1916 by the Roumanian American Congregation, which held the building until the 1960s when membership began to decline as the children of immigrants moved to the suburbs. The property was deed-

ed to a new congregation formed by a union of the Roumanian American Synagogue and the Hungarian American Synagogue, which took the name Society Hill Synagogue in 1967. Throughout the 1970s and 1980s the present Conservative congregation has raised funds to restore and expand the monumental building. In 1985 Philadelphia architect James O. Kruhly designed a successful back building to provide offices for the rabbi and cantor and to accommodate other support services.

Recent renovations of the main auditorium respect the simplicity of Walter's original design and focus attention on the aron kodesh, *or holy ark, which contains the Torah scrolls.*

OLD FIRST REFORMED CHURCH

Fourth and Race Streets
Philadelphia, PA 19106

Andrew D. Caldwell, builder, 1837

Telephone for visitor information:
215.922.4566

www.oldfirstucc.org

Old First Reformed Church may be the most peripatetic congregation in the history of Philadelphia. Like many colonial churches, it kept moving west, abandoning one building after another in a futile effort to keep pace with its migrating members. But ultimately it would find comfort by returning to its roots in Old City near the banks of the Delaware River.

On September 21, 1727, the sloop *William & Sarah* arrived at Philadelphia with four hundred immigrants from the Palatinate—a German language area on the French border—in the care of the Rev. Mr. George Michael Weiss. These were not the first nor would they be the last such band attracted by Pennsylvania's environment of religious toleration. Ultimately Germans would constitute the largest white, non-British group in the United States—and a third of Pennsylvania's population. (Because of a 1934 merger of the Evangelical and Reformed Churches and a later merger of that group in 1957 with the Congregational Christian Churches, the congregation is now part of the United Church of Christ.)

Weiss's flock first erected a brick church in the shape of a hexagon with hipped roof and lantern. This was replaced by an elegant two-story Middle Georgian church—65' x 95', fronting directly on what is now Race Street—designed by master builder William Colladay (1738–1823). When this colonial building in turn proved inadequate, a three-story church set back 45 feet from Race Street was commissioned from the builder Andrew D. Caldwell in 1837. All three churches were erected on the same ground at Fourth and Race streets in response to a growing congregation.

When the neighborhood began to deteriorate, the church followed its congregation west, moving first to Tenth and Wallace Streets (1882) and then to Fiftieth and Locust Streets (1917). By the 1960s the church leaders reported, "our neighborhood is rapidly changing from the original ethnic tradition, greatly limiting our present ministry." The church building was sold to an African American Baptist congregation and the original Fourth and Race site was purchased from the Philadelphia Redevelopment Authority.

The building the congregation abandoned in 1882 and reclaimed in 1967 had been in the hands of the Lucas Paint Company. This firm, founded in 1849 by John Lucas (1823–1901) at Front and Arch Streets, manufactured paint and varnish in Gibbsboro, New Jersey. New structures to accommodate the company's Philadelphia business offices were erected in front of the former church and the sanctuary was converted into a distribution warehouse. Mr. Lucas seems to have respected the original uses of the building; he protected the altar surround with partitions and, as the Sesquicentennial of the Revolution approached, the company proudly referred to the historical character of its headquarters site.

☞ *The present Old First Reformed Church building dates from 1837. It replaces a two-story Middle Georgian building erected in 1772, which greatly influenced the design. Andrew D. Caldwell, the builder, lived nearby on Front Street.*

The restored building has been returned essentially to its 1837 appearance. Master builder Caldwell seems to have followed the pattern of Colloday's Middle Georgian church of 1772 and may have reused the bricks and other elements of the colonial church, unfortunately omitting the Venetian window that dominated the north façade of the earlier structure. The similarity of the two buildings has caused them to be conflated by those who are unaware that a later building replaced the colonial one. To add to the confusion, Robert Smith, builder of St. Peter's, Old Pine, and the steeple of Christ Church, has often been credited with the 1772 church building, an attribution finally laid to rest by recent research.

As at Old Pine, the British occupied First Reformed Church during the winter of 1777–1778 as a hospital, and they imprisoned the minister (Caspar Weyberg) for his rebellious support of the Revolution.

Today the congregation operates a wide range of outreach programs for the community to aid the homeless and provide summer day camp and youth hostel facilities. For many years the Old First Christmas crèche with live animals has been a popular part of the congregation's seasonal celebrations.

⤳ *While the church was used as a warehouse by the Lucas Paint Company (1882–1967), the sanctuary was divided into two floors for storage of paint and varnish. During the restoration, the original altar surround was discovered behind partitions. See also page i.*

OLD SAINT GEORGE'S CHURCH

235 N. Fourth Street
Philadelphia, PA 19106

Robert Smith (?), master builder,
1763–1769

Telephone for visitor information:
215.925.7788

www.gophila.com/culturefiles/
sacredplaces/stgeorges

☞ *America's oldest Methodist church in continuous service, Saint George's dates from 1763. It was nearly destroyed in the 1920s to make way for the Delaware River (Benjamin Franklin) Bridge. To pass under the new bridge, Fourth Street had to be lowered, forcing the construction of the retaining wall shown here.*

Few sacred places are more meaningful to Methodists than Old Saint George's, the "oldest continuously used Methodist church building in America," or, as it is often called, "the Cradle of American Methodism." The church building itself started inauspiciously. Commissioned in 1763 by a group of German Calvinists, this large structure (53' x 82') bankrupted the congregation before it could be completed. It may have been designed by the Scottish-born master builder Robert Smith (1722–1777), who is responsible for Saint Paul's (pages 10–11), Saint Peter's (pages 60–65), and the steeple of Christ Church (pages 40–45)—but this speculative attribution is based solely on a similarity of roof truss design. No other documentation is known to survive. Regardless who designed the building, it ultimately passed to the Methodists, who retained the name it had already been given, Saint George's Church.

The first "class" of Philadelphia Methodists had been organized by Thomas Webb in 1767. This colorful former British army officer—he wore a green eye patch, preached in his regimentals, and often laid his sword across the pulpit Bible for dramatic emphasis—had been converted by John Wesley and licensed as a lay preacher. He proved to be a natural orator; John Adams called him "one of the most fluent men I have ever heard." By the time Joseph Pilmoor (1739–1825) arrived from England to take charge of the Methodist society, there was already a need for larger quarters. Saint George's was purchased for £650 in 1769.

In 1771 Francis Asbury—destined to be known as "the father of American Methodism"—arrived from England. He preached his first American sermon at Saint George's (October 29, 1771) and over a career spanning forty-five years of itinerant preaching would travel 270,000 miles and deliver 16,900 sermons. He personally ordained more than 4,000 preachers. In 1784, when the Methodist Church was organized, Asbury would become the first American bishop. It is also significant that in the same year Richard Allen, a former slave who had purchased his freedom, received a license to preach from Saint George's, the first African American Methodist to be so licensed in America. He organized Bethel Church (pages 112–115) and in 1816 became the first bishop of the African Methodist Episcopal Church.

Of course, all this was still in the future when Asbury arrived in Philadelphia on the eve of the American Revolution. Following the Battle of the Brandywine, Washington's defeated army fell back across the Schuylkill River, leaving Philadelphia to be occupied by General Howe's legions on September 26, 1777. During the winter of 1777–1778, with the Americans uncomfortably encamped at Valley Forge, the British hibernated in the city—and their cavalry occupied Saint George's. With its unfinished dirt floor, the church made a perfect indoor riding academy.

Early Methodist churches are typically meeting house plain, and apparently

Saint George's suffered little from its rude treatment by the occupying army. Interior renovations after the Revolution included floors and pews, plus the addition of galleries in 1792. Like most colonial churches in Philadelphia, the main sanctuary of Saint George's was two stories high with a gable roof and no basement. To expand the building in 1804 a basement was excavated to provide classrooms, and additional excavation in 1836 created the present ground level assembly room. (By 1836 Saint George's had a membership of nearly 3,000.) Unfortunately a fire on August 12,

The sanctuary, designed to seat 1,000 worshipers, is appropriately chaste. The spiral stair
pulpit is a replica of the original said to have been used by Francis Asbury when preaching his first
sermon in America, October 29, 1771.

1865, burned off the roof and did extensive damage to the interior, requiring fairly extensive redecoration.

Saint George's, like Saint John's and Saint Augustine's (pages 86–90), fell in the path of the Delaware River (Benjamin Franklin) Bridge and was scheduled to be acquired by eminent domain and demolished in the early 1920s. Already recognized for its role in the earliest days of American Methodism, Saint George's was able to bring suit and force the bridge to be moved fourteen feet to the south, although the rush of traffic between Camden and Philadelphia is uncomfortably close to the church building.

Connected to the church is a museum of American Methodism containing memorabilia such as the chalice sent to America by John Wesley and the Francis Asbury Bible. There is also a research library on Methodism that may be consulted upon application.

The basement story was excavated to provide class meeting rooms wherein were installed these semicircular benches.

SAINT AUGUSTINE'S CHURCH

*Fourth Street, south of Vine Street
Philadelphia, PA 19106*

*Napoleon LeBrun, architect, 1847–
1848; Edwin F. Durang, architect,
steeple, 1867*

*Telephone for visitor information:
215.627.1838*

In 1790 there were only 35,000 Catholics in the United States—out of a total American population of nearly 4,000,000—located mainly in Maryland and Pennsylvania, all organized into one diocese headed by Bishop John Carroll in Baltimore. In Philadelphia the rapidly expanding Catholic population was served by Saint Joseph's (pages 50–53), Saint Mary's (pages 54–59), and Holy Trinity (pages 116–119). Then, in 1796, the Irish-born Augustinian friar Matthew Carr (1755–1820) arrived in the city to assume his priestly duties at Saint Mary's Church. Within a few weeks he published a handbill addressed "To the Inhabitants of Philadelphia" calling for the establishment of a new Roman Catholic church in the Northern Liberties. The gratifying response to this appeal included gifts from President George Washington, Commodore John Barry, and financier Stephen Girard. With these resources Father Carr purchased land on north Fourth Street between Vine and Sassafras (Race) Streets and laid the cornerstone of what would become the first Saint Augustine's Church. By 1804 the new parish had been incorporated as the "Brothers of the Order of Hermits of Saint Augustine," but construction of the new church designed

☛ *The first Saint Augustine's Church
(1796–1844). Lithograph by C. G. Childs
(1830). American Catholic Historical
Society Collection.*

☛-☛ *The main façade of Saint
Augustine's Church by Napoleon LeBrun
with Edwin F. Durang's recently recreated steeple. When Fourth Street was
lowered in the 1920s, the pedimented
front door of the church was lowered
and stairs added to the vestibule in the
tower.*

On either side of the sanctuary and high altar are paintings by Filippo Costaggini of Saint Joseph, patron of the Augustinian Order, and Our Mother of Consolation, both signed and dated 1882. The white marble statues, Saint Augustine (left) and Saint Monica (right), both date from the early twentieth century.

by Nicholas Fagan moved slowly. The galleries were not finished until 1824, and William Strickland added a belfry in 1829.

Father Carr's church succumbed to the deadly riots of May 1844, when an American nativist anti-Irish mob, incited to violence by working-class fears of largely Catholic immigrants, burned the building to the ground. To quell the rioting, the governor of Pennsylvania ultimately called out troops supported by the crew of the U.S.S. *Princeton*. As historian Sam Bass Warner has pointed out, the 1844 riots ultimately brought about consolidation of Philadelphia County's crazy quilt of twenty-nine legal jurisdictions, the emergence of a professional metropolitan police force able to control riots, and a reaffirmation of Catholic rights to equal protection of the law.

But for the moment Saint Augustine's parish was left with smoldering ashes and charred brick rubble where once had stood a hard-won church, pastoral residence, and library. (A lawsuit against Philadelphia County for failure to protect the church

ultimately led to a court-ordered settlement for approximately half the estimated loss.) To replace Saint Augustine's Church the parish turned to Napoleon LeBrun, who had already designed a church for the Saint Philip Neri parish in Southwark, which only narrowly escaped destruction by fire at the hands of another nativist antipapal mob (pages 98–101). The cornerstone was laid on May 23, 1847, and the new building was consecrated on November 5, 1848.

The simplicity of LeBrun's design is probably a response to the limited budget. He extended and reused the original foundations for a brick auditorium box relieved only by unadorned recesses flanking a projecting tower with stone quoins, the entire composition capped by a modillion cornice. LeBrun had also proposed a steeple, which was not constructed until 1867. For this project the parish turned to architect Edwin F. Durang (1825–1911), who extended the brick tower and added a steeple in a Georgian Revival mode of diminishing stages from square to octagon to circle with clock faces. While not following LeBrun's design exactly, Durang

The high altar of carved white marble and Mexican onyx dates from the 1920s. Fortunately it escaped the misinterpretation of Vatican II that led to the destruction of so many altars. The large Crucifixion was painted by Hans P. Hansen in 1926.

respected his elder's intent, which may also reflect the desire of the Augustinian friars for a style that conformed with familiar Philadelphia Protestant Georgian architecture.

The Delaware River (Benjamin Franklin) Bridge (constructed in 1920–1926) threatened three churches: Saint John's Evangelical Lutheran (1808–1809), Saint George's Methodist (pages 82–85), and Saint Augustine's. Saint John's was demolished and salvaged elements reconstructed at Sixty-First Street and Columbia Avenue, while the others were saved. The level of Fourth Street had to be depressed to pass under the new bridge, forcing the Methodists to add a retaining wall and a flight of steep new steps. The Catholics lowered the pedimented entrance of Saint Augustine's to the revised street level. To compensate for the grade change they created a new rise of steps in the vestibule of the tower (the ghost of the original doorway location can be seen in the brickwork).

Durang's steeple proved to be no more resistant to weather and decay than its colonial predecessors in Society Hill. Despite efforts to reinforce the structure and seal out water, a December storm in 1992 began pulling it apart, forcing its removal. The restored steeple—recreated in aluminum rather than wood and copper—was lifted into place in 1995.

We know little of LeBrun's interior beyond one description:

> The interior is arranged in the usual manner of modern churches; the sanctuary, however, is novel in design and arrangement. It is much admired. The columns supporting the dome over [the altar] are of Scagliola marble, the capitals of which, together with the entablature over them, are richly carved and gilded. The design of this beautiful feature of this church is copied from the much-admired remains of the Temple of Jupiter Olympus at Rome.

The large central panel of the ceiling and the two large paintings on the west wall of the sanctuary are by the Italian artist Filippo Costaggini, who also worked at Old Saint Joseph's church (pages 50–53) and at the United States Capitol after the death of Constantino Brumidi. The interior was substantially redecorated in the 1890s in preparation for the parish centennial celebration of 1896.

By the late twentieth century the Augustinian friars could see little future for their handsome church with its shrinking congregation. Then Saint Augustine's became the American shrine for Santo Niño de Cebu and center for the large Filipino community of the Delaware Valley. The Holy Child has great significance to Filipinos, and the statue in the Our Lady of Good Counsel shrine is representative of the one brought to the Philippines by Magellan in the sixteenth century and now in the care of Augustinians in the Philippines.

⚊ *To the right (north) of the sanctuary is the shrine of Our Lady of Good Counsel. Erected in 1891, most of the current decoration—marble, mosaic, painting—dates from 1911–1912. The shrine now contains a statue of the Santo Niño de Cebu.*

SAINT NICHOLAS CHURCH

(formerly Second Dutch Reformed Church)

817 North Seventh Street Philadelphia, PA 19123

Architect unknown (Stephen Decatur Button?), 1852–1853

Telephone for visitor information: 215.922.9671

In the mid-nineteenth century, there were two Dutch Reformed churches erected in the Northern Liberties of Philadelphia. The First Dutch Reformed Church (now demolished) stood at the corner of Spring Garden and Seventh Streets and was designed by Stephen Decatur Button (1813–1897) in what he called the "Roman Corinthian Style," with a giant order portico of six columns forty feet high and pilasters of a similar scale on the flank elevations between round-headed windows. That Button designed the building there can be little doubt; both his specifications and a handsome signed lithograph document the commission. Not far away, however, in the 800 block of Seventh Street, stands a nearly identical structure that once housed the Second Dutch Reformed Church. It, too, presents a handsome giant order portico of six columns, but these are in what Button would probably have called the "Roman *Ionic* Style," a subtle but important difference. For many years these two buildings have been confused, and consequently the Second Dutch Reformed Church has often been attributed without corroborating evidence to Button. For the time being, the building must remain without attribution.

In many ways the Second Dutch Reformed Church is a typical late classical structure, more Italianate than Greek or Roman Revival in style; it is a simple rectangular box, save for the portico of fluted columns in the Ionic order supporting an unadorned entablature and pediment. More like John Haviland's earlier work than Button's nearby First Reformed Dutch Church, the Second Reformed Dutch Church is elevated on a high platform reached by a dozen steps behind iron gates. Entrance to the vestibule was originally by three flat-headed doorways with lintels supported by scrolled brackets. (To accommodate a later reconfiguration of the vestibule, these doorways were replaced by a tall pedimented entrance.) The exterior stucco over masonry (rough cast) was originally scored with lines to simulate stone blocks (ashlar) and finished with paint onto which sand was blown to heighten the stone-like effect.

In the late nineteenth and earlier twentieth centuries, Eastern European immigrants began arriving in large numbers to join the Germans and Irish in the great workshop of mills and factories that Philadelphia had become. Largely Jewish or Orthodox Catholics, they settled into communities along the Delaware River, particularly in what are now called Society Hill, Queen Village, and the Spring Garden district. Hardworking, strongly faithful, lacking substantial resources to erect sacred places, yet wishing to gather to worship in their own languages, they often acquired churches being abandoned by English-speaking Protestant congregations moving west. Just as John Haviland's Saint Andrew's Episcopal Church would became a Greek Orthodox church in 1922—and, ultimately, the Greek Orthodox Cathedral of Saint George (pages 120–123)—so the Second Dutch Reformed con-

The pedimented main façade of Saint Nicholas Church features six giant order fluted columns with Ionic capitals. The building was originally commissioned by a Dutch Reformed congregation in the 1850s. It became an Orthodox church in 1917.

gregation sold their building in 1917. The Russian Orthodox Independent Congregation and Church of Saint Nicholas became the new owner. This congregation consisted of 782 families, and nearly 5,000 persons attended the dedication of the newly named Saint Nicholas Church. Prior to dedication, the modest Protestant interior of the Second Dutch Reformed Church had been modified to conform to the Orthodox liturgical service. The iconostasis replaced the pulpit, and iconographer George Novikoff began converting the interior into the richly decorated space seen today. He would work at the church over the following twenty-five years. To the visitor unfamiliar with the role of the icon in Orthodox worship, a visit to the church of Saint Nicholas is a rich visual feast.

The simple Protestant interior of the 1850s has been transformed over the several decades into a sanctuary embellished with rich Orthodox iconography. The stained-glass windows, designed by Matthias von Reutlinger, date from renovations in the 1970s.

SOUTH PHILADELPHIA

⇥ Samuel S. Fleisher Art Memorial. The sanctuary is lined with limestone statuary from Samuel S. Fleisher's collection. The Italian and Spanish marble pulpit was inspired by examples in southern Italian basilicas admired by Henry Robert Percival. The marble rood screen was manufactured in Paris and is based on one at Saint Mark's, Venice; the fourteenth-century crucifix is carved wood from Germany. The oak choir stalls have flip-up seats called misericords, which in medieval churches allowed monks to support themselves when required to stand for long periods. See pages 102–105.

SAINT PHILIP NERI ROMAN CATHOLIC CHURCH

218 Queen Street,
Philadelphia, PA 19147

Napoleon LeBrun, architect, 1840;
Frank R. Watson, architect, 1897–1899

Telephone for visitor information:
215.468.1922

Situated in the historic Southwark district of Philadelphia, Saint Philip Neri Roman Catholic Church is directly across Queen Street from Mario Lanza Park, surrounded by a lively neighborhood of renovated row houses and loft condominiums carved from low-rise commercial buildings. So peaceful is this residential setting today it is difficult to believe this modest church was for a brief time the focal point of vicious anti-Catholic rioting in 1844 resulting in more than fifty casualties.

The Roman Catholic population of Philadelphia, largely Irish and German at the time, grew rapidly in the decades prior to the Civil War, requiring that many new parishes be created. In 1840 there were five Roman Catholic churches in the city; by 1850 there were thirteen; and by 1865 there were thirty-three. Most of these were of modest scale, speedily and inexpensively erected of stuccoed brick, and without lavishly expensive interior embellishment. Saint Philip Neri Church is the best surviving example of these early efforts to relieve the burden on Saint Mary's and Saint Joseph's parishes in Society Hill (pages 50–59).

The new church took for its patron Philip Neri, a sixteenth-century Italian saint born in 1515 and ordained in 1551. Eventually he attracted a congregation of secular priests (without vows and devoted to popular preaching and education), which he named the Oratory. He died in 1595 as an apostle of Rome and was canonized by Pope Gregory XV in 1622.

To design the new Southwark church the parish turned to Napoleon LeBrun (1821–1901), son of French-born Catholic parishioners of Saint Mary's. Four years earlier he had entered the office of Thomas Ustick Walter (1804–1887) as an apprentice, there being no schools of architecture at that time. During this period Walter's expanding office was busy at work on Moyamensing Prison, Girard College, and Andalusia, among many other projects. By 1840 LeBrun—although not yet twenty—might have been ready to strike out on his own as an independent practitioner, or he might have designed the church while still in Walter's office. More likely, Walter laid him off due to the economic depression of the late 1830s and early 1840s. (Walter would declare bankruptcy in 1841.) Regardless, Saint Philip Neri is the first building we can definitely attribute to LeBrun. Subsequently, he would design churches for Presbyterians and Episcopalians as well as Roman Catholics. In 1847 he was called on to rebuild Saint Augustine's (pages 86–91) after an earlier structure had been burned during the same anti-Catholic riots that nearly destroyed his first church. Ultimately he was awarded the commission for the Cathedral of Saints Peter and Paul on Logan Square (pages 152–157). LeBrun's most important and widely known contribution to Philadelphia secular architecture is the Academy of Music (1855) on Broad Street.

By 1840 the need for a parish south of Spruce Street had been recognized, a lot secured, and LeBrun hired. The cornerstone was laid on July 31, 1840, and nine

🎺 *Main façade of Saint Philip Neri Roman Catholic Church in the Southwark district of Philadelphia, directly opposite Mario Lanza Park. It survives essentially as designed by Napoleon LeBrun in 1840.*

months later the new church—albeit not yet plastered—opened its doors for services. But storm clouds of hate loomed ominously.

In the 1830s and 1840s an anti-Irish and antipapal political movement took root in Philadelphia. Variously known as the Native-American Party, American Party, or Know-Nothing Party, it lobbied for repeal of naturalization laws and the banning of public office for non-natives. The most violent criticisms were reserved for Irish Catholics, who—it was popularly believed—wished to exclude the Bible from public schools. During anti-Catholic riots in 1844 Saint Michael's Church at Second and Jefferson Streets was destroyed, along with Saint Augustine's Church. Two months later the rioters descended on Saint Philip Neri Church with heavy arms and incendiary intent. The church was protected by units of Philadelphia militia, but the rioters attacked with artillery. By the time the smoke cleared, the casualties amounted to fifteen killed and forty-four wounded, but the embattled church building had been saved.

Saint Philip Neri Church was not so fortunate in October 1897, when a fire started in an adjoining livery stable. The roof and ceiling of the church burned, but the exterior "showed little damage," although "the interior was ruined" according to church records. To repair and redecorate the interior the parish engaged the prominent Roman Catholic architect Frank R. Watson (1859–1940), who had trained with the eminent Catholic church architect Edwin F. Durang. The new altars were consecrated on January 26, 1899. The interior today is essentially as installed by Watson, while the exterior is largely unchanged from LeBrun's 1840 design.

The upper sanctuary of Saint Philip Neri is largely the result of a post-fire redecoration by architect Frank R. Watson, 1897–1899.

SAMUEL S. FLEISHER ART MEMORIAL

(formerly Episcopal Church of the Evangelists)

709–721 Catharine Street
Philadelphia, PA 19147

Louis C. Baker, Jr., for Furness, Evans and Company, architects (alternatively, Charles M. Burns, architect, 1886)

Telephone for visitor information: 215.922.3456

Web site: www.fleisher.org

Finding appropriate uses for redundant or insolvent sacred places is not exclusively a twenty-first-century problem. For example, the Episcopal Church of the Evangelists had been established in the 1840s on Catharine Street between Seventh and Eighth Streets to minister to the poor. By 1880 the parish faced insolvency and planned to sell the building, an action headed off by a young clergyman, Henry Robert Percival (1854–1903), who asked for an opportunity to revive the parish. By 1885 he had attracted a following, paid off the debt, and pulled down the old church building to make way for something new.

What Dr. Percival had in mind was a church in the Italian basilica style, which he described as "Romanesque, much favored in Italy and Spain between the years 900 and 1400 and is the most ancient style of the Christian Church." To design his new building, Percival turned to the popular firm of Frank Furness and Edmund C. Evans. This architectural practice had grown so large by 1886 that they decided to bring into partnership some of the younger men in the office and adopt the name of Furness, Evans and Company. One of the new partners was a Princeton graduate and former draftsmen, Louis C. Baker, Jr. (1859–1915), who had joined Furness and Evans in 1880. It is Baker who actually executed the design and was specifically thanked by Percival at the dedication. (Recently a case has been made for Charles M. Burns, Jr., as architect, a discrepancy yet to be resolved.)

According to Percival's instructions, the new church was to have the relative proportions of the cathedral at Pisa, square pillars like those in Saint Mark's, Venice, and a square sanctuary as in the cathedral at Orvieto (see pages 96–97). The portal was inspired by the church of San Zeno Maggiore, Verona. What the architect thought of this romp through Baedeker is not of record.

Without the vitality and enthusiasm of Dr. Percival, who died in 1903, the parish once again failed and the building was sold in 1922 to Samuel S. Fleisher, who had established the Graphic Sketch Club in 1898. This club offered free art instruction to all comers and by 1915 had settled into the abandoned Saint Martin's College for Indigent Boys building to the west of Dr. Percival's basilica. By purchasing the former church and linking it to his school, Fleisher obtained an appropriate "sanctuary" to display his collection of ecclesiastical art. He rededicated the deconsecrated basilica "to the patrons of the busy streets of Philadelphia," whom he invited "to enter this Sanctuary for rest, meditation and prayer."

Just as Percival had embellished his church with works by artist Robert Henri, tile maker Henry Mercer, and stained-glass and mosaic artist Nicola D'Ascenzo, Fleisher commissioned iron gates from Samuel Yellin and an altarpiece from the muralist Violet Oakley (1874–1961). As a young woman, Oakley studied with Cecilia Beaux at the Pennsylvania Academy of the Fine Arts and Howard Pyle at the

☜ *The sanctuary porch of the Samuel S. Fleisher Art Memorial has marble columns supported by lumps of stone left rough to suggest lion sculptures weathered over the centuries. The gates were commissioned by Samuel S. Fleisher from the Polish-born Philadelphia master metalworker Samuel Yellin (1885–1940).*

Drexel Institute. In 1902 she was commissioned to paint thirteen murals in the Governor's Reception Room of the new Pennsylvania State Capitol in Harrisburg. Fleisher commissioned Oakley to create a massive backdrop for the high altar in the sanctuary—a reredos to replace the one removed when the Church of the Evangelists was deconsecrated—as a memorial to his mother. Intended as a work devoted to Moses, the central subject is actually Pharaoh's daughter holding the infant Moses.

Following Fleisher's death in 1944, the Graphic Sketch Club was renamed the Samuel S. Fleisher Art Memorial to be managed by the Philadelphia Museum of Art, with the Sanctuary to become an ecclesiastical museum. While many of the works of art collected by Fleisher have been moved to the Philadelphia Museum of Art, where they can be protected from extremes of temperature and humidity, much remains to justify a visit.

☞ *Violet Oakley's* Life of Moses *(oil on canvas in gilded wood frame, 18' x 7', 1929) was commissioned by Samuel S. Fleisher as a memorial to his mother.*

SHRINE OF SAINT RITA OF CASCIA

1166 South Broad Street
Philadelphia, PA 19146

George I. Lovatt, and Ballinger and Perrot, architects, 1907–1915

Telephone for visitor information:
215.546.8333

www.saintritashrine.org

The visitor intent on negotiating South Broad Street traffic could easily miss the Shrine of Saint Rita of Cascia. That would be attributable to the pace of twenty-first-century life, not to the vigorous Baroque styling of this much beloved church. It stands directly on the street, like its town house neighbors, and fully utilizes its mid-block site. Yet there can be few churches in Philadelphia so Roman in their ambiance and brilliance of execution. The exterior of Saint Rita's is all façade, a triumphal arch of light-colored brick, limestone, and terra cotta with a large pedimented entrance

The Baroque façade of the Shrine of Saint Rita of Cascia on South Broad Street is one of the finest compositions by the young architect George I. Lovatt in collaboration with the firm of Ballinger and Perrot.

The National Shrine of Saint Rita of Cascia with its reliquary in the lower church has recently been renovated and expanded to accommodate the large visitation of pilgrims from around the world who come to petition Saint Rita to intercede in their behalf.

supported by pairs of engaged Tuscan columns flanked by niches containing statues of Saint Augustine on the north and Saint Patrick on the south. The nave projects above the ground floor entablature with paired pilasters supporting a segmental pediment bracketed by two gigantic scrolls.

The church is named for Saint Rita of Cascia (1381–1457), known as the "Advocate of the Hopeless and even of the Impossible" and one of the most popular saints in the Roman Catholic Church "because of her amazing answers to prayer, as well as the remarkable events of her own life." Cascia is a small town near Spoleto in Umbria. Pope Leo XIII canonized this Augustinian nun in 1900, and the Augustinian Friars have established a shrine in her honor in the lower church.

Saint Rita's church and shrine were designed by George I. Lovatt (1872–1958), who ranks with Edwin F. Durang and Henry Dagit among Philadelphia leaders in late nineteenth- and early twentieth-century Catholic church work. Lovatt studied at the Pennsylvania Museum and School of Industrial Art, opened an office in 1894, and launched a successful career. He received a commendation for the Church of the Most Precious Blood (Twenty-Sixth and Diamond Streets) at the International Exhibition in Barcelona (1926), and a gold medal for his Church of the Holy Child (Broad and Duncannon Streets) from the Philadelphia Chapter of the American Institute of Architects (1930). Lovatt shares credit for Saint Rita's with the architecture and engineering firm of Ballinger and Perrot (Walter F. Ballinger and Emiel G. Perrot), who pioneered in the use of reinforced concrete.

Established as an Augustinian parish to serve a predominantly Irish congregation, the ethnicity of Saint Rita's gradually changed to Italian in the 1920s. In the following decades membership grew to 13,000 families, only to decline rapidly after World War II to fewer than a thousand families today.

⊂⊷ *The striking interior of Saint Rita's reflects a major redecoration undertaken in the 1990s. The church and shrine to Saint Rita are visited by thousands of pilgrims annually, although the largely Italian American congregation is now smaller than in earlier decades.*

EAST OF BROAD

St. John the Evangelist Church. The sanctuary embellishments date from the early twentieth-century redecoration following the fire of 1899. See pages 136–139.

MOTHER BETHEL AFRICAN METHODIST EPISCOPAL CHURCH

419 South Sixth Street
(Richard Allen Avenue)
Philadelphia, PA 19147

Hazelhurst and Huckel, architects,
1889–1890

Telephone for visitor information:
215.925.0616

www.motherbethel.org

To the casual visitor strolling south from Independence Square, the handsome but relatively modest rough-hewn stone-fronted church of Mother Bethel may not seem extraordinary—just another Romanesque Revival Style Victorian building. But such an impression is misleading. This National Historic Landmark is venerated by Americans of all races and creeds who are committed to the struggle for individual rights and black self-determination in Philadelphia and the nation. The present Mother Bethel is the fourth building to stand on this site since the eighteenth century. It houses a large, active congregation and also maintains a public shrine to Richard Allen (1760–1831), the former slave who founded the African Methodist Episcopal Church in America.

John Wesley's charge to Methodists left little doubt on the issue of slavery. "Buying or selling the bodies and souls of men, women, and children, with an intention to enslave them," he declared, would result in eternal damnation. As a consequence, early Methodist classes openly opposed slavery. Unfortunately, by the late eighteenth century, many white Methodists retreated from what they perceived as the excessive zeal of the abolition movement. At the same time, the number of blacks attracted to Methodism dramatically increased. One historian claims that "the number of black class members equaled or exceeded that of white members" in the eighteenth century. This frightened white Methodists, who began to segregate congregations by restricting black worshipers to the balconies. In Philadelphia—then the largest city in the nation with a substantial free black population—discrimination at Saint George's Church (pages 82–85) set off a chain reaction leading ultimately to the formation of the African Methodist Episcopal Church. Following a confrontation in November 1787, the black members of Saint George's Church walked out of services and founded their own congregation.

Black Philadelphians had left Saint George's, but not the Methodist Episcopal Church. That move to independence would only come in 1816, when Richard Allen invited black congregations from New Jersey, Maryland, Delaware, and Pennsylvania to send delegates to a general convention in Philadelphia. Out of that meeting would emerge an independent denomination with Allen as the first bishop. Today the African Methodist Episcopal Church consists of 8,000 congregations worldwide with 3,500,000 members.

In 1787, of course, all this remained in the future. Philadelphia's rebellious black Methodists had left Saint George's. But where would they worship? In 1793, Allen purchased a small wooden blacksmith shop and moved it to a lot he had previously acquired in 1791 at Sixth and Lombard Streets. On this sacred ground—the oldest real estate continuously owned by blacks in the United States—three churches, each larger than its predecessor, were subsequently erected to replace the humble shed. On November 7, 1889, the cornerstone of the present church was laid, and on Octo-

✎ Mother Bethel is the mother church of the African Methodist Episcopal Church. The present building (erected 1889–1890) stands on land continuously owned by blacks since the eighteenth century.

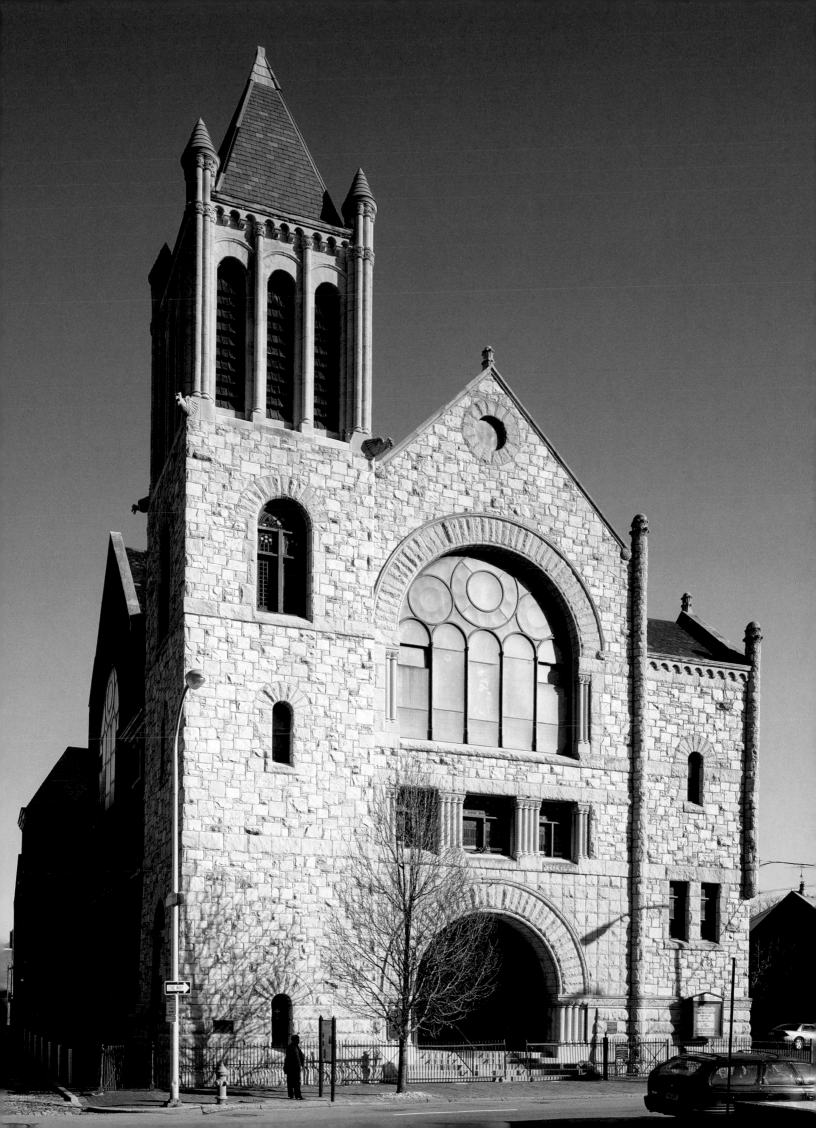

ber 26, 1890, the granite-faced Romanesque Revival style Mother Bethel Church was dedicated.

As architects the congregation had selected Hazelhurst and Huckel, a firm founded in 1881 by Edward P. Hazelhurst (1853–1915). He had worked in the offices of T. P. Chandler and Frank Furness before establishing a partnership with Samuel Huckel, Jr. (1858–1917), who served his apprenticeship with Benjamin D. Price, church architect and stained-glass purveyor. The style of the new church is generally associated with the influential American architect Henry Hobson Richardson (1836–1886), who popularized the Romanesque style with his Trinity Church, Boston (1872), and Allegheny County Courthouse in Pittsburgh (1884–1888). Romanesque buildings—Mother Bethel is a typical example—were usually constructed of rough-textured stone pierced by round arches framing deep-set windows and recessed door openings. Usually there was a single tower—in Mother Bethel's case rising four stories. The overall effect is grave and substantial; this is a building for the ages. Here a congregation might gather to worship in safety.

The interior is more dramatic. Shallow transepts with stained-glass windows produced by the Century Art Company provide a flood of light from the north, south, and west. The complex timber framing and the semicircular pews and continuous horseshoe balcony give the auditorium excellent acoustics and focus both eye and ear toward the pulpit, choir, and organ pipes on the east wall behind the altar.

In the basement crypt are the tombs of Richard Allen and his wife, Sarah Allen. There is also a museum—including the wooden pulpit and several pews fashioned by Allen and used in the first church—which is open to the public on a regular schedule.

The auditorium of Mother Bethel Church successfully focuses the congregation on the altar, pulpit, and organ pipes on the east wall. Light floods the space from the north, south, and west.

HOLY TRINITY CHURCH

*Sixth and Spruce Streets
Philadelphia, PA 19106*

*(William Palmer, master builder?),
1788–1789*

*Telephone for visitor information:
215.623.7930*

www.stmaryholytrinity.org

☞·☞ *The first church in the
United States established to house an
ethnic group, Holy Trinity (German
Catholic) Church dates from 1788–
1789. It is an excellent example of
Philadelphia brickwork laid in Flemish
bond—headers and stretchers alternating in the same course—with glazed
headers creating a distinctive decorative pattern. The graveyard is often
identified as the last resting place of
Longfellow's fictional heroine, Evangeline.*

☞· *A set of unsigned architectural
drawings associated with the Philadelphia master builder William Palmer
(fl. 1787–1815) includes this primitive
perspective view of Holy Trinity, which
suggests he may have been the designer. The Athenæum of Philadelphia*

Three Roman Catholic parishes in Philadelphia date from the eighteenth century: Saint Joseph's (pages 50–53), Saint Mary's (pages 54–59), and Holy Trinity. German-speaking Philadelphians had always constituted a large part of the Catholic faithful at Saint Joseph's and Saint Mary's, and both parishes from time to time had German-speaking priests ministering to their needs. By the 1780s, however, a movement to establish a separate German parish developed, leading to the purchase of land for a church (1788) and a petition to the Pennsylvania legislature for incorporation as "The Trustees of the German Religious Society of Roman Catholics, called the Church of the Holy Trinity, in the city of Philadelphia" in 1789. Thus came into being the first American parish church established to serve a national group. In the decades to come other parishes organized by ethnic origin—Irish, Polish, Italian, Lithuanian, and others—would become common.

The simple brick structure oriented east to west may have been designed and built by master carpenter William Palmer (fl. 1787–1815). A set of drawings that descended in his family survives to document the original appearance of the church. Unfortunately, Holy Trinity suffered two serious fires. On July 7, 1860, a smoldering firecracker tossed on the roof destroyed virtually everything but the exterior walls and parts of the high altar, which were rescued from the inferno. The present decorative brick cornice and hipped roof probably date from that rebuilding. Then, on Christmas Day 1890, a fire started in the sacristy that spread throughout the building, requiring yet another redecoration. To add final insult to previous injury, the

ceiling collapsed in 1995. While virtually nothing remains of the simple eighteenth-century interior, the present Victorian altar survived the misguided destruction prompted by Vatican II that was visited on nearby Saint Mary's. A simple oak table placed facing the congregation now serves as an altar, thereby preserving the white and gilt confection that stretches across the apse at the east end.

Ironically, Holy Trinity is associated in popular mythology with a shameful episode in Anglo-American colonial history. The French-speaking Catholic Acadians were expelled from Nova Scotia by the British in 1755 during the French and Indian War. Approximately 2,000 men, women, and children were scattered across

other British colonies, including 453 delivered to the Delaware Valley, where they suffered severely due to local fears they would join with German and Irish Catholics in all sorts of unspecified mischief. Interned for years on marshy Province Island, south of the city, most died of smallpox.

A century later, with the plight of the Acadians in mind, Henry Wadsworth Longfellow wrote the tragic poem *Evangeline: A Tale of Acadie*, in which the lovers Gabriel and Evangeline end badly in Philadelphia. The poem concludes:

> Still stands the forest primeval; but far away from its shadow,
> Side by side, in their nameless graves, the lovers are sleeping,
> Under the humble walls of the little Catholic churchyard,
> In the heart of the city they lie, unknown and unnoticed.

In the generations since Longfellow, the site of the lovers' grave has been variously identified—most often with the churchyard of Holy Trinity. So enduring is this fictional American romance that it is not uncommon to this day to find tourists gazing through the churchyard fence in an attempt to identify the graves.

Twice destroyed by fire, the interior of Holy Trinity was most recently renovated after the ceiling failed in 1995. The Crucifixion over the altar survived the fires. It is by Francis Martin Drexel (1792–1863), who was born in the Tyrol, Austria, and emigrated to America in 1817, plying his trade as a portrait painter until 1837 when he established a brokerage office, the origins of the banking house Drexel and Company.

Lithograph of the interior of Holy Trinity as it appeared in 1880. American Catholic Historical Society Collection.

GREEK ORTHODOX CATHEDRAL OF SAINT GEORGE

(formerly Saint Andrew's Episcopal Church)

248–256 South Eighth Street Philadelphia, PA 19107

John Haviland, architect, 1822

Telephone for visitor information: 215.627.4389

English-born and trained John Haviland (1792–1852) ranks among the most important Philadelphia architects of the early nineteenth century. In short order, after arriving here in 1816, he married the widowed daughter of his first Philadelphia patron, established an architectural office, and promoted himself by producing a book. The landmark *Builder's Assistant: Containing the Five Orders of Architecture . . .* (1818–1821) is significant as the earliest American architectural pattern book to contain both Greek and Roman orders. His earliest important architectural commission was the First Presbyterian Church on South Washington Square (1820–1822). A late and unfortunate loss—it succumbed to the wrecker's ball in 1939—First Presbyterian was the earliest Philadelphia church to have a full Greek temple façade.

With Haviland's next ecclesiastical essay we are more fortunate. In 1822 a new Episcopal congregation formed—including Haviland—determined to erect a church dedicated to Saint Andrew in the rapidly developing neighborhood west of what would soon be named Washington Square. (Originally called Southeast Square when dedicated for public use in 1682 by William Penn's surveyor-general, it was formally laid out and planted as a public promenade in 1816 and officially named for Washington in 1825.) As a member of the congregation, Haviland probably donated the design. The cornerstone was laid on September 9, 1822, by Bishop William White, and the completed church was consecrated by him, May 31, 1823. So rapidly was the church erected that the *Philadelphia Gazette* commented, "nine months ago, the stone which forms part of the fabric, was unquarried—the bricks were unburnt—the wool, out of which the lining of the pews has been made, was on the back of the sheep."

✑ *John Haviland's First Presbyterian Church, on the south side of Washington Square (1820; demolished). The site of this handsome structure is now occupied by the Hopkinson House condominium complex. Presbyterian Historical Society.*

The main façade of John Haviland's design for what is now the Greek Orthodox Cathedral of Saint George is based on the Temple of Bacchus at Teos, reduced to a six-column front. The fence is a noteworthy survival; it continues the Greek Revival detailing.

As at the nearby First Presbyterian Church, Haviland's design source was again the Temple of Bacchus at Teos, uncompromisingly Greek Revival with six (rather than eight) carefully spaced, fluted columns in the Ionic order supporting an enriched entablature. Across the front is a vigorous cast- and wrought-iron fence in the neoclassical style, which protects and elegantly defines the entire composition. This fence is one of the rare Philadelphia survivals of its type, dating from the early nineteenth century. Beyond the fence, the church itself is approached via a platform of six marble steps extending across the entire front, providing an appropriate and desirable setting that Haviland had been unable to realize on the smaller Washington Square lot available to the Presbyterians. The temple front portico is wood painted to simulate marble (sanded) while the body of the church itself is brick that has been stuccoed (rough cast) and then scored to simulate slabs of marble. This ashlar effect originally was heightened by painting the scoring lines. At the west end of the church, tower foundations were provided for a lofty spire of 230 feet to rival that at Christ Church, but the spire was never realized.

Entrance is through a central door fourteen feet wide and twenty-five feet high, divided into seven vertical compartments of four horizontal panels enriched with egg and dart moldings; the stiles and rails of each panel are studded with rivets to lend what Haviland called "character of strength." Only the lower three panels operate as a door.

The interior is arranged in a conventional three-aisle plan with balconies. Today the visitor is struck by the unexpected sight of rustic exposed roof trusses in place of what was originally a flat ceiling with heavily ornamented coffering. A fire in 1930 ignited above the ceiling, destroying the roof and causing the plaster ceiling to fall. The fire-damaged trusses were encased and left exposed against plastered rafters. Also lost in the fire was a classical screen of two freestanding columns and pilasters based on the order of the North Porch of the Erechtheum. The pilasters survived the fire and now frame the apse, the head of which was carried into a curved recess above the original ceiling line.

As Philadelphia expanded westward in the later nineteenth century, and as those with the means to do so fled the city in the twentieth century, the neighborhood around Washington Square became less desirable for residential use. The Episcopal congregation deserted Saint Andrew's Church, and in 1922 the structure became the property of the Greek Orthodox Church, which altered the interior for their liturgical needs. Particularly noteworthy is the stenciled and painted iconostasis installed after the 1930 fire. Which is not to suggest the present congregation does not appreciate the building; they have done much to return the original splendor of Haviland's design. Many original architectural and decorative features remain, most notably what was described in the *Philadelphia Gazette* in 1823 as columns supporting the gallery "composed of a cluster of palm leaves for flutes, running over at the tops and forming a capital. Over each is introduced a wreath, and the whole is bronzed and supports a light entablature."

Today the Greek Orthodox Cathedral of Saint George is an active cultural center and a shrine of living Byzantium for a widespread congregation to which—according to a recent press release—many Orthodox kings, patriarchs, heads of state, leading members of the diplomatic corps, governors, mayors, senators, representatives, famous military men, and world renowned figures of science, literature, and learning have made pilgrimages.

As for John Haviland, he was buried in the crypt below the nave he had designed and where he had worshiped. When the Saint Andrew's congregation abandoned the church, Haviland's remains were exhumed and reinterred in the courtyard of the Philadelphia Divinity School, where, presumably, they still rest.

The Greek Orthodox congregation acquired the church in 1922, and after a fire in 1930 the interior was renovated to meet their liturgical needs. Particularly handsome is the iconostasis, which separates the sanctuary from the congregation.

CHURCH OF SAINT LUKE AND THE EPIPHANY

330 South Thirteenth Street
Philadelphia, PA 19107

Thomas Somerville Stewart, architect,
1839–1840; Furness and Hewitt,
parish house, 1874

Telephone for visitor information:
215.732.1918

www.stlukeandtheepiphany.org

The present congregation of the Church of Saint Luke and the Epiphany provides a metaphor of the trials facing urban parishes formed in the nineteenth century. It results from the uniting of Saint Luke's parish and an earlier parish known as the Church of the Epiphany (founded in 1833), formerly housed in a stately Doric porticoed building by Thomas Ustick Walter on the northwest corner of Fifteenth and Chestnut Streets. The church was built to serve the neighborhood of John Haviland's elegant Colonnade Row (1830) on the south side of Chestnut Street (page 161), but the Epiphany congregation went into decline after the Civil War as commercial enterprises supplanted residential neighborhoods. The final blow came in 1896, when merchant John Wanamaker offered the vestry $600,000 for the church and land. Since none of the parishes in West Philadelphia would agree to a new parish established on their turf, Epiphany joined with Saint Luke's on Thirteenth Street below Locust. At the time Epiphany had 600 communicants and an endowment; Saint Luke's could claim a membership of 260 and a debt.

Saint Luke's had been founded in 1839 to serve the rapidly expanding southwestern section of Philadelphia. In typical nineteenth-century fashion, architects

⊶ The baptismal font is en suite with the Greek Revival interior and was probably designed by Thomas Somerville Stewart.

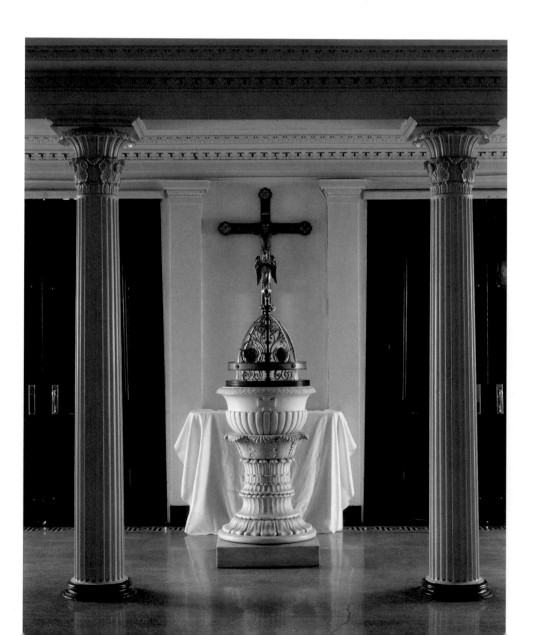

Saint Luke and the Epiphany by Thomas Somerville Stewart (1839–1840) is one of the most important Philadelphia Greek Revival structures to survive from the early decades of the nineteenth century.

were invited to submit designs, resulting in the selection of a relatively unknown contender. Saint Luke's would prove to be Thomas Somerville Stewart's most important essay as an architect. Trained as a master carpenter, Stewart (1806–1889) began to enter major architectural competitions in the early 1830s, where he encountered Thomas Ustick Walter, who was also launching his career. Walter, who would eventually assure his place in American architectural history with designs for the dome and wings of the United States Capitol, bested Stewart in both the Girard College (1832) and Preston Retreat (1837) competitions. Then Stewart secured a commission to design the ill-fated Pennsylvania Hall (1837–1838), gutted by an incendiary anti-abolitionist mob only three days after it opened. The following year, however, he successfully competed for the Saint Luke's commission, where his "Corinthian" design was selected by the vestry over the more expensive "Gothic" proposals of both William Strickland and John Notman.

Saint Luke's marks a turning point in Stewart's career. The completed church was admired by a building committee from Richmond, Virginia, appointed "to visit churches in Northern cities, where the attention of the public is more directed to the science of architecture than in the South." The committeemen were so taken with Stewart's Saint Luke's that they invited him to Richmond to design Saint Paul's Church (1843–1845) near Jefferson's Virginia Capitol, which would come to be

Stewart's ink and watercolor perspective presentation drawing submitted to the Saint Luke's vestry and annotated, "This Steeple excepted in the Church erection 14 January 1839." The Athenæum of Philadelphia, gift of Thomas C. Stewart, 1977.

The stair hall of Furness and Hewitt's parish house (1874) and its adjoining chapel were recently returned to historically sympathetic colors.

called the "church of the Confederacy." It survived the Richmond fire at the close of the Civil War and remains to this day one of the major landmarks of that city.

Saint Luke's gave Philadelphia another excellent example of a Greek Revival temple-front church, on a larger scale than John Haviland's First Presbyterian Church on Washington Square (1820–1822; demolished 1939) or his Saint Andrew's Episcopal Church (1822; now the Greek Orthodox Cathedral of Saint George, pages 120–123). Here is a giant order portico with eight fluted Corinthian columns based on the Choragic Monument of Lysicrates in Athens. The portico rests on a raised platform approached by a flight of steps set behind a stone and stucco fence surmounted by rich wrought-iron cresting. (Philadelphia is fortunate that three of its most important Greek Revival buildings of the early nineteenth century have retained their neoclassical iron fences: the Second Bank of the United States, Saint Andrew's, and Saint Luke's.)

Stewart, like Haviland at Saint Andrew's, offered the vestry a steeple to rise 207 feet above its residential neighbors. To reduce costs, the steeple was not approved. The interior, however, closely follows Stewart's design of tall Corinthian columns and pilasters supporting a chancel dome with stained-glass skylight (subsequently covered). The chancel is elevated with an open work rail; the ceiling is coffered.

Gradually Saint Luke's attracted a large congregation, and by the 1870s the vestry approved the construction of a new parish house and chapel, for which they hired the firm of Frank Furness (1839–1912) and George W. Hewitt (1841–1916) as architects. Unfortunately this handsome addition to church facilities increased the debt burden at the very time the congregation began to decline. By 1898 the merger with the Church of the Epiphany offered a practical solution that saved the parish and an architecturally significant complex of buildings. In the twenty-first century this Center City church has entered a new period of vitality by developing various support programs and community events in addition to its regular services of worship.

☞ *The chancel continues Stewart's Corinthian design. Originally the dome was a skylight with stained glass.*

SAINT STEPHEN'S CHURCH

*19 South Tenth Street
Philadelphia, PA 19107*

*William Strickland, architect,
1822–1823; Frank Furness, north
transept addition, 1878–1879;
George C. Mason and Son, parish
house, 1888*

*Telephone for visitor information:
215.922.3807*

Wedged between high-rise buildings and uncomfortably close to the hustle and bustle of revitalized Market Street, Saint Stephen's Episcopal Church is a forlorn reminder of an elegant residential neighborhood long ago swept aside by temples of commerce and transportation. Yet it deserves to be better known. Architecturally it is one of the earliest surviving Gothic Revival buildings in America, designed by Philadelphia native son William Strickland (1788–1854), who is best remembered for his neoclassical Second Bank of the United States on Chestnut Street, the Merchants' Exchange on Third Street above Walnut, and the recreated tower of Independence Hall. The interior of Saint Stephen's Church is, unfortunately, greatly altered, but the persistent visitor will be rewarded by the discovery of an unexpected and remarkable assemblage of nineteenth-century ecclesiastical art.

The true principles of Gothic architecture were little known in America of the 1820s, nor would they be until two decades later when Philadelphia's Saint James the

☞ Saint Stephen's Church as engraved by Cephas G. Childs and published in his Views in Philadelphia and Its Vicinity *(Philadelphia: Childs, 1827–1830). This shows the church before the north transept and parish house additions. The Athenæum of Philadelphia.*

☞·☞ The Gothic Revival west façade of Saint Stephen's Church (1822–1823) by architect William Strickland survives virtually unchanged except for the tower crenelations—if they were ever installed.

Upon entering from the vestibule, visitors immediately encounter the life-size recumbent effigy of Edward Shippen Burd (1779–1848), principal benefactor of Saint Stephen's Church, carved in marble by Carl Johann Steinhäuser, a student of the brilliant Danish sculptor Bertel Thorvaldsen (1770–1844).

Less (pages 248–254) and Saint Mark's (pages 162–167) were erected under the influence of the Cambridge Camden Society. Strickland's master, English-trained Benjamin Henry Latrobe (1764–1820), introduced Gothicized detailing to Philadelphia at Sedgley (1799; demolished 1857) and the Bank of Philadelphia (1807–1808; demolished 1836)—both buildings young Strickland knew. When Strickland launched his own practice his maiden effort proved to be a Gothic Revival design for Philadelphia's Masonic Hall (1809–1811; burned 1819).

These early Gothic Revival buildings by Latrobe and Strickland—including Saint Stephen's Church—had none of the integral thrust and counterthrust of a true stone structural system. All were conventional rectangular buildings with pitched roofs superficially cloaked in picturesque trappings of crenelated towers, pointed

windows and doors, piers in clusters, and ceiling vaults—often little more than stage sets patched together from wood and plaster. At Saint Stephen's Strickland actually began with an existing symmetrical chapel acquired from a failed Methodist congregation. To this modest box he added a dramatic stone façade defined by paired octagonal towers rising from the pavement in five stages, four of which are pierced by pointed Gothic lancet windows. These towers are connected by a crenelated entrance screen—all executed in coursed granite ashlar—with pointed arch windows over tripartite ground floor entrance doors.

From its earliest years Saint Stephen's Church attracted wealthy parishioners—with socially prominent Philadelphia names like Wharton, Ingersoll, and Hazelhurst—who lived in the neighborhood and embellished the interior with memorials. In the person of founder, vestryman, and lawyer Edward Shippen Burd (1779–1848), Saint Stephen's was particularly fortunate. It was Burd's widow, Eliza Sims Burd, who commissioned a remarkable series of memorials to her husband and their children by the German sculptor Carl Johann Steinhäuser (1813–1879), including a life-size recumbent effigy of Edward Shippen Burd surrounded by a Gothic canopy worthy of a medieval English parish church. (Upon seeing this effigy for the first time, an old friend of Burd's remarked, "The last time I saw Edward Burd was over a game of cards in Paris. What is he doing in this church?" The second rector of Saint Stephen's, Henry W. Ducachet, who was famous for his bons mots, instantly replied, "Sir, he's waiting now for the last trump.")

Believing that the church should nourish a large and rich culture and that the arts can contribute to worship, the nineteenth-century rectors and vestry encouraged the commissioning of works by outstanding artists such as Augustus Saint-Gaudens, Henry Holiday, the Tiffany Studios, and Philadelphia's own D'Ascenzo Studio. In addition to the works illustrated here, visitors should seek out the tall baptismal font (West Wall) held aloft by three children carved in marble, also commissioned from Carl Johann Steinhäuser in 1856.

In the later decades of the nineteenth century, Saint Stephen's underwent several architectural modifications. Frank Furness added a dramatic transept to the northeast and painted the walls turquoise blue stenciled with flowers, doves, and emblems of Saint Stephen, although this decorative scheme has largely been destroyed. A parish house facing Tenth Street was added by George C. Mason and Son, architects, in 1888. Another artistic surprise is the 1889 altar picture of the Last Supper (east wall) by the English artist Henry Holiday (1839–1927), who studied at the Royal Academy and became associated with Dante Gabriel Rossetti, Edward Burne-Jones, and Simeon Solomon. Holiday succeeded Burne-Jones as chief designer of Powell and Sons, the stained-glass makers, fulfilling more than three hundred commissions, including several for American clients. In 1890 he founded his own glassworks in Hampstead, London. His work appears in Westminster Abbey, Trinity College, Cambridge University, Salisbury Cathedral, and Southward Cathedral, London. The commission for Saint Stephen's was underwritten by the children of Mrs. James Magee in memory of their mother.

This unexpected treasure of ecclesiastical art makes Saint Stephen's Church worthy of a special visit. The vestry should be encouraged to resist any action that would detract from this remarkable assemblage.

The extraordinary Burd Memorial (set in its own chapel, north wall), 1852, by Carl Johann Steinhäuser (1813–1879), memorializes three Burd children who died and are depicted asleep at the feet of the angel of resurrection who is about to blow her trumpet. The upper inscription reads "IN THE CRYPT BENEATH THIS CHAPEL REPOSE THE REMAINS OF ELIZABETH BURD BORN NOV. 6, 1815 DIED JULY 25, 1845. OF MARGARET COXE BURD BORN SEPT 2. 1819 DIED APRIL 27.1844 AND OF WOODDROP SIMS BURD BORN MAY 2.1822 AND DIED MAY 11.1837." *The lower inscription reads:* "THIS MONUMENT IS ERECTED IN ACCORDANCE WITH THE WILL OF EDWARD SHIPPEN BURD, TO COMMEMORATE THE VIRTUES AND RELIGIOUS CHARACTER OF HIS CHILDREN, AND TO PERPETUATE THE EXAMPLE OF THEIR PIOUS LIFE AND HAPPY TRANSITION, IN THE SANCTUARY WHERE THEY WERE TRAINED FOR HEAVEN. WHEN CHRIST, WHO IS OUR LIFE SHALL APPEAR, THEN SHALL WE ALSO APPEAR WITH HIM IN GLORY. COL 3.4." *The base is signed:* "C. Steinhäuser Fec. Roma 1852."

One of the most significant artistic works adorning Saint Stephen's Church is an eight-foot marble relief (east wall, north side of the reredos) by the American sculptor Augustus Saint-Gaudens (1848–1907) commissioned by Dr. Silas Weir Mitchell (1829–1914) and his wife, Mary Cadwalader Mitchell, as a memorial to their daughter, 1902. The standing winged figure holds aloft a tablet inscribed "BLESSED ARE THE PURE IN HEART FOR THEY SHALL SEE GOD." Below the figure is a plinth inscribed "IN MEMORY OF MARIA GOUVERNEUR MITCHELL BORN MARCH XXI MDCCCLXXVI DIED JANUARY XXIV MDCCCXCVIII." Saint-Gaudens had previously used this figure for his Amor Caritas, which was among his works that won the grand prize at the Exposition Universelle (1900). Saint-Gaudens wrote to Dr. Mitchell in 1901 that the relief for his daughter's memorial would be similar to the earlier work, which he called "one of the things I care for most that I have done."

SAINT JOHN THE EVANGELIST CHURCH

*21 South Thirteenth Street
Philadelphia, PA 19107*

*William Rodrigue, architect, 1831;
Frank R. Watson, architect, 1899*

*Telephone for visitor information:
215.563.4145*

By 1830, conflicts between the trustees of Saint Mary's Church and the bishop of Philadelphia caused Father John Hughes to be chosen to form a new Catholic parish and erect a church in the "western" part of the city. As architect Father Hughes selected William Rodrigue (1800–1867), son of French Catholic émigrés who had been baptized at Saint Mary's. After studies in Paris, Rodrigue returned to Philadelphia in 1823 to enter the office of William Strickland. (Rodrigue later married Father Hughes's sister, and when Hughes was named coadjutor bishop of New York the Rodrigue family moved with him, settling in Brooklyn, where he continued to practice, specializing in structures for the Catholic Church there.)

According to one church account, "St. John's was the first of the Catholic churches in Philadelphia to take on something of the embellishment common to the churches of Europe. Congregations like St. Joseph's, St. Mary's, St. Augustine's, and the Holy Trinity, in all of which for a long time the membership included but few rich families, worshiped in edifices simple in their architecture and comparatively unadorned." Catholic churches before Saint John's certainly did not architecturally declare their ecclesiastical purpose. Like Strickland at nearby Saint Stephen's Church—designed for a new Episcopalian congregation in 1822 (pages 130–135)—Rodrigue gave the Catholics a Gothic style church with twin towers rising in three stages on either side of a recessed tripartite entrance. Father Hughes wrote to Archbishop Purcell of Cincinnati that the new church

> will cause those who give nothing towards its erection to "murmur" at its costliness and those who did contribute to be proud of their own doing. As a religious edifice, it will be the pride of the city. The leading Protestants and infidels proclaim it the only building that is entitled to be called a church, inasmuch as its appearance indicates its use and there is no danger of mistaking it for a workshop.

✎ *The exterior of Saint John the Evangelist preserves the overall form of William Rodrigue's original church. After the church was extensively damaged by fire in 1899, the towers were extended and the building resurfaced with rough-faced stone. Along the north wall are fifty-four burial vaults containing the remains of Catholics from diverse backgrounds, for example, Philadelphia essayist Agnes Repplier, Anna Maria Huarte de Iturbide (widow of the Mexican emperor Augustín de Iturbide), and Thomas Penn Gaskell, great-great grandson of William Penn.*

Saint John the Evangelist Church is Rodrigue's only major commission known with certainty. This makes it particularly unfortunate that in 1899 a fire in adjoining buildings spread to Saint John's rectory and then to the church itself. Heavy snow and winds hampered firefighting, and by the time the flames were extinguished the roof had collapsed and the interior was gutted. Virtually all the contents—statuary, pews, stained-glass windows, altars, paintings, and frescoes—were destroyed. And yet, standing undamaged amid the ruins, was the pure white Carrara marble statue of the Blessed Virgin Mary which today is one of the most venerated objects in the reconstructed church. A few days later the *Catholic Standard and Times* reported:

> The new St. John's is already assured. While the water was still streaming from the walls of the burned church, the parishioners and their friends gathered in

Horticultural Hall on Sunday afternoon and within one short hour subscribed $5,000. While old St. John's, as is the way of parishes in the centres [of the city], has lost much prestige of its former fashionable attendance, a few of the first families still remain within its boundaries. Its newer congregation is as loyal to the tradition of the historic church as are the descendants of the pew holders of the 30's.

To rebuild following the fire, Saint John's Church turned to the prolific architect Frank Rushmore Watson (1859–1940), who had worked with the prominent Catholic church architect Edwin F. Durang. Watson subsequently formed a partnership with (William) Samuel Huckel, Jr. (1858–1917), who had specialized in Protestant churches while in the office of Benjamin D. Price. Saint John the Evangelist is usually credited to the firm of Watson and Huckel because of renovations done at the church in 1906–1907, but it seems likely that the original commission belongs to Watson alone because Huckel did not join him until 1901 or 1902.

Watson's solution was to preserve Rodigue's walls and towers which survived the fire and later to clad the entire church in rough-faced granite toped by more dramatic pinnacles (now unfortunately removed)—what the rector called "Not a new St. John's, but the old St. John's in a new dress" on October 7, 1900, when the church first reopened.

To replace statuary destroyed in the fire, two life-size Carrara marble figures of Saint John and the Sacred Heart of Jesus were commissioned from the Italian sculptor Cesare Aureli (dated Rome, 1903) for either side of the sanctuary. Through additional redecoration in 1906–1907—when the balconies were removed—and several later campaigns, mostly recently in 1990, the interior has been lightened and embellishments reduced (see pages 110–111). The altar rail and gates have been removed and the altar itself brought forward, but the delicate white marble reredos and statuary dating from the early twentieth century survive.

Now in the care of Capuchin Franciscan Friars, Saint John's has a small parish but attracts thousands of Catholics who work in or visit Center City and are welcomed at all hours to worship in this historic church.

⟿ The Carrara marble statue of the Blessed Virgin Mary of the Immaculate Conception was commissioned from Rome in 1857 for Saint John's Church. It survived the 1899 fire virtually unscathed and was reinstalled in the reconstructed church. The gold crown studded with jewels was fashioned by J. E. Caldwell and Company from jewelry set with precious gems, coins, and medals contributed by Saint John's Sodality to celebrate the Golden Jubilee of that charitable association's founding in 1852.

ARCH STREET UNITED METHODIST CHURCH

Broad and Arch Streets
Philadelphia, PA 19107

Addison Hutton, architect, chapel,
1864–1865; main church, 1868–1870

Telephone for visitor information:
215.568.6250

www.archstreetumc.org

Arch Street United Methodist Church with its "paper white walls and silvery, weathered arches" stands at the very heart of Philadelphia and declares the nineteenth-century realization of William Penn's dream for a city centered between its two rivers. This marble church is the first building of what would eventually become our finest gathering of Victorian public architecture. It stands next to James H. Windrim's Masonic Temple (1868–1873) and John McArthur's City Hall (1874–1901) and not far from the Pennsylvania Academy of the Fine Arts by Furness and Hewitt (1871–1876).

Arch Street Methodist Church is also one of Addison Hutton's finest surviving buildings. Hutton (1834–1916) gained his architectural experience in the office of Samuel Sloan (1815–1884) and was in charge of building the famous octagonal house called "Longwood" in Natchez, Mississippi, when the Civil War burst upon the nation. In independent practice he would later design the Philadelphia Savings Fund Society building (1868) on Washington Square, the Ridgway Library on South Broad Street (1870–1878), and the Historical Society of Pennsylvania building (1902), in addition to Arch Street Methodist Church. Why the Methodists selected this young and not yet celebrated Quaker architect is unknown; perhaps he had worked for a member of the congregation while in Sloan's office.

Dedicated on November 17, 1870, the new church made a significant impression from the first. "The building is of florid Gothic style of architecture," the *Public Ledger* declared, "with transepts, formed by the chapel, which was erected several years ago, rendering the completed structure cruciform in shape." The congregation had formed in 1862 to provide a Methodist church to serve the residential neighborhood then emerging near Broad and Arch. The chapel was completed by 1865, and the main church begun in 1868. Given a building site advantageously located at the intersection of two major streets, Hutton designed two façades and placed the 233-foot tower and steeple at the corner, through which worshipers entered, rather than providing the principal entrance in the center of the main façade and hence on a direct line with the nave, the typical plan of urban churches at the time. The choice of Gothic style architecture for a Methodist church is also a dramatic departure from the traditional, understated "meeting house plain" structures favored by Methodists and other nonconforming denominations. Not only is this the first Gothic Methodist church in Philadelphia, it is a dramatic statement that John Wesley's heirs had realized economic and social success on an equal footing with other Protestant denominations.

The Methodists were not alone at this important intersection. The First Baptist and the Lutheran Church of the Holy Communion congregations were already ensconced across Broad Street in handsome buildings by Stephen Decatur Button and Frank Furness respectively. But within a few decades—as the neighborhood

☞ *The slender, tapering, octagonal spire supported by flying buttresses of Arch Street United Methodist Church, together with the towers of the Masonic Temple and City Hall, dramatically proclaim the center of Philadelphia at the crossing of Market and Broad Streets.*

lost its residential character—attendance at services in all three churches declined and developers of commercial real estate began to circle around. In 1899 the Baptists moved to Seventeenth and Sansom Streets (pages 184–187), and in 1901 the Lutherans sold out, ultimately occupying a former Episcopal church at Twenty-First and Chestnut Streets (pages 206–209). Several offers for the Methodist site in the first decade of the twentieth century were publicized in the press, and by 1920 it was reported that "the most valuable piece of church property in this city, perhaps, is that owned by the Arch Street Methodist Episcopal congregation at the southeast corner of Broad and Arch streets." Offers of $1,250,000—a substantial sum at the time— were ultimately rejected.

The Arch Street Methodist Church held on during the Depression and World War II years. No longer was there talk of abandoning the Center City crossroads; rather than flee the city, the church would recognize and respond to change. A radio ministry reached out to the region, while a modern transportation system allowed parishioners to travel greater distances to attend services. If students and immigrants now populated Center City, then programs tailored to their needs would be launched.

Taking as its motto, "Indebted to the Past . . . Committed to the Future," the congregation has maintained Hutton's handsome building. After having been insensitively painted in a misguided effort to "modernize" the interior in the 1950s, the sanctuary has been restored by recreating the original decorative scheme. Once again this congregation proved to be far-sighted. Preserving, restoring, or recreating the original decoration after decades of neglect has repeatedly been demonstrated to have a salutary effect on our historic sacred places. Speaking to a reporter at the time of the 1987 restoration, the pastor is quoted as saying,

> we believe we are called to be at this strategic Center City location. But then we want the appearance of our building to be inviting and winsome, and to reflect the care that extends beyond the building itself to the people for whom it exists. A shabby looking building may suggest a careless ministry, but our commitment is such that everything about our presence at this prominent crossroads of our city expresses the renewal and hope that is the essence of the gospel of Jesus Christ which we proclaim.

The Victorian decoration in the sanctuary was recreated in the 1980s.

WEST OF BROAD

⚏ One of the great treasures of Saint Mark's Church is the groin-vaulted stone Lady Chapel at the east end of the south aisle, designed by Cope and Stewardson. The chapel and its fittings were donated by Rodman Wanamaker in memory of his wife Fernanda, who died in 1900. The chapel was consecrated in 1902. Originally fitted with a white and green alabaster altar and reredos designed by English church decorator Charles E. Kempe, it was refurnished in 1909 with a marble altar created by English jeweler Carl Krall and entirely encased in silver. See pages 162–167.

ARCH STREET PRESBYTERIAN CHURCH

(formerly West Arch Street Presbyterian Church)

1724 Arch Street
Philadelphia, PA 19103

Joseph C. Hoxie, architect, 1853–1855

Telephone for visitor information:
215.563.3763

Philadelphia at the beginning of the nineteenth century experienced a flurry of new building as the population swelled and new residential neighborhoods marched westward toward Broad Street. To serve the residents of these late Federal brick and marble-trimmed or brownstone-faced row houses, most denominations needed to establish new sacred places. The Presbyterians had already inched west from Robert Smith's colonial Old Pine (pages 66–69) with the construction of John Haviland's neoclassical First Presbyterian Church on Washington Square (pages 120–122). To serve what was then called the "northwestern part of the city," the Presbytery of Philadelphia authorized a new congregation, which in 1823 constructed an imposing late Georgian brick church, named Arch Street Presbyterian, that boasted a 165-foot steeple.

The original Arch Street Presbyterian Church on Arch above Tenth Street erected 1823, demolished 1902. In 1897 the congregation united with West Arch Street Presbyterian Church, which then adopted the present name. Presbyterian Historical Society.

Designed by Joseph C. Hoxie, the present Arch Street Presbyterian Church was built in 1853–1855 to serve a rapidly growing Victorian neighborhood. Now it is surrounded by the high-rise buildings of Philadelphia's commercial center.

Designed to seat 1,100 worshipers, the neoclassical sanctuary continues the Corinthian order used on the exterior, complete with a pedimented podium and a coffered ceiling. Altogether Arch Street Presbyterian is one of the most handsome architectural compositions in the city.

This edifice on Arch Street west of Tenth Street would eventually suffer the fate of most Presbyterian churches erected between the Delaware River and Broad Street in the nineteenth century. Arch Street Presbyterian's decline was caused—according to the official history—by "the death of older members and the increased changes in the locality [that] seriously weakened the congregation," which had dwindled to fewer than 250 souls. Ultimately the church building would be demolished in 1903 to make way for an eight-story publishing house, but not before the surviving congregation had moved westward to Eighteenth Street, where it joined in 1897 with what had been known until then as the West Arch Street Presbyterian

Church. (Keeping track of Presbyterian church genealogy is an exercise only an ecclesiastic could love.)

West Arch Street Presbyterian Church, built by a congregation organized in 1828, was another effort to serve Presbyterians who were moving westward as the riverfront wards became increasingly commercial. The elders selected as architect Joseph C. Hoxie (1814–1870), a native of Rhode Island who had worked in Connecticut and New Jersey before relocating to Philadelphia. In 1848 he formed a partnership with his brother-in-law, the architect Stephen Decatur Button; about the time Hoxie secured the Presbyterian commission (1853) the partnership seems to have dissolved by mutual agreement, although they continued to work together on various projects. It seems clear that Hoxie was in independent practice when working on West Arch Street Presbyterian Church, which remains his most celebrated surviving work. He would later design Presbyterian churches in Easton, Norristown, and Harrisburg, Pennsylvania. What little we know of Hoxie suggests a leaning toward bizarre eclecticism and picturesque design drawn from a wide spectrum of historical styles.

The Arch Street commission permitted Hoxie to pull out all the stops, causing

Arch Street Presbyterian Church as the exterior appeared in 1869 before architect Hoxie's Baroque towers and lantern were removed. Notice the streetscape of late Federal and Italianate row houses whose prosperous residents the large church was built to serve. The Athenæum of Philadelphia.

Presbyterian magazine to declare that this "will probably be the most imposing church edifice which has been erected in Philadelphia." The cornerstone was laid on May 21, 1853, and construction under the supervision of Joseph Denegre required two full building seasons to complete; the new church was dedicated on October 15, 1855. Stylistically the result might be called Roman Corinthian. Here are pedimented portico and projecting pediments facing north, west, and east with monumental Corinthian columns and pilasters. Rising from the center of this symmetrical composition is a handsome dome.

Today Arch Street Presbyterian exhibits an understated classicism. But this restraint is a product of radical surgery around 1900. Photographs of the church taken shortly after its completion expose Hoxie at his most eclectic and the mid-Victorian Presbyterians in a moment of unexpected flamboyance. Could it be that the church elders had their eye on the nearby Roman Catholic Cathedral of Saints Peter and Paul then under way? John Notman's design for the main façade, in what he called "pure Roman style," boasted flanking towers that were later omitted, probably to economize (pages 152–157). But the Presbyterians got their twin towers, which rise above the northeast and northwest corners of the roof on either side of the main portico and from the dome—as Notman had planned for the Catholics—a matching lantern. A mid-nineteenth-century guidebook agrees with the designation of Arch Street Presbyterian as "one of the finest church edifices in the city. It is of the Corinthian order of architecture, with a magnificent portico on Arch street, a central dome, 170 feet high, and richly ornamented cupolas, each 115 feet high, in the *minaret style*" (emphasis added). English Baroque, perhaps, but clearly in the eyes of this critic, Italian Byzantine. The handsome interior, designed to seat 1,100 in the sanctuary, continues the Corinthian classicism of the exterior. The effect of Hoxie's coffered dome ceiling, pedimented pulpit platform, and organ case is dramatic and unexpected.

Today Arch Street Presbyterian Church is surrounded by commercial high-rise buildings; there is little hint of the residential neighborhood that caused the church to be erected in the mid-nineteenth century, although the recent construction of nearby high-rise residential buildings and retirement facilities offers hope of a residential population returning to that part of Center City. In addition to the union of the two Arch Street churches in 1897, the Girard Avenue Welsh Presbyterian Church merged with Arch Street in 1970, which continues to give the congregation ties to the Welsh Society of Philadelphia and special Welsh programs.

☛ *This view looking north in the sanctuary shows Hoxie's effective use of skylights, the galleries, and the pedimented organ case that balances the podium at the south end. Henry and William Pascoe, who lived nearby at Schuylkill Eighth (Fifteenth) Street and Sassafras (Race) Street executed the complex decorative plasterwork.*

CATHEDRAL BASILICA OF SAINTS PETER AND PAUL

Eighteenth Street and Benjamin Franklin Parkway, opposite Logan Circle Philadelphia, PA 19103

Napoleon LeBrun, architect, 1846–1864; John Notman, façade design, c. 1852

Telephone for visitor information: 215.561.1313

The building history of the Roman Catholic Cathedral Basilica of Saints Peter and Paul is the most complex of any sacred place in Philadelphia. Church historians like to attribute the design to Mariano Maller and John B. Tornatore, who served as the original building committee. Indeed, these priests may have suggested a Romanesque/Baroque prototype, inspired by Santi Ambrogio e Carlo Borromeo dei Lombardi al Corso, popularly known to tourists in Rome as San Carlo al Corso. Beyond the reputed source, all evidence for the design points to the young Philadelphia-born architect Napoleon LeBrun (1821–1901), whom we've already encountered at Saint Philip Neri (pages 98–101) and Saint Augustine's (pages 86–91).

☞ *The original cathedral plan by Napoleon LeBrun dates from 1846 and shows the location of the high altar until the extensive renovations of 1956–1957, which extended the cathedral to the east. The Athenæum of Philadelphia.*

☞☞ *The stately brownstone Roman Catholic Cathedral Basilica of Saints Peter and Paul facing Logan Circle was designed by Napoleon LeBrun and erected in 1846–1864. The main façade, however, is by John Notman and dates to the early 1850s.*

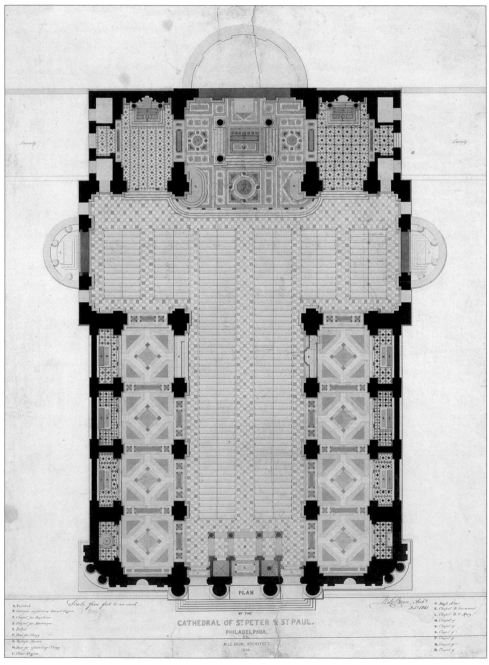

According to LeBrun's account of the cathedral, his "original design [was] made in 1846, in September of which year I supervised the laying of the corner-stone, and continued to direct the work until 1851."

Church officials found fault with LeBrun's "simple, yet majestic" proposal for the main façade and began to shop around for a less expensive alternative. Bishop Francis Patrick Kenrick admitted in a private letter from 1850 that "work on the Cathedral building is going ahead well enough; but the cost of the front will be very great." At least two non-Catholic architects were consulted. An alternative elevation and plan survives, dated April 5, 1850, by the architect of Girard College, Thomas

This view looks down the vaulted nave toward the transept crossing to the sanctuary, which was extended during the 1956–1957 renovations to provide a semicircular apse and to accommodate a new altar with a thirty-eight-foot marble and bronze domed canopy (baldachin). The black and white marble floor dates from the early twentieth-century renovations.

Ustick Walter—for which he received $25.00 (Athenæum of Philadelphia Collection). We also know from LeBrun's account that "a disagreement between myself and [the] clients then caused a suspension of my connection with the building for several years, during which time the present façade was erected . . . according to an amended design by Mr. John Notman. This was his sole connection with the work."

Notman's recent successes at Saint Mark's Church (pages 162–167) and Calvary Presbyterian Church had firmly established his reputation as a sympathetic architect of Protestant sacred places. These commissions would ultimately result in his being invited to design Holy Trinity and Saint Clement's (pages 168–173). The drawings

for Notman's cathedral façade do not survive, although a lithograph of his design, a newspaper description from 1852, and his official reports to the cathedral building committee provide a fairly detailed idea of his intentions. Notman probably was responsible for the giant order portico of four Corinthian columns, sixty feet high and six feet in diameter—in contrast to the attached columns and pilasters of the San Carlo al Corso prototype. His design also called for Baroque corner towers and a tall dome resting on columns, expensive embellishments never realized for a client constantly strapped for funds. Like LeBrun, Notman argued with the building committee, and in 1857 he was accused of inflating costs and fees and dismissed. John T. Mahony supervised the remaining work on the façade, which was dedicated in 1859.

LeBrun does not give a date for his reappointment as cathedral architect ("the walls . . . were not yet brought up to the roof level"), but his surviving drawings at the Athenæum are all updated after March 1860. "I was engaged to resume charge of the work, and carried it to completion in 1864, entirely according to my own designs and original plan," LeBrun concludes. Throughout the Civil War, church officials struggled to raise funds and keep workmen on the job. The new cathedral was dedicated on November 20, 1864, although the interior remained incomplete and unembellished for decades.

In 1913, on the eve of the First World War, Henry D. Dagit (1865–1929) received the commission to renovate and redecorate the cathedral interior and design a new Italianate Renaissance Revival palazzo next to the cathedral, facing Race Street, as a residence for the archbishop. Progenitor of a multigeneration firm of successful architects, Dagit developed a practice in Catholic institutional structures, especially after his appointment in 1898 as architect for the Archdiocese of Trenton, a position he held for a decade. His best-known commission remains Saint Francis de Sales Church in the Byzantine Revival Style (see pages 222–227).

In the mid-twentieth century the cathedral launched the most extensive architectural campaign since the 1850s. For this work the New York firm of Otto R. Eggers and Daniel P. Higgins, two graduates from the office of John Russell Pope, was hired. Eggers and Higgins designed the Chapel of Our Lady of the Blessed Sacrament on the north side of the cathedral campus (1954) and extended the sanctuary to the east by providing a coffered semicircular apse. In this additional space was erected a marble altar under a bronze canopy (1956–1957).

Following the Forty-First International Eucharistic Congress, held in Philadelphia in 1976, Pope Paul VI designated the Cathedral of Saint Peter and Saint Paul a basilica. This title is conferred on churches with special historical or religious significance.

The principal side chapels, entered from the transept on the north and south sides of the sanctuary, can be seen on LeBrun's original plan. The altars in these chapels date to 1887 and are dedicated respectively to the Sacred Heart of Jesus and the Blessed Virgin Mary. In 1917 the chapels were further embellished when Venetian glass mosaics of the Vision of Blessed Margaret Mary Alacoque and the Assumption of the Blessed Virgin Mary were installed above the altars. The Gorham Studios of New York executed the mosaics.

THE NOTMAN CHURCHES

The Scottish-born architect John Notman (1810–1865)—like Scottish master builder Robert Smith in the eighteenth century and native-born architect William Strickland in the early nineteenth century—is a conspicuous figure in the history of Philadelphia's ecclesiastical architecture. During the last and most creative years of his life Notman designed and built four major Center City churches west of Broad Street. Three of these—Saint Mark's, Saint Clement's, and Holy Trinity—continue to nurture congregations drawn largely from the remarkable neighborhoods they were built to serve.

A native of Edinburgh and son of a stonemason, Notman served an apprenticeship to a carpenter and then probably worked in the office of William Henry Playfair (1790–1857), the leading architect of public buildings in Edinburgh, who often designed in the picturesque Italianate Revival style Notman would bring to the United States. Notman immigrated to Philadelphia in 1831, where he may have found work as a carpenter or draftsman. His first major architectural commission was Laurel Hill Cemetery, where he created the ground plan and designed a Doric gateway, a Gothic chapel, and several tombs (1836–1839). These were widely publicized in several books and periodicals that brought Notman's work to the attention of the Episcopal bishop of New Jersey, the Rt. Rev. George Washington Doane (1799–1859), who became Notman's patron. For Bishop Doane he designed Riverside, overlooking the Delaware River near Burlington, New Jersey, the first fully developed picturesque Italianate villa in America (1839, demolished).

The Academy of Natural Sciences building (1839–1840, demolished) may be Notman's first important public commission in the city. It certainly introduced him to The Athenæum of Philadelphia building committee, given the close relationship between the two societies. For the Athenæum he designed and built a library in the Italianate palazzo mode on Washington Square (1845–1847) based on London club architecture popularized by Robert Smirke, Decimus Burton, and Charles Barry. Notman's widely published Athenæum proved to be the seminal structure in the style and one of the earliest Philadelphia buildings to be erected of brownstone rather than the more common marble or stuccoed brick.

During the 1830s and 1840s Notman also competed with other Philadelphia architects for church commissions; the earliest of which we can be certain is Saint Luke's, which he lost to Thomas S. Stewart (1839; pages 124–129). In 1845 Bishop Doane secured for him a small but significant commission to design the Chapel of the Holy Innocents for Saint Mary's Hall in Burlington, New Jersey, one of the earliest buildings in the United States to take into account guidelines of the Cambridge Camden Society, of which Bishop Doane was the sole American patron member. The *Ecclesiologist* published a favorable notice of this chapel, calling it an admirable first beginning for an American church. (For a discussion of the Camden Society

→ *Portrait of John Notman (1810–1865) by Samuel Bell Waugh (1814–1885), Philadelphia, circa 1849–1850. Private collection.*

and the *Ecclesiologist*, see below and pages 248–250.) Other small church commissions followed: Saint Thomas's Church, Glassboro, New Jersey (1846–1847), the Church of the Ascension, Lombard Street above Eleventh in Philadelphia (1846–1850, demolished), a chapel for the College of New Jersey (1847, demolished), and Green Hill Presbyterian Church, Girard Avenue above Sixteenth Street in Philadelphia (1847–1849, now Christ Temple Baptist Church).

Then, in 1847, Notman secured the Saint Mark's commission, which would be his ecclesiastical chef-d'oeuvre and a major boost to his reputation. Thomas Ustick Walter, when at work on the United States Capitol in Washington, would write to a Philadelphia friend who had inquired for an architect:

You wish me to recommend some one to you in whose taste I have confidence. My own impression is that Mr. Notman (Spruce above Broad) is the best Archt in Philada. I am not personally acquainted with him, but his works, as The Athenæum, St. Mark's Church, and other things I have seen of his, indicate taste, genius, and practical skill.

What more could one want in an architect?

New Jersey church commissions continued to come his way: Second Presbyterian, Princeton, New Jersey (1848–1849, much altered), and Saint Paul's Church, Trenton (1848–1851). But the major commissions now came from the rapidly expanding Philadelphia neighborhoods west of Broad Street. In 1851 Notman was ask to design Calvary Presbyterian Church on Locust Street west of Fifteenth Street (demolished, see pages 149–150), and the same year he took over from LeBrun at the Cathedral of Saints Peter and Paul (pages 196–197). Then, nearly simultaneously, came commissions for two large Episcopal churches: Saint Clement's (1855–1859)—north of Market and therefore not technically a part of Rittenhouse—and Holy Trinity (1856–1859) on Rittenhouse Square. Together with Saint Mark's, these mid-nineteenth-century churches are among the most important surviving Victorian sacred places in Philadelphia.

The Rittenhouse neighborhood—where John Notman lived and designed so many architecturally notable churches—embraces the southwest quadrant of Penn's original city, bounded on the east by Broad Street, on the west by the Schuylkill River, and on the north and south by Market and South Streets. Central to this area is one of Penn's public squares, designated on the original city plan as "Southwest Square" but not laid out as a pleasure garden until 1825, when it was named for David Rittenhouse. In the eighteenth and early nineteenth centuries development was sparse west of Broad Street, except for clay pits, brickyards, coal-yards, and modest manufactories of earthenware, porcelain, glass, and paint. In the 1830s and 1840s the commercial development of Philadelphia east of Broad began to displace residential neighborhoods, and middle-class Philadelphians decamped for new developments such as Clinton Row (southeast corner of Broad and Chestnut) and Colonnade Row (Chestnut Street at Fifteenth), while the Victorian "merchant aristocracy" erected major freestanding mansions. As a consequence, Presbyterian and Episcopal churches began to spring up. A second wave of settlement occurred in the 1850s following construction of Notman's Saint Mark's Episcopal and Calvary Presbyterian, both commissioned for new congregations then being formed. Brownstone rows by the likes of architects Thomas Ustick Walter and Samuel Sloan as well as builders such as John McCrea were rising on all the principal streets. By 1865 Rittenhouse Square had been entirely enveloped by residential development

and large city houses were spreading west along Walnut, Locust, Spruce, and Delancey. Occupants of these houses provided congregations for the new churches, and their wealthy owners willingly contributed to embellishing their sacred places in the decades prior to the Great Depression and World War II. After a brief period of decline, these neighborhoods recovered their allure as attractive places to live, although most of the wealthy patrons had abandoned Center City in favor of Chestnut Hill and the Main Line.

While Philadelphia's cityscape has suffered successive architectural intrusions of astounding beauty and unmitigated ugliness, the Rittenhouse neighborhoods manage to retain their historicity, humane scale, and livability. Here the trend toward declining population that plagues many urban centers of the northeast and upper midwest has been reversed, and the pews of Notman's churches are once again occupied, if not to capacity.

Artist Frank H. Taylor recreated Colonnade Row, designed by John Haviland at Chestnut and Fifteenth Streets, for real estate speculators Charles and George Blight in 1830 (demolished). To the right is Epiphany Episcopal Church, designed by Thomas Ustick Walter (demolished). This congregation would later join with Saint Luke's Church (pages 124–128). Library Company of Philadelphia.

SAINT MARK'S CHURCH

1625 Locust Street
Philadelphia, PA 19103

John Notman, architect and contractor, 1847–1852; Cope and Stewardson, architects, Lady Chapel, 1900–1902

Telephone for visitor information: 215.735.1416

www.saintmarksphiladelphia.org

☞ *Viewed from this elevated angle, the tower of Saint Mark's appears almost out of scale with the church itself. It rises from a square base in buttressed stages to an octagonal spire with an overall height of 175 feet. Entrance to the church is through the first level of the tower. During the 150th anniversary of the parish the ring of eight bells was restored.*

A visitors' guidebook to Philadelphia published for the Centennial Exposition in 1876 describes Saint Mark's Church as "the property of one of the wealthiest congregations in the city, and its services are grand and impressive." While the congregation is no longer so wealthy, the church and its services are certainly impressive, and modern visitors should put Saint Mark's high on their short list of significant historic sacred places of Philadelphia worth going to see.

Saint Mark's and Saint James the Less (pages 248–253) were the first Episcopal churches in the Philadelphia area deliberately designed with the restoration of the Anglo-Catholic form of worship in mind. Saint Mark's vestry organized on June 28, 1847, and appointed a building committee to erect a church in the western section of Philadelphia. (At the time, the Church of the Epiphany on the northwest corner of Chestnut and Fifteenth Streets was the only Episcopal church west of Broad Street.) They invited Notman to submit plans, but may have been uncertain whether his proposal would be appropriate for a high church liturgy. They recorded,

> In order to secure a better choice of plans application was made by letter to the Ecclesiological Society of England, from whom was obtained a plan, which from certain peculiarities it was not considered desirable to adopt. Mr. Notman since offered a plan including some improvements from the English drawings, which met with the approbation of the committee.

What the committee received from the Ecclesiological Society was a Gothic design by Richard C. Carpenter (1812–1855), based on his All Saints Church, Brighton (demolished). Through his friendship with Augustus Welby Northmore Pugin, Carpenter became associated with the Cambridge Camden Society (later the Ecclesiological Society), founded in 1839 to restore and reconstruct the outward signs and symbols of the Anglican church. Pugin had criticized early nineteenth-century English ecclesiastical design for its lack of Christian meaning. He argued for a return to medieval structures, particularly those dating from the fourteenth century. Camden Society leaders thought the Gothic style of medieval parish churches particularly appropriate for sacramental, liturgical worship. Like Saint James the Less, Saint Mark's would consist of two distinct parts: the nave to accommodate the laity and the chancel reserved for the clergy, separated by a rood screen. The *Ecclesiologist* stated flatly, "every church of whatever kind, size, or shape, should have a distinct Chancel at least one-third of the length of the Nave, and separated from the latter, internally at least, if not externally, by a well-defined mark, a chancel-arch if possible, or at least by a screen and raised floor." At the eastern end of the chancel is the sanctuary—raised from the floor of the chancel—housing the stone high altar backed by a reredos. The western end of the chancel would contain seats

The famous red doors of Saint Mark's combine the artistry of the Polish-born ironworker Samuel Yellin (1885–1940) and the Italian-born stained-glass and mosaic artist Nicola D'Ascenzo (1871–1954). The polychrome tympanum figures depict Christ in Majesty and the legend "Come unto me, all that are heavy-laden, and I will give you rest."

for the clergy and choir. The reintroduction of this plan from pre-Reformation parish churches constituted a rejection of the Protestant "priesthood of all believers," which had brought worship out to the nave and placed greater emphasis on preaching than on the sacraments.

Carpenter's plans for a "town-church" approved by the Cambridge Camden Society were received by the Saint Mark's vestry and given to Notman, who altered them to better suit the climate and site. (Carpenter had created a three-gabled roof, which would have been impractical in a climate where heavy snows are likely.)

🕯 *This view looks east toward the chancel and the high altar, above which is a stained-glass window by Meyer and Company depicting the Ascension of Christ. The carved alabaster altar of Saint John the Evangelist is on the left (north) aisle behind the pulpit. Originally created for the Lady Chapel, the altar and reredos were moved to this location when the chapel was redecorated. The rood beam was designed by the distinguished ecclesiastical architect Henry Vaughan (1845–1917).*

While the Saint Mark's design is partly based on Carpenter's church, architectural historians have also pointed out its similarity to Saint Stephen's, Rochester Row, Vincent Square, Westminster, which the *Illustrated London News* published on July 24, 1847.

The cornerstone of Saint Mark's was laid in 1848, the first services were held in 1849, and the tower and steeple were finished in 1851. Notman's plans must have been sent to London, because the *Ecclesiologist* (April 1848) published an approving notice of the church. In Philadelphia the *Public Ledger* (March 22, 1849) published rapturous praise and described the new church in the following words:

> This church edifice is composed of brown free stone [sandstone] of the most pleasing tone of color, in the decorated style of Gothic architecture that prevailed in the last quarter of the thirteenth and the beginning of the fourteenth centuries; a period in which it may be said to have attained the highest point of graceful proportion and luxuriant beauty.... The church comprises a chancel, a nave and aisles, an organ or choir aisle with a convenient vestry.... An open screen of oak will mark the division of the church and chancel. The window over the altar is of five lights, and will be of painted glass of an appropriate design.

Like those of Saint James the Less, the interior walls are unplastered hammer-dressed stone in the manner approved by Pugin and Carpenter. The interior is simple and not over-ornamented. In the words of architectural historian Phoebe B. Stanton,

> Beneath the dark, open timber roof, in the limited light of the nave, the capitals of the arcades, alternately foliated and molded, assist in the composition of *the finest church interior of its period in the United States*. In Philadelphia ecclesiology had brought a new church style and a new sophistication to American architecture. (emphasis added)

Gradually the spare interior began to attract embellishments. The most significant of these is the Lady Chapel designed by Cope and Stewardson, given by Rodman Wanamaker, son of department store magnate John Wanamaker, in memory of his wife Fernanda, who died in 1900. The principal designer was Charles E. Kempe (1838–1907), whose alabaster altar and polychrome black oak reredos were later moved to the end of the north aisle and rededicated to Saint John. In its place Wanamaker donated another altar of marble encased in silver. The Lady Chapel by Cope and Stewardson is so intricate in its execution and redolent of Christian

The carved marble pulpit, designed by Ralph Adams Cram, represents Saint Paul, Saint Francis of Assisi, and Saint John Chrysostom; the railing is carved with the heads of beasts representing the four Evangelists: Matthew, Mark, Luke, and John. Cram is also responsible for the choir rail and gates, the latter made by Tiffany Studios and depicting angels kneeling in adoration. The carved oak choir stalls were designed by Henry Vaughan. The organ loft can just be seen; it holds an Aeolian-Skinner organ with 104 ranks of pipes.

iconography that sitting with a brochure in hand (provided by the church) is time well spent (see pages 144–145). The altar alone contains 144 individually sculpted figures of saints. In 1913 Ralph Adams Cram (1863–1942), the celebrated architect of Saint John the Divine in New York, designed the marble pulpit and the adjoining choir rail and gates, the latter manufactured by the Tiffany Studios; they show facing angels kneeling in adoration.

SAINT CLEMENT'S CHURCH

*2013 Appletree Street
(between Arch and Cherry Streets)
Philadelphia, PA 19103*

*John Notman, architect and
contractor, 1855–1859; Horace Wells
Sellers, architect, 1897–1933*

*Telephone for visitor information:
215.563.1876*

While there could be little doubt of the Anglo-Catholic yearnings of the Saint Mark's vestry, Notman's next two Episcopal churches appear—initially at least—to have been created for low church congregations. Both Saint Clement's and Holy Trinity are in the Norman Romanesque style revived by English architects in the 1830s and 1840s for nonconforming congregations with an allergic reaction to neomedieval Gothic styling. English ecclesiastical architecture following the Norman Conquest was influenced by late Romanesque round-arch buildings of France prior to the evolution of the pointed Gothic arch in the thirteenth century. These churches typically had massive walls following the ancient Roman structural system—often sculpted and molded with round-headed arcades, horizontal stringcourses, and narrow windows with semicircular heads. The interiors were usually without aisles, and the sanctuary occupied a rounded apse rather than the fully developed chancel that would come later. According to the late Henry Russell Hitchcock, who made a considerable study of these churches,

Since almost all of them are provided only with basilican apses, or else with very shallow rectangular eastern projections, in evident avoidance of the deep

☞ *The picturesque entrance porch with its rope-turned columns leads to the vestibule. The porch dates from the construction of the parish house (1864).*

☞☞ *Saint Clement's Church is in the Norman Romanesque Revival style, with its arcaded apse facing east onto Twentieth Street. The first level arcade is original; the second level was added by Horace Wells Sellers when the sanctuary was expanded in 1908. Originally there was a tall spire on the tower; as so often happened in Philadelphia, it was declared unsafe and demolished in 1869.*

chancels insisted on by the Camdenians, one may assume that their sponsors were all Low Churchmen intentionally eschewing Decorated Gothic as well as ritualistic planning.

The land on which Notman would erect his third church west of Broad Street was donated to the vestry by William S. Wilson, a Presbyterian related to the first rector, but also a speculator in land and a developer of property with a keen instinct for attracting prosperous Philadelphians moving west from the commercial center of the rapidly expanding Victorian city. The cornerstone was laid in May 1856, but a financial panic the next year delayed completion of the church until late 1859. As patron the parish selected the martyred Clement of Rome, patron saint of mariners, stonecutters, and sick children.

In plan the resulting church has neither side aisles nor interior columns. A handsome blind-arcaded, semicircular apse is at the east end facing Twentieth Street; the entrance vestibule is at the west end, accessed by a picturesque arcaded porch with spiral-turned columns.

Ironically, within a decade of its first services, Saint Clement's would undergo a "Catholic awakening" triggered by the election of the Rev. Mr. Herman Batterson as rector in 1869. His efforts to introduce Anglo-Catholic liturgy and services put him into direct conflict with the Rt. Rev. William B. Stevens, bishop of Pennsylvania, described as "an uncompromising Protestant and militant low churchman." The conflict spilled into the press and ultimately into the Court of Common Pleas. Eventually the Anglo-Catholics prevailed. *The Illustrated History of the Centennial Exhibition* commented in 1876 that Saint Clement's "is a handsome edifice, richly decorated within. It is an Episcopal church, and is noted as the most extreme ritualistic establishment in the City."

In no small part the subsequent alterations to the interior of Saint Clement's Church are in response to this successful campaign to bring the congregation into

↢ *The Gothic high altar, designed by Horace Wells Sellers and carved by Belgian sculptor Edward Maene, was consecrated in 1908. The reredos is oak in the form of a triptych surmounted by a baldachin. To accommodate the altar the sanctuary ceiling had to be raised approximately fifteen feet; the lancet windows were created at the same time, as were the choir stalls.*

↢ *New York architect Wilfred E. Anthony (1878–1948), known mainly for his Roman Catholic churches, designed the Shrine of Our Lady of Clemency, dedicated in 1943. From behind Our Lady golden rays of glory radiate, and above the figure is a carved wood valance surmounted by a tall spire. Henry Beretta sculpted the shrine, which was gilded and painted by Robert Robbins.*

In 1929 the City of Philadelphia widened Twentieth Street. Rather than demolish the church, the Saint Clement's vestry acquired two properties to the west, raised the 5,500-ton church onto rails, and pushed it back forty feet onto new foundations. All costs for the relocation were covered by the city. This photograph shows the church elevated on its cribbing ready to be moved back. Urban Archives, Temple University.

the Anglo-Catholic fold. Where the vestry of Saint Mark's had introduced several nationally and internationally celebrated architects and designers to embellish their Notman church, Saint Clement's relied on Horace Wells Sellers (1857–1933), a Philadelphia architect and engineer who devoted more than a quarter century of service to the church.

Great-grandson of the artist Charles Willson Peale, Sellers studied at the University of Pennsylvania and launched a career as both architect and engineer. He had a lifelong interest in historical architecture and served on advisory committees for Independence Hall, Christ Church, and Washington's Headquarters at Valley Forge. His contributions to Saint Clement's Church are substantial: the Crypt Chapel (1889), clergy house (1903), parish house (1907), altar and reredos (1908), and other alterations and additions, including the Lady Chapel (1915). He also designed the Lea Memorial Pulpit and its canopy (1921).

The greatest challenge to the vestry, congregation, and architect arrived in the form of the City Beautiful Movement of the 1920s, which transformed Logan

Square and created a monumental boulevard lined with cultural institutions stretching across Philadelphia's unrelieved grid plan from City Hall to the Philadelphia Museum of Art. Grand early twentieth-century civic projects in Philadelphia—the Benjamin Franklin Parkway and the Delaware River Bridge, for example—levied a costly toll on the city's sacred places. One project related to the parkway was the widening of Twentieth Street from fifty to ninety feet. In the words of a brochure published by Saint Clement's at the time, "here was a historic Church, known among Churchmen throughout the length and breadth of the land, a shrine for Anglo-Catholics for those from abroad as well as from home, face to face with possible destruction or removal. What could be done?" The answer came from architect Horace Sellers, who suggested physically moving the 5,500-ton church onto new foundations forty feet to the west. This complex engineering feat was accomplished without mishap, and Notman's Saint Clement's Church was literally pulled back from the brink of disaster.

The groined ceiling, altar, and reredos of the Lady Chapel are English red stone. There are three canopied niches in the reredos containing statues of the Virgin and Child (center) flanked by Saint Joseph and Saint Elizabeth with the child Saint John the Baptist. The extraordinary gates are by the Polish-born master ironworker Samuel Yellin (1885–1940).

CHURCH OF THE HOLY TRINITY

1904 Walnut Street at Rittenhouse Square, Philadelphia, PA 19103

John Notman, architect and contractor, 1856–1859; John Fraser, tower architect, 1868

Telephone for visitor information: 215.567.1267

www.htrint.org

As already discussed, Saint Mark's was intended from the beginning to be an Anglo-Catholic church, and Saint Clement's became one within a decade of its opening, notwithstanding the low church resonance of its Norman Romanesque ancestry. Holy Trinity, however, was intended to be a low church and proudly remains so to this day. In June 1855 a vestry was formed to organize a new congregation and to erect a church in the vicinity of Rittenhouse Square. The building committee examined designs in several styles—including Gothic—but ultimately followed the lead of Saint Clement's, selecting John Notman's design in the Norman Romanesque style. Orientation of the chancel is problematical for a high church confronted with an east-facing lot; if the chancel is to face east as dictated by Anglo-Catholic tradition, the church must turn its back on the street, as happened at Saint Clement's. Since the Holy Trinity vestry evidenced no strong feelings on this matter, Notman could take full advantage of the Rittenhouse Square east-facing lot and let the chancel fall where it might, in this case on the west wall.

The elaborately ornamented Connecticut brownstone principal façade of Holy Trinity faces on Rittenhouse Square. A deeply recessed central doorway is flanked by towers to the north and south. These towers have similar, albeit smaller entrances—all with clustered columns and carved capitals. Above the central bay of the main façade is an interlaced blind arcade; above the arcade is a wheel window; and above the window is a pediment with triplet windows and corbeled cornice. The towers flanking the central bay are virtually identical at the lower levels, but due to their difference in height they are picturesquely asymmetrical. The south tower is shorter and terminates in a central pediment. The north tower was not executed during Notman's life; it was added in 1868 by John Fraser (1825–1906), who had just formed a partnership with George W. Hewitt and Frank Furness. It roughly follows Notman's design, which is preserved in his professional papers at The Athenæum of Philadelphia.

As for the interior of Holy Trinity, the *Daily Evening Bulletin* (March 28, 1859) reported,

> The interior of the church is no less imposing than the outside, and the mediæval style of the arrangement of the building, with its immense rafters, and galleries supported on massive brackets of grained wood is not violated by the appliances which modern taste and luxury demand. The auditorium occupies the entire main building. . . . The chancel is at the western end of the church, and the organ gallery is at the other extremity. . . . The chancel is a marked feature of the church. It is semi-circular in form, having a width of 34 feet and a depth of 17 feet. It is ornamented with an arcade on columns, supporting a semi-domed ceiling radiated to the chancel arch. It is lighted through stained glass at the apex.

☞ *The picturesque Norman Romanesque façade of John Notman's Holy Trinity Church (1855–1859) faces Rittenhouse Square from the southwest corner of Walnut and Nineteenth Streets. The north tower was added in 1868 and houses a twenty-five-bell carillon.*

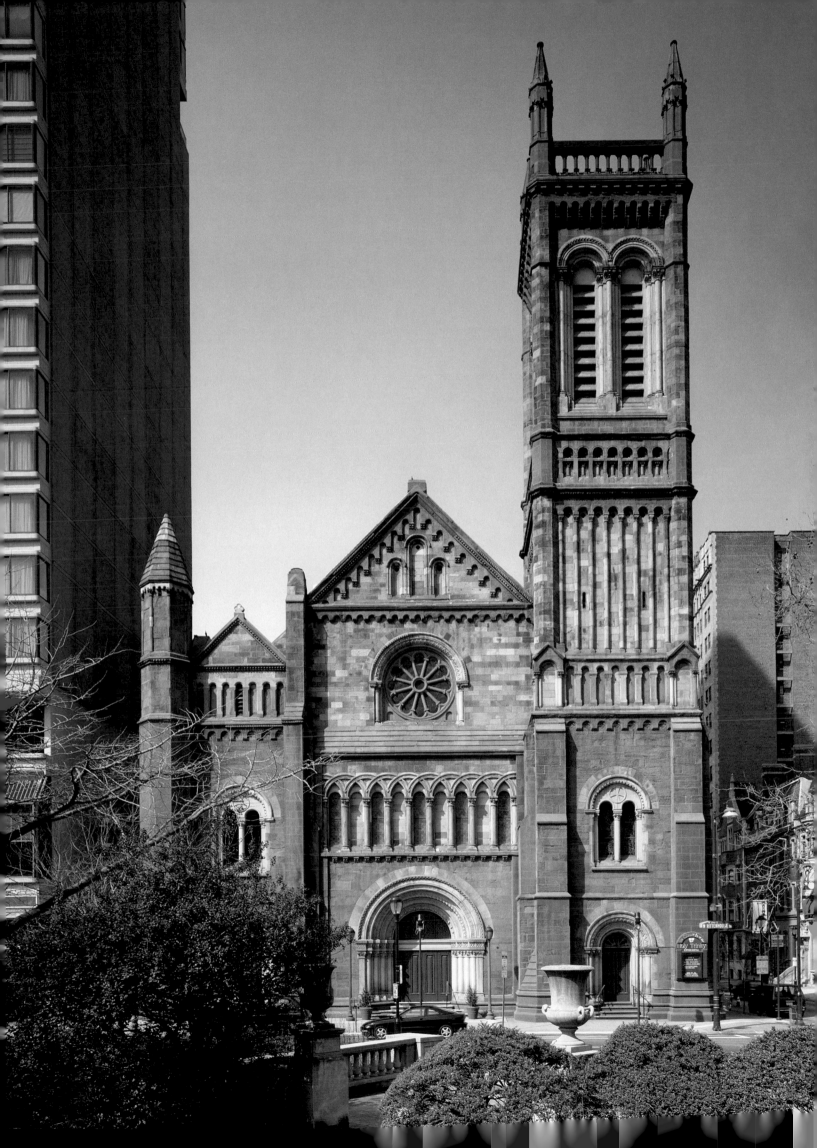

During the Civil War a new rector arrived at Holy Trinity: Phillips Brooks (1862–1869), whose ability as a speaker filled the pews several times on Sunday and on Wednesday evenings as well. In 1868, after spending two weeks in Jerusalem, Brooks wrote the words to his famous carol, "O Little Town of Bethlehem," set to music by the Holy Trinity organist Lewis Redner, whose composition is principally credited by musicologists for the enduring success of the carol. The following year, Brooks accepted the call to Trinity Church, Boston, where—after twenty-two years of service—he became bishop of Massachusetts. (Four rectors of Holy Trinity have been elevated to the episcopate, a remarkable record.)

The only major alterations to Holy Trinity came in 1880. The interior was extensively renovated and updated under the direction of Boston architect Henry Van Brunt (1832–1903) and Philadelphian James Peacock Sims (1849–1882). According to one newspaper account,

> The present alterations and renovation consist principally in re-forming the roof into a barrel vault in the centre. . . . The chancel has also been very much altered. The old dome has been preserved, but below the space has been squared by the opening of large arches into spaces previously lost. In the chancel a Bishop's chair, and ten stalls have been placed, all in handsomely carved black walnut. The pulpit and reading desk are of the same material, and are very elaborate in design and decoration. . . . The old pews have been removed and new ones put in.

Three years later Joseph E. Temple donated chimes for the main tower as a memorial to his wife, Martha Anna Kirtley. Cast by the Severin van Aerschodt Foundry, Louvain, Belgium, the chimes were played for first time on October 3, 1883. By the mid-twentieth century the chimes were no longer functional; contributions by friends and parishioners of the church—most notably Emilie Busch de Hellebranth—permitted the carillon to be put in working order for the year 2000 celebrations.

In 1942 the mural artist Hildreth Meiere (1892–1961) was commissioned to decorate the chancel apse with scenes from the nativity in honor of Phillips Brooks, second rector of Holy Trinity. An artist of no little renown, Meiere's public murals and mosaics can be seen in the Nebraska State Capitol, the Saint Louis Cathedral, Rockefeller Center, the dome of the National Academy of Sciences in Washington, and Saint Bartholomew's Church in Manhattan. The central panel of her Holy Trinity Church murals depicts the nativity, the panel on the Gospel side the shepherds scene from Luke and the Epistle side the Magi bearing offerings from Matthew.

By the late 1960s the congregation had severely declined and the vestry seriously entertained a proposal to lease the site to a developer, thereby guaranteeing that the church would be demolished. Fortunately a last-minute protest by watchful

The nativity murals in the chancel, by Hildreth Meiere, date from 1942. The Phillips Brooks Memorial Pulpit, dating from 1880, can be seen on the right.

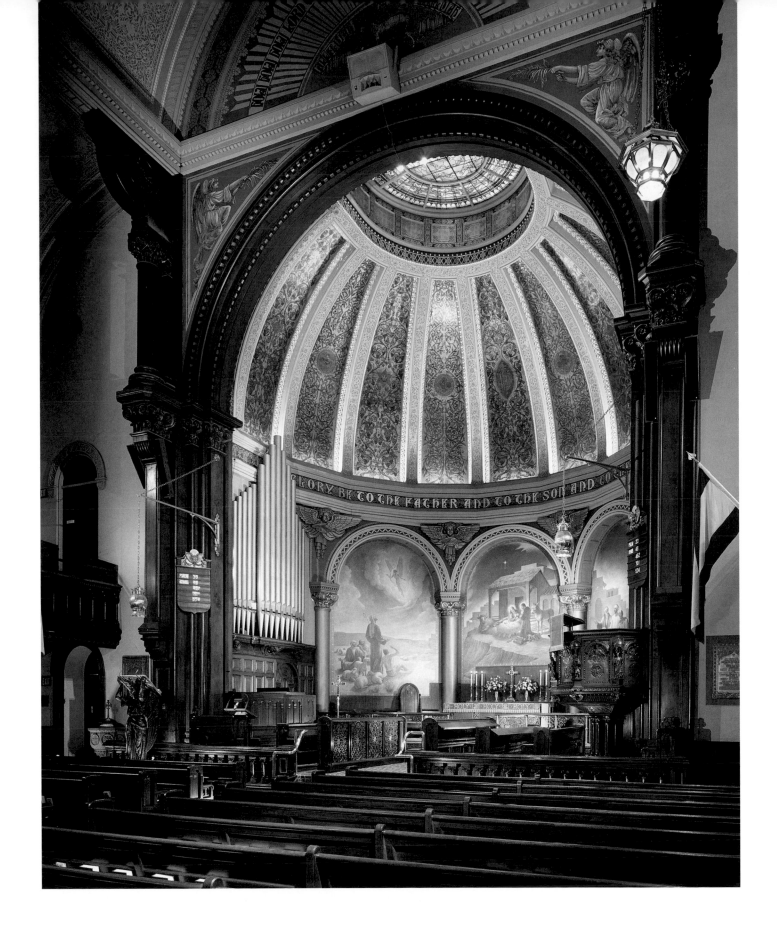

members of the congregation, vigorously supported by the preservation community, saved Holy Trinity, which has subsequently enjoyed substantial support for restoration and has seen an increase of interest from neighborhood residents. (For a more detailed discussion of the preservation debate, see Preface, pages x–xi.)

TENTH PRESBYTERIAN CHURCH

(West Spruce Street Presbyterian Church)

Seventeenth and Spruce Streets Philadelphia, PA 19103-6714

John McArthur, Jr., architect, 1855–1857; Frank Miles Day, architect, 1893

Telephone for visitor information: 215.735.7688

www.tenth.org

The building now sheltering one of the largest and most vibrant Center City Presbyterian congregations was constructed originally for the West Spruce Street Presbyterian Church. By the mid-nineteenth century, many residents of Philadelphia were moving (in the words of one church historian) "to suburban districts in . . . the southwestern part of the city, west of Broad Street, across the farms that covered what is now the central part of the city." The closest Presbyterian church to this rapidly developing area was a substantial congregation known as Tenth Presbyterian, housed in a neoclassical building designed for it by William Strickland (1828–1829, demolished) at Twelfth and Walnut Streets. By 1852 the Tenth Presbyterian elders recognized the need for a new church farther west; they consequently developed and colonized a new congregation, to be known as West Spruce Street Presbyterian Church, with a new building on the southwest corner of Seventeenth and Spruce erected in 1855–1857.

⌖ The original McArthur towers and steeples of West Spruce Street Presbyterian Church are shown in this dramatic photograph. They were reduced in 1912 due to structural failure and may someday be reconstructed. Presbyterian Historical Society.

⌖⌖ John McArthur, Jr., architect of Philadelphia City Hall, designed the Italianate West Spruce Street Presbyterian Church in 1855–1857. Later the congregation adopted the name Tenth Presbyterian Church.

The Memorial to Gustavus S. Benson (1806–1883), president of the corporation of Tenth Presbyterian Church, was "erected by his children upon the walls of the church which he loved well and served faithfully, and in reverent assurance that he worships now in a Temple not made with hands, eternal in the Heavens."

Fortunately for the new congregation, the Scottish-born architect John McArthur, Jr. (1823–1890) was both congregant and deacon. He would design the church, in exchange for a building lot on which he later erected a substantial town house. McArthur is remembered today as the architect of Philadelphia City Hall, the tallest public building in the United States at the time of its completion in 1901. What is not generally known is that prior to City Hall tower the tallest building in Philadelphia was the steeple of West Spruce Street Presbyterian Church, taller even than the famous steeple of Christ Church.

McArthur came to Philadelphia at the age of ten, and studied architecture and building at Carpenters' Hall and at the Franklin Institute, where he attended lectures by Thomas Ustick Walter. By 1848 he had won his first architectural competition, the Philadelphia House of Refuge. From that point he secured a steady stream of commissions ranging from hotels to private residences, commercial structures, and churches. During the Civil War he designed and supervised the erection of twenty-four temporary hospitals as architect for the Quartermaster General's Department in Philadelphia. The Philadelphia City Hall commission that occupied the last fifteen years of his life must be considered the foremost achievement of a long and successful career.

The popularity of the Italianate Revival style was at its height in the years prior to the Civil War, and McArthur's West Spruce Street design is often called a "free adaptation of the Lombard Romanesque" style, with characteristic round-headed windows and doors and decoratively corbeled cornice. The cornerstone of the brick and sand-painted wood-trimmed building was laid on April 26, 1855, and the completed building was dedicated on January 4, 1857. The most dramatic features of the design were the two brick towers with their wooden steeples flanking the main Spruce Street entrances to the auditorium. The east tower and steeple, stepped back from the Seventeenth and Spruce corner, rose nearly 250 feet, while the squat west tower and steeple was half as high. Unfortunately, structural decay in the steeples forced the congregation to truncate both in 1912. (The current congregation recognizes the desirability of recreating these essential elements of McArthur's original conception, and there are plans to reproduce the steeples.)

McArthur's interior design also suffered over time. Early photographs show an Italianate interior with a pedimented framing to a semicircular apse behind a central pulpit flanked by columns and pilasters in the Corinthian order. This scheme was swept away in 1893, when the firm of Frank Miles Day and Brother updated the interior. This dramatic change was brought about by the decision of the presbytery to merge the declining Tenth Presbyterian congregation with its sibling West Spruce Street Presbyterian. In deference to the role of the mother church in founding West Spruce Street , the congregation at Seventeenth and Spruce adopted the name Tenth Presbyterian Church. The Strickland-designed church at Twelfth and Walnut Streets was sold and demolished.

The principal architect of these renovations, Frank Miles Day (1861–1918), was born in Philadelphia and studied at the South Kensington School of Art, the Royal Academy, and, ultimately, as part of the Walter Millard atelier—all in London. He returned to Philadelphia and established his own office in 1887, where he was joined in 1893 by his older brother, H. Kent Day (1851–1925). The younger Day's work departs from the idiosyncratic architecture of earlier Philadelphia architects Frank Furness and Willis G. Hale; nonetheless, one wonders at the motivation of a Presbyterian congregation to sweep aside a modest Italianate interior in favor of a neo-Byzantine design featuring stenciled geometric and symbolic designs. Windows and paneling were also replaced and stained-glass windows by the Tiffany Studio were installed. More explicable is the installation of slip pews in place of box pews to accommodate the larger combined congregation.

The current congregation of 1,400 members is evangelical conservative; in 1984 they voted to leave the United Presbyterian Church (USA) and join the Presbyterian Church in America (PCA).

⟜ The neo-Byzantine interior reflects extensive remodeling by the firm of Frank Miles Day and Brother, 1893, in response to the merger of the Tenth and West Spruce Street congregations.

FIRST BAPTIST CHURCH

*123 South Seventeenth Street
Philadelphia, PA 19103-5499*

Edgar V. Seeler, architect, 1899–1900

*Telephone for visitor information:
215.563.3853*

fbcphila@aol.com

☛ *Edgar V. Seeler's handsome adaptation of Romanesque and Byzantine architectural styles in gray Holmesburg granite and Worcester sandstone (1899–1900) can no longer be fully appreciated from ground level due to the surrounding commercial towers. The design owes much to H. H. Richardson's Romanesque Trinity Church, Boston.*

Baptists had arrived in Philadelphia from Newport, Rhode Island, by 1684, and Welsh Baptists from the Pennepek (Lower Dublin) Baptist Church began to drift into town after 1688. The first formal congregation drew together for worship in 1698. They met in a storehouse with the Presbyterians, and then in a brewhouse until 1707, when they took over a simple Quaker meeting house near Christ Church (pages 40–45) abandoned by the followers of George Keith. A brick meeting house replaced the frame building in 1731 and was in turn enlarged in 1762 and again in 1808. Finally, in 1856, the congregation elected to move to the northwest corner of Broad and Arch Streets, the first of what would be three nonconforming Protestant congregations to settle on that key intersection near Center Square, future site of City Hall (pages 140–143, 206–209).

As architect the Baptists selected Stephen Decatur Button (1813–1897)—their probable architect of choice, co-religionist Thomas Ustick Walter, being otherwise engaged in Washington, D.C., designing the wings and dome of the United States Capitol. Button's eclectic Romanesque style church with its impressive steeple may have encouraged the Methodists to a similar exclamation a few years later when they hired Addison Hutton to design the first Philadelphia Methodist Gothic style church across Broad Street. But just as the Baptists were the first to make the jump to that central intersection, they were the first to move again. In the words of one Baptist historian, "in 1898, the church having celebrated its bi-centennial anniversary in significant and appropriate manner, promptly proceeded with the sale of its increasingly valuable property at Broad and Arch Streets." With the advantage of hindsight, it is easy to question the wisdom of this move. Yet it was prompted in part by the union of First Baptist and Beth Eden Church at Broad and Spruce Streets, in addition to the rapidly expanding commercial environment of Broad and Arch. On the eve of the twentieth century, the Seventeenth and Sansom Streets area remained residential; the towering commercial structures that would later cast their shadows over the site were as yet not imagined.

As architect the Baptists selected Edgar V. Seeler (1867–1929), a Philadelphia native who received his basic education at the Massachusetts Institute of Technology and final polish at the École des Beaux-Arts in the atelier of Victor Laloux. Seeler returned from France in 1893 to establish his own practice without serving an apprenticeship in the office of an established Philadelphia architect. The rigorous École des Beaux-Arts experience equipped its graduates to design with facility in a wide variety of historical styles. Study abroad also offered the singular opportunity to observe the architecture of many ages and cultures; these students did not learn their history of architecture from photographs in books. In later years Seeler would design suave Georgian and classical revival buildings for the Curtis Publishing Company (1912) and the Penn Mutual Life Insurance Company (1916), both on Independence Square, among many other Center City projects.

It seems unlikely that Seeler would have proposed for a Baptist church a free adaptation of Byzantine and Romanesque architecture with a sanctuary dome reminiscent of Hagia Sophia in Constantinople, even for a congregation coming from Button's mid-nineteenth-century, eclectic Romanesque edifice. In fact, the style can be traced to a prominent member of the congregation who had recently returned from the Middle East. "Build something wonderful," he is recorded as having said, "like the incomparable Santa Sophia in old Constantinople." Undaunted, and probably with H. H. Richardson's Romanesque Trinity Church in mind from his student days in Boston, Seeler produced a cruciform auditorium in a Greek cross arched over by barrel vaults richly embellished with Christian emblems and symbols. The stained-glass windows were supplied by the studio of Otto Heinike and Owen J. Bowen, New York City. Remarked one member, "some have inquired as to whether it is not a bit elaborate and ornate for Baptists! It is true that they have had a tradition of simplicity rather than ostentation and that they have often referred to their

When the First Baptist Church moved to Broad and Arch and then to Seventeenth and Sansom, the congregation preserved the grave markers of its early pastors. The oldest of these is the tombstone of Abel Morgan, pastor from 1711 to 1722.

places of assembly and worship as meeting houses." Without actually explaining the apparent inconsistency, the response was that, since the means to build well were available, the congregation "could and under the impress of the Spirit they should erect a structure of surpassing tribute to God Whose leading they humbly sought and earnestly followed." The resulting architectural essay, one of the most arresting of its style in Philadelphia, was dedicated October 14, 1900, having required less than one year to erect.

On January 13, 1949, First Baptist Church was nearly destroyed by fire. Flames gutted the chancel, destroying the organ and pulpit. Smoke and water ruined the decorative stenciling and painting; the stained-glass windows in the dome were lost. Restoration required nearly a year; before and after photographs show how successful the sanctuary has been returned to its former splendor. Only the stained glass in the dome has not yet been restored.

Directly behind the pulpit in the chancel area of the sanctuary is the oval baptistry lined with Pavonnezza marble, reached by concealed stairs connected with robing rooms below.

CHURCH OF THE NEW JERUSALEM

(adaptive reuse as corporate offices)

*2129 Chestnut Street
Philadelphia, PA 19103-3146*

*Theophilus Parsons Chandler, Jr.,
architect, 1881–1883; angel staircase,
1908; Mark B. Thompson, architect,
1989*

*Telephone for visitor information:
215.977.1700*

Congregations usually select sites for their sacred places based on proximity to members' homes and availability of transportation. For that reason several denominations are occasionally found clustered together. The intersection of Broad and Arch Streets was once a showcase of large Baptist, Methodist, and Lutheran city churches, and the immediate area of Chestnut and Twenty-Second Streets is another concentration, including the Center City Lutheran Church of the Holy Communion (pages 206–209), the First Unitarian Church (pages 200–205), and the Church of the New Jerusalem. All these were erected in the span of a few years; two continue to house active congregations while one does not.

What happens when a congregation relocates or can no longer support its architecturally significant building? Ideally another congregation steps up to assume the responsibility. But in too many instances demolition follows. There are, however, successful alternative uses for redundant sacred places. For example, the Fleisher Art Memorial occupies the former Church of the Evangelist (pages 102–105) and Tabernacle Presbyterian Church (pages 212–215) now serves the University of Pennsylvania as a theater. But the poster child for a successful adaptive reuse in Philadelphia is the Swedenborgian Church of the New Jerusalem, located on a landscaped corner lot in Center City, a masterwork of architect Theophilus Parsons Chandler, Jr.

The Swedenborgian denomination teaches the Bible as illuminated by the eighteenth-century Swedish scientist, philosopher, and mystic Emanuel Swedenborg (1688–1772). His followers believe, to quote a late nineteenth-century definition,

> The Lord, Jesus Christ, is the One God of heaven and earth, in whom is the Divine Trinity. When man looks to the Lord and shuns evils as sins against Him, he is redeemed and saved by the Lord's divine power. The Sacred Scripture is Divine, and a source of life and strength to men, because it contains within its letter infinite depths of spiritual truth. Man is a spiritual being; at death he lays aside the material body, and according to his character formed by life on earth finds his abode in heaven or in hell. The second coming of the Lord has already taken place; it is not a personal coming, but a new revelation of the Lord through deeper understanding of His Word; it is the beginning of a new era of progress among men.

Originating in England, congregations built on the teachings of Swedenborg (often called the New Church for short) began appearing in North America after the Revolution; the first was established in Baltimore. In 1816 the first General Convention of American congregations came together in Philadelphia. That same year William Strickland designed a "Saracenic-Gothic Revival" domed temple for the

Philadelphia Swedenborgians at George (Sansom) and Twelfth Streets, which they later sold to the Academy of Natural Science—certainly an early adaptive reuse of a sacred place. By the mid-nineteenth century they were in a building by the German-trained architects Edward Collins and Charles Autenrieth at the southeast corner of Broad and Brandywine Streets, which the congregation sold to Spring Garden Unitarian Church when the forceful preaching of the Rev. Mr. Chauncey Giles began to attract large crowds of worshipers. In 1881 the church council acquired a stoneyard at the northeast corner of Twenty-Second and Chestnut Streets on which to erect a larger Gothic Revival church designed by Theophilus P. Chandler, Jr. Ground was broken on August 22, 1881, and the completed church was dedicated on March 11, 1883.

Theophilus Parsons Chandler, Jr. (1845–1928) is not well known today, but few architects have had greater influence on Philadelphia architecture. Born in Boston and educated at Harvard, he also studied at the Atelier Vaudremer in Paris. Return-

The Church of the New Jerusalem occupies an important corner on Chestnut Street at Twenty-Second. Designed in 1881–1883 by Theophilus Parsons Chandler, Jr., the church was sold to developers in the mid-1980s with protective covenants to assure its preservation.

A glass partition has been inserted into the original sanctuary, creating an atrium effect that visually opens the three levels of office space to the former chancel.

The top floor offices enjoy the high ceilings and visually exciting cherry trusses and varnished narrow board decking.

A double helix circular staircase designed by project architect Mark B. Thompson provides access to the sanctuary floor from the upper two office levels. Notice that the chancel fittings have been retained as features of the lounge area. All the interior woodwork of the church is American cherry. See page 292.

ing to Boston, he worked in several offices until moving to Philadelphia in 1872 to establish his own firm. Family ties to Philadelphia—his grandfather was William Schlatter, a founder of the First New Jerusalem Society of Philadelphia—and northern Delaware, where he ultimately married into the Dupont family, practically guaranteed that he would have a successful practice. Chandler was celebrated in particular for his ecclesiastical designs, including Calvary Presbyterian Church in Washington, D.C., First Presbyterian Church in Pittsburgh, Tabernacle Presbyterian Church in West Philadelphia (pages 212–215), and one of his most significant Philadelphia essays, the Church of the New Jerusalem. Chandler is most often remembered as the founder of the University of Pennsylvania Department of Architecture, which has trained and nurtured legions of young architects. He also served as president of the Philadelphia chapter of the American Institute of Architects.

Chandler's "early English Gothic" design for the low, sprawling church and adjoining parish house at Twenty-Second and Chestnut Streets was executed in brownstone from Trenton and Newark, New Jersey. These two structures form an

L on the north and east sides of the lot, leaving an open court that provides a rare garden setting for a late nineteenth-century city church. A cloister-like gallery connects the church and parish house, and behind the parish house is the so-called angel staircase added by Chandler in 1908. The church interior is virtually square, with entrance gained through a dramatic vaulted stone porch. On the east wall there are three stone Gothic arches, the largest central bay forming a shallow chancel with a Gothic carved limestone altar. On the north and south walls are large stained-glass windows set in gables, which give the appearance of transepts and flood the interior with light. All the woodwork and furniture—some of which Chandler designed— is American cherry. The parish house is finished in butternut.

By the mid-1980s the Swedenborgian congregation could no longer afford to maintain so large and expensive a complex. Active membership had declined to fewer than fifty souls. Nor was there a substantial endowment. As one member remarked, "In the past when the church suffered an operating or maintenance shortfall, the Council passed the hat amongst themselves. After World War II there were no wealthy church leaders." In 1985 the congregation began working with the Philadelphia Historic Preservation Commission, the Preservation Fund of Pennsylvania, and the Preservation Coalition to market the property with assurances that the buildings would not be demolished for yet another faceless Center City highrise. With protective covenants against demolition or significant alteration, the congregation willingly sacrificed monetary value to preserve what all parties recognized as an artistic treasure. (The church council had been offered substantially more than the asking price if the congregation would first secure a demolition permit or promise not to object if the new owner applied for one.)

A private developer saw the potential to create something unusual and "harmonious with the neighborhood," which includes the adjoining College of Physicians to the north and Furness's Unitarian church to the east (pages 200–205). Having acquired the property and located a lead tenant, the developers retained architect Mark B. Thompson to design a respectful and sensitive adaptation that yielded a 16,000-square-foot corporate office facility in the church and parish house. The conversion of the nave into three levels of offices gives all areas visual access to the chancel area, where the altar, pulpit, and some original furniture have been preserved. However, the insertion of two additional floors in the nave made the project ineligible for the Federal Preservation Tax Credit.

Not every redundant sacred place lends itself to such adaptive reuse. But in this instance—given the attractive Center City location—the road from endangered architectural monument to successful commercial property of great character through private investment illustrates it is possible for the preservation community to work with owners and developers to achieve a mutually acceptable result.

⟜ In 1908 Theophilus P. Chandler, Jr., returned to the New Church and added the famous angel staircase to the back of the parish house. This is his romantic presentation drawing now preserved in the architectural archives of The Athenæum of Philadelphia. The carved angels have been removed.

THEOPHILUS P. CHANDLER
ARCHITECT

The Angel Staircase
THE NEW CHURCH

FIRST PRESBYTERIAN CHURCH

(Second Presbyterian Church)

*Twenty-First and Walnut Streets
Philadelphia, PA 19103*

*Henry Augustus Sims, architect, 1869–
1872; Furness and Evans, architects of
the tower, 1900*

*Telephone for visitor information:
215.567.0532*

www.fpcphila.org

The Presbyterians established their first Philadelphia congregation in 1698 and, in 1704, erected a meeting house on the south side of High (Market) Street at White Horse Alley (Bank Street). This simple frame building—familiarly called "Old Buttonwood" after a nearby grove of trees—was expanded several times and finally replaced in 1794. The resulting church, erected on the same site and illustrated in the famous Birch view of 1800, boasted a giant order portico with Corinthian capitals—one of the earliest Roman neoclassical revival structures in the city (see page 196).

Earlier in the 1730s, a schism triggered by the Great Awakening had rent the Presbyterians into the conservative "Old Side" believers and the revivalist "New Side" converts, brought on in part by the evangelical preaching of George Whitefield and Gilbert Tennent. (One Presbyterian historian said of Whitefield that "under the spell of his matchless oratory, men wept, women fainted, and hundreds professed conversion.") At First Presbyterian the excessive emotionalism associated with the Great Awakening seemed vulgar and inappropriate. This disagreement led to the formation of a Second Presbyterian Church in 1743. After worshiping peripatetically, the New Side congregation commissioned its own church structure on the northwest corner of Third and Arch Streets in 1750. As carpenter-builder the they selected Robert Smith (1722–1777), a recent immigrant from Scotland destined to become the most famous master builder of colonial Philadelphia. The church was originally erected without a steeple because of costs; this embellishment was added in 1762, designed by the church elder and master builder Thomas Nevell (1721–1797). The "neat and ornamental" steeple was thought by some of the congregation, according to John Fanning Watson, "too much like aspiring to the airy honors just before acquired by Christ Church" (pages 40–45). It gave rise to the anonymous satirical couplet:

> The Presbyterians built a church,
> And fain would have a steeple;
> We think it may become the church,
> But not become the people.

Second Presbyterian abandoned Smith's brick colonial building in 1837 for a simple classical marble box at Seventh Street below Arch. Finally, in 1872, the congregation moved to a new church at Twenty-First and Walnut Streets, to which this narrative will shortly return.

In the meantime, what of the First Presbyterian congregation? They did not remain long in their rebuilt church on Market Street. By 1818 the distinctive wood columns were so decayed and the roof structure so weakened by rot that the building was "in imminent danger of falling down." Doubtless the westward relocation

☞ First Presbyterian Church, originally designed by Henry Augustus Sims for the Second Presbyterian Church (1869–1872), combines several shades of red sandstone. The tower was not completed to Sims's design; the present tower is by the firm of Furness and Evans, 1900.

of church members and the rapid commercialization of the nearby Delaware River waterfront contributed to the decision to move rather than to repair the twenty-four-year-old building. The congregation engaged a young English-born and -trained architect, John Haviland (1792–1852), to design a Greek Revival replacement sited on the south side of Washington Square, this time with a portico in the Ionic rather than the Corinthian mode (see page 120).

The First Presbyterian congregation had probably not moved far enough west when it abandoned the colonial site for Haviland's classical temple. By 1928 the decline in congregation and deterioration of the building forced them to unite with Calvary Presbyterian Church on Locust west of Fifteenth Street. The combined congregation would henceforth be known as First Presbyterian, but would worship in the newer Calvary Church designed by John Notman in 1851. Calvary may have been the first major Presbyterian church in Philadelphia to be built in the newly fashionable Victorian Gothic style. The interior, however, according to one description, probably drafted by Notman, "is at once simple and impressive; its simplicity not arising from want of decoration . . . but the decoration it has is constructive, and therefore harmonious and pleasing." The floor plan reveals a traditional rectangular box without transepts or apse. Calvary differed in another sense from the expected. Presbyterians—like Methodists, Baptists, and virtually all nonconforming denominations, for that matter—placed the main emphasis on preaching rather than celebration of the sacraments. Consequently all these churches traditionally placed the pulpit directly on the central axis, rather than placing an altar there, as is found in pre-Reformation European churches and in Roman Catholic and high Episcopalian churches. At Calvary, however, the pulpit was placed off to one side and the communion table occupied the center of the chancel.

During the Depression of the 1930s, several church leaders suggested an additional union, this time between First and Second Presbyterian. Nothing came of this proposal until after World War II, when protracted negotiations resulted in an agreement to merge the congregations and occupy Second Presbyterian's handsome Gothic Style church at the corner of Twenty-First and Walnut Streets. On March 8, 1949, the Presbytery of Philadelphia approved the merger. The new congregation would share a double heritage but continue under the name First Presbyterian Church in Philadelphia.

The newly renamed First (formerly Second) Presbyterian Church had been erected on a lot "in the midst of a cultivated and rapidly increasing population" from designs obtained from the engineer and architect Henry Augustus Sims (1832–1875). A native of Philadelphia, Sims spent most of his early career in Canada, returning to Philadelphia in 1866. His buildings in both Ottawa and Philadelphia reflect his interest in the Gothic Revival. Ground was broken in March 1869 and the church was dedicated in October 1872. Funds were not adequate to erect the 225-foot steeple Sims designed; the present tower with its asymmetrical pinnacles, designed by Furness and Evans, would not be added until 1900.

Sims designed a traditional nave and transept cruciform plan with a tall clerestory nave and aisles. In a period when it was not uncommon to simulate Gothic details with lath and plaster, Second Presbyterian made liberal use of a variety of stone, as well as brick and terra cotta. The columns supporting the arches on either side of the nave are polished marble with capitals carved by Alexander Milne Calder, sculptor of the William Penn statue on Philadelphia City Hall. The church also is embellished with an excellent assemblage of stained-glass windows by J. and G. H. Gibson, Magee and Smith, Tiffany Studio, Cox and Son of London, Wailles of Newcastle-upon-Tyne, Jean Baptiste Capronnier of Brussels, and others.

First Presbyterian Church on High (Market) Street, as illustrated by Thomas and William Birch, The City of Philadelphia . . . *(Philadelphia, 1800). The artist John Trumbull (1756–1843) may have been responsible for the design. John Adams, who attended the First Church during his vice presidency, thought the new building "much larger, higher, more light, airy and elegant" than the previous meeting house. This handsome structure would be abandoned in 1820 for a new building on the south side of Washington Square designed by John Haviland (illustrated on page 120). The Athenæum of Philadelphia.*

That the Presbyterians would fly in the face of their low church liturgical tradition by selecting a Gothic design with Anglican (if not Roman Catholic!) echoes, rather than a simple preaching box, reflects a shift in fashion occurring in other denominations as well (see Arch Street United Methodist, for example, pages 140–143). It may well be that this issue was already moot by 1872. Calvary Presbyterian had embraced the Gothic style twenty years before and had even moved the pulpit off to one side. At Second Presbyterian, however, the ornate pulpit was placed squarely in the center as the focal point of the nave.

By 1953, liturgical sensibilities had shifted again. The congregation engaged Philadelphia architect Harold Eugene Wagoner (1905–1986) to update the sanctuary. Wagoner specialized in religious buildings. He was employed by the Methodist Bureau of Architecture in the late 1920s and early 1930s and would later write, "my firm is one of the few, perhaps the only one in the U.S. which has devoted all its efforts to Religious Architecture. We have had commissions in 36 states. . . . We have designed over 500 religious buildings." At Wagoner's hands the entire front of the sanctuary was remodeled to provide a "split" or divided chancel that removed Sims's pulpit from its central location in favor of the communion table, which was moved to the rear of the apse, between choir stalls. At First Presbyterian this Italian marble communion table with reredos leans dangerously close to becoming an altar, a liturgical faux pas by nineteenth-century standards of Presbyterian church design.

The six polished marble columns supporting the clerestory nave have carved capitals by Alexander Milne Calder (1846–1923) and represent tobacco, grapes, wheat, cotton, corn, and sugar. Recent renovations in the organ loft have permitted the stained-glass window by Magee and Smith in the north façade—which celebrates the making of joyful noise—to be seen for the first time since 1904.

FIRST UNITARIAN CHURCH

2125 Chestnut Street
Philadelphia, PA 19103

Furness, Evans and Company,
architects, designed 1883,
erected 1885–1886

Telephone for visitor information:
215.563.3980

www.firstuu-philly.org

⚲ *This photograph of the First Uni-
tarian Church, designed by Furness,
Evans and Company, on Chestnut
Street between Twenty-First and
Twenty-Second, shows the tower porch
and rock-faced ground floor stonework.
The tower was removed in the 1920s
and the stone smoothed in the 1950s.
The Athenæum of Philadelphia.*

Unitarian belief in a single God—as opposed to the orthodox Catholic view of the
Trinity—appealed to eighteenth-century intellectuals such as English scientist,
author, and educator Joseph Priestley (1733–1804), the discoverer of oxygen. Priestley's growing heterodoxy and republican leanings in favor of the French Revolution
caused his home to be firebombed during the Birmingham riots on Bastille Day,
1791. Fearing for his life, Priestley vowed to seek sanctuary in the United States. He
arrived in Philadelphia to great acclaim among members of the American Philosophical Society, and he would reside henceforth in Pennsylvania.

Priestley inspired a small group of largely English-born merchants residing in
Philadelphia to organize in 1796 as the Society of Unitarian Christians, the first congregation in the United States to take that name. By 1812 the congregation had commissioned an octagonal church building from Robert Mills (1781–1855), who called
himself the first American-born architect. This structure at Tenth and Locust
Streets seated 300 persons, adequate for the congregation's needs when built but
woefully inadequate after William Henry Furness arrived as pastor in 1825. By 1828
William Strickland had been engaged to demolish Mills's octagon and replace it

with an 800-seat Greek Revival church embellished with a Doric portico of reused columns from Benjamin Henry Latrobe's demolished Philadelphia waterworks pump house formerly located in Center Square (now the site of City Hall).

The coming of the Rev. Dr. William Henry Furness (1802–1896) is central to the history of Unitarianism in Philadelphia. Born in Boston and graduated from Harvard Divinity School, he fully expected to serve a New England congregation; instead the call came from Philadelphia. "This church," he later wrote, "composed almost exclusively of persons from the Old Country . . . , was looked upon pretty much as a settlement of a small company of Mahometans, an exotic, having no root in the soil." For all Philadelphia's Protestant liberality, the Unitarians were "about as obscure and despised as any company of Methodists or such like are in Boston." Nonetheless, Furness's considerable intellect and winning personality rapidly attracted favorable attention. His boyhood schoolmate and lifelong friend Ralph

The south-facing façade of the First Unitarian Church as altered in the twentieth century. The rose window is by John LaFarge; it replaces a clear-glass geometric rose window designed by Furness, Evans and Company.

Waldo Emerson said Furness had "a face like a benediction and a speech like a benefaction, and his stories more curative than the Phila. Faculty of Medicine."

After half a century at the helm of the Philadelphia Unitarians, Dr. Furness retired, although he remained a respected voice (see page v). Within a decade of his retirement, the congregation determined to erect a third church building, this one closer to Philadelphia's upscale residential center on Chestnut Street between Twenty-First and Twenty-Second Streets. As architect the congregation selected the firm of Furness, Evans and Company, which included Dr. Furness's youngest child, Frank Furness (1839–1912), who had been raised, according to one of his biographers, "in a cultured, middle-class domestic atmosphere that was Unitarian and abolitionist, intellectual and artistic."

In 1870 Dr. Furness had addressed the American Institute of Architects, admonishing his audience to avoid conformity and be willing to experiment. However, he warned, in America

with all our freedom, we do not tolerate oddness. We insist, in this country, upon everything's being cut to one pattern. Only think what a long day of it, one particular style of building (the Quaker style—marble steps and wooden shutters) has had here in Philadelphia.

Rather, he argued, architects should be adventurous, willing to create "new orders of architecture" and "new styles of building" fitted to new materials then coming into use. But they should be prepared to suffer from critics who would fail—or be unwilling—to understand their intention.

Presumably Frank Furness heard his father's remarks, and must have greeted them with wry humor. His first commission, the Germantown Unitarian Church (1866–1867, demolished) was a fairly conventional English Gothic design influenced by Saint James the Less (pages 248–253), but by the time of his Rodeph Shalom Synagogue at Broad and Mount Vernon streets (1868–1869; demolished) he was already out of the conventional box that would soon find opportunity at the Pennsylvania Academy of the Fine Arts (Furness and Hewitt, 1871–1876). Dr. Furness rose again on the subject of architecture when invited to speak at the Academy cornerstone ceremony, where he celebrated: "the monotony of our streets is disap-

The First Unitarian Church has a notable collection of stained-glass windows, including works by Henry Holiday, John LaFarge, and the Tiffany and D'Ascenzo studios. The artist of this Pre-Raphaelite-inspired memorial window for Helen Kate Furness has not yet been identified

pearing; the spirit of beauty is beginning to brood over our city, over its private dwellings and public edifices."

The parish house and church designed for the Unitarians a few years later is the best surviving Center City ecclesiastical commission by Furness, Evans and Company, although it has suffered several unfortunate mutilations, particularly to the exterior. Originally the picturesque façade had been dominated by a massive, high-peaked porch or semidetached tower, and the stonework had been rustically rock-faced. Both these exotic features offended later architects associated with the church. R. Brognard Okie (1875–1945)—the colonial revivalist responsible for the Betsy Ross House and Pennsbury Manor—must have found Furness, Evans and Company's work particularly egregious. He removed the tower in 1921. Then, during the 1950s, when the firm's reputation was at its nadir, the rock-face masonry walls were smoothed in an unfortunate effort to tame First Unitarian Church into bland conformity with American taste at the time.

Nor did the interior with its elaborate hammer-beam trusses escape the twentieth century. Originally the plastered walls were painted blue and the ceiling red with gold leaf stencils. In the early 1920s the artist Thornton Oakley (1881–1953) repainted the interior in a "dignified" neutral gray to replace the "strident" original colors. Fortunately, the Furness, Evans and Company color scheme has now been replicated so visitors can appreciate the architect's intention.

On the west wall of the sanctuary is a memorial to the English scientist Joseph Priestley, designed and executed by the Boston firm of Andrews, Jacques, and Rantoul. Both Robert D. Andrews and Herbert Jacques had been trained in the office of H. H. Richardson, Priestley's great-grandson.

🕯 *Six timber trusses support the hipped roof of the sanctuary. The original paint scheme has been replicated after having been painted over in the 1920s.*

CENTER CITY LUTHERAN CHURCH OF THE HOLY COMMUNION

(formerly Saint Paul's Reformed Episcopal Church)

2110 Chestnut Street
Philadelphia, PA 19103

Isaac Pursell, architect, 1879–1880

Telephone for visitor information:
215.567.3668

www.lutheranchurchphiladelphia.org

⌒⊷ *The Romanesque style Center City Lutheran Church of the Holy Communion was designed by Isaac Pursell in 1879 for Saint Paul's Reformed Episcopal Church. In 1903 the Lutheran congregation purchased the building, which for more than a century they have embellished and maintained.*

Like other denominations, Philadelphia's Lutherans responded to the inexorable westward shift of population in the middle decades of the nineteenth century. To Saint John's Lutheran Church at Sixth and Race Streets near Old First Reformed Church (pages 78–81), Old Saint George's United Methodist (pages 82–85), and Saint Augustine's Church (pages 86–91), the rapid commercialization of the neighborhood strongly suggested the need to establish a new congregation in the "western part" of the city. In 1870 the Lutherans settled on a lot at the intersection of Broad and Arch Streets. This was hardly an adventuresome choice. Two other nonconforming Protestant congregations were already well positioned there; the Methodists (pages 140–143) and the Baptists (pages 184–187) occupied two of the corner lots at the same intersection. For an architect the Lutherans turned to the firm of Fraser, Furness, and Hewitt, with George W. Hewitt as lead architect; he gave them a handsome polychromatic green serpentine Gothic pile that was dedicated in early 1875.

Once City Hall neared completion on Center Square, business shifted westward again. Attendance at services in all three churches at Broad and Arch declined. Developers of commercial real estate eyed the prime corners occupied by the churches and made tempting offers. The Baptists were the first to move in 1899, followed by the Lutherans in 1901. Only the Methodists would remain as a reminder of what had once been an important concentration of sacred places.

The Lutheran congregation met temporarily for services in the Witherspoon Building until they were able to purchase Saint Paul's Reformed Episcopal Church in 1903. This robust Romanesque style building had been commissioned from the architect Isaac Pursell in 1879 and occupied for less than twenty years by the Episcopal congregation. One of Philadelphia's most prolific church architects, Pursell (1853–1910) apprenticed with Samuel Sloan, and like his master—and not a few architects of a later age—came to public attention as much through his published designs as his executed commissions. He worked with the Presbyterian Board of Church Erection to advance "approved" plans for churches (many of which he created) and as staff architect for *Mrs. Rorer's Household News*, producing plans for readers.

Which is not to disparage his genuine talent. Shortly after the completion of Saint Paul's, *Illustrated Philadelphia* described Pursell as

a thoroughly qualified and able architect who has evinced great skill and ability in the practice of his profession, designing and superintending the construction of many prominent buildings. . . . He has made a specialty of the building of schools and churches . . . , [and] many of the buildings erected by this responsible architect are much admired for their beauty.

Immediately the Lutherans set about putting their own stamp on the building. A second floor gallery was removed and fittings from the Broad Street church were installed, most notably the pulpit, baptismal font, organ panel, altar, railing, and carved reredos. Subsequently the reredos was modified to permit the installation of a large stained-glass window by the Tiffany Studios, given by Caroline, Florence, and Percival Foerderer in memory of Robert H. Foerderer.

Having moved twice in its long history, the Center City Lutheran Church of the Holy Communion has occupied Pursell's building for a century and, given its active mission programs of social services, takes as its motto: "In the City for Good."

⬤⟶ *The focal point of the sanctuary is the Tiffany window and the altar, rail, and pulpit brought from the congregation's previous church designed by Fraser, Furness, and Hewitt.*

WEST PHILADELPHIA

⤚⤙ *Philadelphia Cathedral: The full intent of the 2000–2002 building campaign is revealed here. Maximum flexibility has been achieved by replacing the permanent slip pews with chairs. The lightweight, wooden liturgical furniture—the altar and ambo (combined lectern and pulpit)—can also be moved to exploit the nave for a wide variety of religious or secular purposes. According to a 2002 Cathedral press release, "the altar table stands on the floor of the nave, in the midst of the people of God and accessible to all. The altar table is neither fenced off by rails, nor distanced from us by steps, for it belongs to the whole people of God." See pages 216–221.*

TABERNACLE UNITED CHURCH

(and Iron Gate Theater, adaptive reuse of the former Tabernacle Presbyterian Church)

*3700 Chestnut Street
Philadelphia, PA 19104*

Theophilus Parsons Chandler, Jr., architect, 1883–1886; addition, 1890

Telephone for visitor information: 215.386.4100

www.tabunited.org

The circuitous history of Tabernacle United Church follows the familiar Philadelphia pattern of congregational mergers and westward architectural relocations. Its roots can be traced to the Independent Tabernacle Church established in 1804 and housed in Ranstead Court (west side of Fourth Street below Market Street where the Bourse now stands). In 1819 the Presbytery of Philadelphia received the congregation as the Seventh Presbyterian Church, which moved in 1843 to Broad Street at Penn Square and subsequently merged with the Sixth Presbyterian Church in 1873 under the name Tabernacle Presbyterian Church. In 1885 Tabernacle moved yet again, from its pedimented neoclassical temple into a new Gothic Revival style building at 3700 Chestnut Street. The cornerstone was laid on October 30, 1884, and the completed building was dedicated May 2, 1886.

The church commissioned by Tabernacle Presbyterian was widely admired and declared by critics "one of the most beautiful Gothic edifices in the New World." One observer wrote,

> it is now, confessedly, the most complete and most beautiful edifice, for religious worship, in the city, or indeed, as far as our observation has extended, in the United States. The dimensions and proportions of the building are consistent with the best taste, the interior arrangements neat, convenient and elegant, and the *tout ensemble*, as a specimen of architecture, highly honourable to the construction.

The architect of this "comely temple" was Theophilus P. Chandler, Jr. (1845–1928). Born in Boston, he studied at Harvard and the Atelier Vaudremer in Paris; after returning to the United States, he apprenticed with several Boston firms. In 1872 he moved to Philadelphia, where the Chandlers had strong family and financial connections. Chandler regularly traveled abroad and owned an extensive library and collection of photographs illustrating the chief European architectural monuments—sources on which he drew heavily for inspiration. Gradually Chandler developed a reputation as a designer of richly detailed buildings. Admired chiefly as an ecclesiastical architect, his major commissions include the Church of the New Jerusalem (see pages 188–193), Calvary Presbyterian Church in Washington, D.C., and First Presbyterian Church in Pittsburgh, Pennsylvania. Chandler also contributed to raising the standards of the architectural profession; he founded the Department of Architecture at the University of Pennsylvania, and served as president of the Philadelphia chapter of the American Institute of Architects.

Chandler characterized the style of his Gothic design as "Decorative English." Constructed of tinted Maryland granite and Indiana limestone, the tower at the intersection of Chestnut and Thirty-Seventh Streets rises 130 feet. The main

☞ Theophilus P. Chandler, Jr.'s Tabernacle Presbyterian Church of 1883–1886 occupies an important intersection at the corner of Chestnut and Thirty-Seventh Streets on the edge of the University of Pennsylvania campus. The main auditorium is now used for student theater productions.

entrance is through a deeply molded and enriched arch closed by a finely detailed pair of wrought-iron gates in the base of the tower. A delicate cloistered porch connects the main auditorium to the minister's residence and a three-story chapel. The auditorium has a vigorous hammer-beam wood truss roof enriched with carved angels.

Unfortunately, the congregation gradually declined in the years following World War II. The University of Pennsylvania acquired the church for student productions as the Iron Gate Theater. The chapel continues to be used for religious services. In 1982 a United Church of Christ congregation joined with the Presbyterians to form a "union church," which describes itself as "free-thinking individuals of all races, ages and sexual orientations who experience God in a variety of ways." Concern for peace and justice has involved Tabernacle United Church in international activism, rights for minorities and women, economic justice, AIDS ministries, rights for sexual minorities, and confronting ageism.

This detail of the finely cut Indiana limestone pinnacles, cornices, and gargoyles demonstrates the skills of master stonemason Michael F. Scully and the architect's eye for appropriate detail.

Chandler's mature handling of the Gothic Revival style is amply demonstrated by the main tower entrance to the auditorium with its handsome wrought-iron gates, which give the theater its name.

PHILADELPHIA CATHEDRAL

(formerly Church of the Saviour)

3723 Chestnut Street
Philadelphia, PA 19104

Charles M. Burns, architect, 1889,
1906; George Yu, architect, renovations,
2000–2002

Telephone for visitor information:
215.386.0234

www.philadelphiacathedral.org

The Cathedral Church of the Saviour near the University of Pennsylvania campus in West Philadelphia has experienced a checkered and—some might say—ill-fated history. In 1889, the Philadelphia architect Charles M. Burns received the commission to rebuild and expand an existing mid-nineteenth-century church at Thirty-Eighth and Chestnut Streets. Devastated by fire on April 17, 1902, little survived of Burns's church except the asymmetrically arranged bell tower and gabled main façade. The congregation invited Burns to return as architect to rebuild the rugged brownstone Romanesque structure and expand it to a width of 84 feet and a length of 150 feet, making it one of the largest Episcopal churches in the city.

Charles M. Burns (1838–1922) had studied at the University of Pennsylvania, but the Civil War interrupted his academic career. After the rebellion had been suppressed he returned to his native Philadelphia to launch what would become a highly successful practice specializing in Episcopal churches. His surviving drawings for such significant commissions as the Church of the Redeemer, Bryn Mawr, and the Church of the Advocate at Eighteenth and Diamond Streets, Philadelphia (pages 244–247) clearly demonstrate Burns's considerable artistic ability. Armed with the rich palette of late Victorian tertiary colors, he lavishly orchestrated murals, stained glass, and stenciling. The resulting interior of the rebuilt Church of the Saviour may be Burns's masterwork.

At the time of its dedication in 1906, the interior—called Norman in style by Burns—had not yet been fully ornamented. According to the *Public Ledger*, "two rows of polished granite columns, capped with Minnesota limestone, support a Flemish oak roof, whose hammer beams in the clerestory are carved with winged cherubim. All the woodwork is of polished Flemish oak, and the floors are of mosaic." Soon thereafter the American artist Edwin Blashfield applied the mural decorations, which are generally considered the principal treasure of the church. One modern art historian calls the Church of the Saviour "one of Blashfield's finest achievements."

Edwin Howland Blashfield (1848–1936) had trained and painted in Paris; he gained widespread attention after returning to the United States in the 1890s to decorate neoclassical buildings at the Columbian Exposition in Chicago. Working from his studio in New York, Blashfield developed a distinguished reputation, especially for blending architecture and murals characterized by elegant line, classically beautiful women, and rich color. These murals, he wrote, present "beauty applied to utility" as "a supreme teacher, through the arts of patriotism, morals and history."

Dedicated as a memorial to Anthony J. Drexel, Blashfield's murals for the Church of the Saviour occupied the semidome and lower walls of the chancel and consist of a choir of angels surrounding a figure holding the Grail. Behind the altar eleven figures holding lilies represent various types of humanity. The art critic of the *Public Ledger* wrote of the semidome,

⊷ The Thirty-Eighth Street façade and bell tower of Charles M. Burns's brownstone Romanesque Church of the Saviour survived a fire in 1902. Both features were reused in the present church dedicated in 1906. This parish church officially became the cathedral of the Episcopal Diocese of Pennsylvania on January 1, 1992.

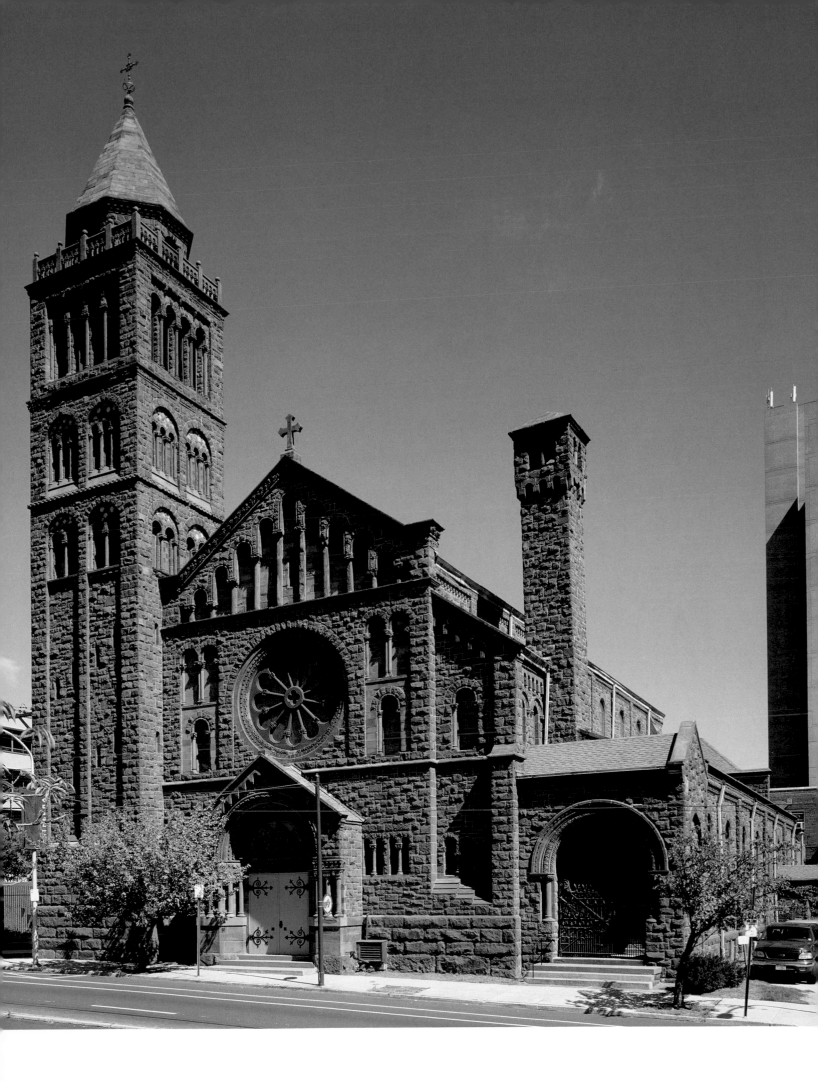

≈ *The chancel and semidome decorated by Edwin H. Blashfield in 1906 are here shown as they appeared prior to the renovations of 2000–2002. Originally the side walls of the nave had been ornamentally painted in red and gold; by the time of this photograph (c. 1983) they had been painted white. The notable collection of stained-glass windows includes examples by Tiffany Studios, William Willet, Horace J. Phipps and Co., John Hardman and Co., and several other artists. Most of these windows were conserved between 1978 and 1985. Photo courtesy of H. Mather Lippincott.*

≈–≈ *The chancel and semidome are shown here after the renovations of 2000–2002. Notice that the Blashfield scrollwork pattern decorations below the semidome have been painted out, and the carved marble altar (c. 1925) by Philadelphia physician, educator, and sculptor R. Tait McKenzie (1867–1938) has been removed, as have the choir stalls, chancel rail, and Flemish oak pulpit. In their place has been erected a stone bench, or presbyterium—incorporating the bishop's chair—for the elders of the church.*

the color scheme ultimately resolves itself into a burst of golden light, although blues predominate amidst a related mass of pale tints, the latter serving to modulate the color into rich harmony. Gold has been freely used everywhere. The flat massing of the halos and the simple treatment of the figures suggest the old masters studied by the pre-Raphaelite school, Mr. Blashfield's treatment being thoroughly modern, however. What the old art has to teach is here assimilated and made part of an art new and beautiful and strong.

During the 1920s the wealthy congregation further embellished the interior with memorials in stained glass and marble. However, as its West Philadelphia neighborhood declined after World War II, the Church of the Saviour parish suffered the loss of congregation common to many sacred places in the city. Gradually the maintenance of so large a church—handsome embellishments notwithstanding—became a burden. Nonetheless, the interiors were cleaned, stained-glass windows conserved, and lighting upgraded in the 1970s and 1980s. Then, in 1992, the bishop of the Episcopal diocese—who had never had an official cathedral—selected the Church of the Saviour as his seat. In 1999 a new dean arrived to take charge, and shortly thereafter a structural survey disclosed weakness in the nave floor. In 2000 the church closed for repairs. What followed casts in high relief the twenty-first-century division between individuals and organizations dedicated to the preser-

vation of our artistic heritage and once numerous and prosperous congregations struggling with declining membership and the costly burden of maintaining an expensive and often historic sacred place.

Dean Richard Giles, styled as "one of the world's leading experts on the design and use of liturgical space," is an articulate and published spokesman for reordering church buildings for worship and mission. Formerly canon theologian of Wakefield Diocese in England, Giles staked out his position on historic churches before arriving in Philadelphia. "The fossilization of worship spaces is not confined to ancient buildings nor to England," he wrote in the late 1990s. "Faith communities in the United States are equally prone to this disease, and the Episcopal Church . . . is in imminent danger of drowning in varnish." Anticipating the humphing and breast beating of potential critics, he argued, "Our work to proclaim the living God is . . . undermined and repudiated by buildings which speak of a geriatric God incarcerated in an old folk's home, the kind of rambling Victorian building that real families gave up living in years ago." And if the sacred place happened to be architecturally or artistically significant, the preservationists—"who have no understanding of the Christian vocation"—would impose unrealistic constraints so congregations "are hampered and hindered as no previous Christian generation ever was by the buildings erected to serve them but which now subdue them." When faced with a "desire to preserve intact the interior of a church building as a received inheritance, sacrosanct and untouchable, we forget what message these moth-balled interiors communicate to those from outside our community who are sufficiently brave and persistent to enquire within."

Confronted with a church from this "faded past"—fit "only for the heritage trail"—Giles admits he always daydreamed: "if only I could get my hands on it! The whole process, from the gutting of the church building through its refurbishment to the grand re-opening is achieved within the space of an hour." Now, with the Cathedral Church of the Saviour in need of structural work, and with the cathedral doors barred, he had an opportunity to realize his dream. Assisted by architect George Yu, the dean and chapter "repitched the tent" with a vengeance. To facilitate shoring up the nave floor, the pews were removed, discarded, and replaced with simple blond wood chairs that can be reconfigured according to the uses of the assembly hall (nave). In the chancel the choir stalls, altar rail, wood paneling, pulpit, and R. Tait McKenzie altar suffered a similar fate (see page 210).

With the slate wiped clean, a portable altar table and reading desk (*ambo*), both of which now stand on the floor of the nave, "in the midst of the people of God and accessible to all," were fabricated. On the elevated chancel—once occupied by the choir stalls and altar—a perimeter stone bench incorporating the bishop's cathedra now wraps around. The baptismal font (incorporating elements from the nineteenth-century font) has been turned into a baptismal pool.

Most students of modern churches recognize the need to accommodate a living liturgy. With reluctance, church traditionalists and the historic preservation community might have accepted replacement of the pews and removal of some chancel fittings (excepting the McKenzie altar, which might easily have been left in place). But the wanton destruction of the Blashfield decorative scheme tipped the scales. Dean Giles was demonized in the press by the preservationists, who were in turn accused of attempting "to pickle a building in formaldehyde, embalming it in a previous state . . . , with just a little sprucing up here and there."

Only time will tell whether the renovations at the Philadelphia Cathedral constitute a brilliant response to a modern need or insensitive vandalism sanctimoniously cloaking itself, in the dean's words, with "a conviction that the mission of the Church should always take precedence whenever architectural layout conflicts with the Church's current needs in liturgy or ministry." And yet, at churches such as Saint Martin-in-the-Fields (pages 282–287), recent adjustments to conform to the living liturgy have been successfully coupled with restoration of original wall surfaces— enhanced by modern lighting—to achieve a pleasing compromise between the two extremes.

Portrait of Philadelphia architect Charles M. Burns by John McLure Hamilton (1853–1936), oil on canvas, circa 1919. In addition to his successful architectural practice, Burns studied with Thomas Eakins and later taught drawing and design at the Pennsylvania Museum and School of Industrial Art. The Athenæum of Philadelphia.

SAINT FRANCIS DE SALES CHURCH

4625 Springfield Avenue
Philadelphia, PA 19143

Henry D. Dagit, architect, 1907–1911

Telephone for visitor information:
215.222.5819

www.stfrancisdesales-parish.org

Saint Francis de Sales Church surprises many first-time visitors. Its Byzantine dome looms over the low-rise southwest Philadelphia neighborhood it serves like a latter day Hagia Sophia. To meet the needs of a rapidly growing Irish immigrant population in the large territory from the Schuylkill River to Chester, a new parish was founded in 1890 under the patronage of Saint Francis de Sales, who had been born Francis Bonaventure (1567–1622) at the Chateau de Sales in Savoy, France, and ordained in 1593. He was consecrated bishop of Geneva in 1602 and canonized in 1665.

Work immediately began on a chapel and school designed by Adrian W. Smith (1860–1892), who had served his architectural apprenticeship with the successful designer of Protestant churches Charles M. Burns (see pages 216–221). Smith's building provided for parish needs for several years until a new church could be

Henry D. Dagit's original drawing for the south elevation of Saint Francis de Sales Church, 1907. Dagit Collection, The Athenæum of Philadelphia.

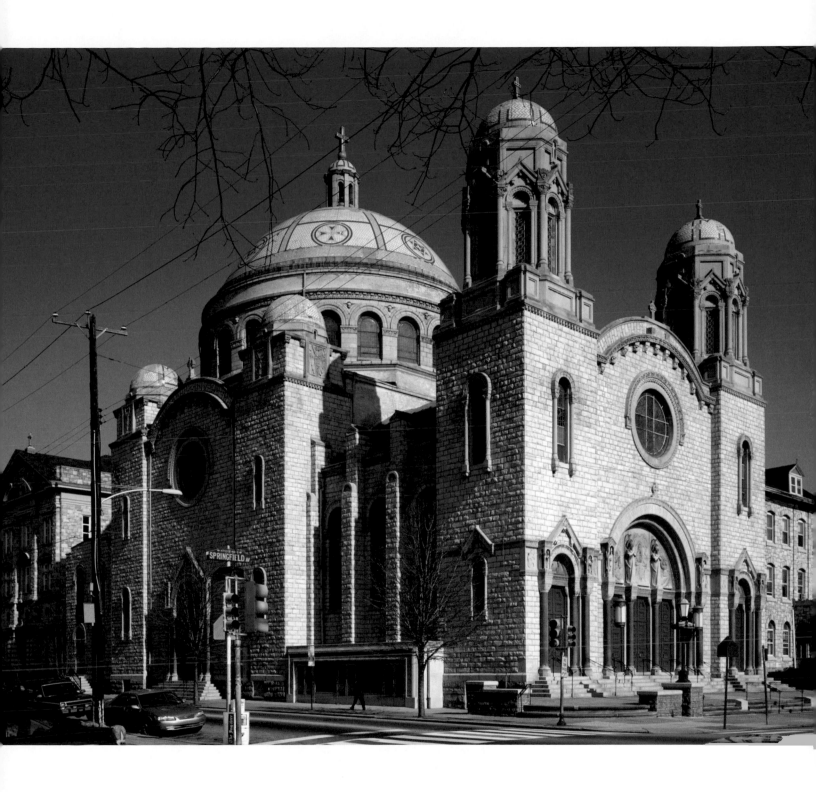

⚱ *The striking Byzantine domes of Saint Francis de Sales Church were covered with polychro-matic glazed Guastavino tiles during construction, 1907–1911. These gradually delaminated from the underlying layers and were covered with concrete in 1955. The present tile covering is similar in decorative pattern to the originals.*

constructed. For that responsibility the pastor turned to Henry D. Dagit (1865–1929), one of the dominant figures in the field of Roman Catholic church and institution design in Philadelphia and patriarch of a multigenerational family of architects. This stature was yet to come in 1898 when Dagit secured the appointment as architect for the Archdiocese of Trenton, New Jersey, a position he held for a decade. With his reputation as a Catholic architect firmly established, Dagit secured the Saint Francis de Sales commission from the Rev. Michael J. Crane, who gave him the formidable charge to design a church

> in which beauty of art would mingle with splendor and stateliness of proportion; one in which rare marbles would be wrought into an illustration of some religious truth; one in which the soul would be lifted up to exaltation; an edifice in which the liturgy would be carried out in all its mystical beauty; a church rich with storied windows, enduring for ages, a perpetual witness of the faith of His people.

The resulting church, for which the cornerstone was laid on October 6, 1907, stands as Dagit's most famous work. Four years in construction, it was dedicated on November 12, 1911.

A Catholic church tracing its architectural genealogy to medieval Byzantine-Romanesque churches of southern France—as opposed to the more common Gothic or Italianate prototypes—is unusual in Philadelphia. Nonetheless, there is a certain logic at work. A Catholic revival movement among mid-nineteenth-century French intellectuals had embraced the Byzantine-Romanesque style as an alternative to the Gothic style, which they thought tainted by association with English Protestants of the Oxford Movement. The premier architectural expression of this revival is the basilica of Sacré Coeur in Paris (1874–1884) designed by Paul Abadie (1812–1884) and influenced by Saint Front at Périgueux. (Whether a similar anti-English sentiment influenced the architectural views of the Saint Francis de Sales clergy must remain a subject for speculation.)

Throughout the Middle Ages, Byzantine architecture associated with the Eastern Roman Empire spread along the Mediterranean basin from Constantinople. The most distinctive characteristics of the style are large exterior domes, interior modules of domed space, and round-headed arches—all highly colored and ornamented. Romanesque architecture is a descendant of the Byzantine, but introduces vaults rather than domes, which solves the need of Catholic liturgy for linear spaces.

The dome of Saint Francis de Sales is more than a rare example of the Byzantine Revival style in Philadelphia. It is also one of our three landmark examples of

⊷⧁ The main south entrances are set in walls of rusticated white marble ashlar embellished with Indiana limestone and polished granite columns. Bas relief carvings above the doors depict scenes in the life of Christ. Directly above the main entrance there once was a niche and statue of Saint Francis de Sales; the location is now marked by a small cross.

Guastavino tile construction, a vaulting technique utilizing interlocking terra-cotta tiles set in mortar to form self-supporting arches to span large, unsupported spaces. (The other examples are the Girard Bank at Broad and Chestnut Streets—now the Ritz Carlton Hotel—and the Museum of the University of Pennsylvania.) This construction technique—traditional in the Catalan region of Spain—was brought to the United States by Rafael Guastavino y Moreno, who arrived in 1881 and founded the Guastavino Fireproof Construction Company in 1889. His arching system of cohesive fireproof construction immediately became popular with American architects because it allowed rapid building without expensive forms and braces. Most important, the Guastavino dome contributes greatly to the stunning impact the Saint Francis de Sales interior has on worshipers and visitors alike. The dome is 62 feet in diameter, rests on four reinforced concrete arches, and begins 90 feet from the floor. It is surmounted by an open lantern, on top of which the original cross reached a height of 126 feet. The dome is pierced by twenty-four openings set with ornamental mosaic glass windows. Four smaller domes bracket the main dome.

Liturgical changes following Vatican II created a quandary for Saint Francis de Sales Church. Desiring to protect the neo-Byzantine architecture of Dagit's original design, a happy compromise of creating a new altar advanced toward the nave was adopted, thereby permitting the priest to face the congregation during the Mass. In 1968 this commission was given to Robert Venturi and John Rauch, architects, who designed a new altar, reading table, and chair of one-inch-thick opaque plexiglass. The entire choir was then illuminated by a curved, white cathode light described by one sympathetic critic as a "wall that is not a wall, an invisible wall, a symbolic line which defines the new space; it recognizes the history and aesthetic value of the traditional altar, yet defines it as history, a past out of which we are now reaching toward something new." To the congregation, however, the light suggested offensive commercial architecture, and it was removed.

☞ *The interior is richly embellished with four polychromatic sculptured terra-cotta arches springing from polished green granite columns to support the Guastavino tile ceiling. There are three Carrara marble altars. Arts and Crafts movement grace notes include the Pre-Raphaelite angels on either side of the main altar. The original communion rail gates were removed as part of the Venturi and Rauch reconfiguration of the sanctuary in 1968.*

NORTH PHILADELPHIA

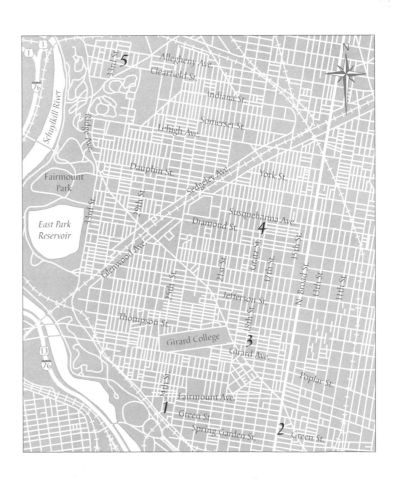

↝⚭ *Rodeph Shalom Synagogue: The main sanctuary is the finest surviving D'Ascenzo Studio interior, and possibly the finest ever. See pages 234–237.*

SAINT FRANCIS XAVIER CHURCH

Twenty-Fourth and Green Streets
Philadelphia, PA 19130-3196

Edwin F. Durang, architect, 1893–1898;
rebuilt following a 1906 fire,
rededicated 1908

Telephone for visitor information:
215.765.4568

Sited on a gentle rise of land next to the Philadelphian and diagonally opposite the Philadelphia Museum of Art, Saint Francis Xavier Church is the oldest Roman Catholic parish in the Fairmount district of Philadelphia. Every day thousands of commuters on the Benjamin Franklin Parkway rush by this commanding asymmetrical Romanesque structure built of randomly coursed blocks of Port Deposit granite with contrasting lighter limestone string courses, quoins, and window surrounds. Yet few Philadelphians beyond its faithful congregation have ever ventured inside this prominent church; fewer still know its history.

As Philadelphia expanded north and west from the historic city core, Saint John the Evangelist Church on Thirteenth Street below Market (see pages 136–139) found it increasingly difficult "to accommodate all the Catholics of the western portion of the city." Consequently, Bishop Francis Patrick Kenrick authorized a new parish on May 27, 1839, to serve "a large Catholic population [that] now exists in the western portion of the district of Spring Garden" and to be named for Saint Francis Xavier (1506–1552). Xavier had been recruited by Ignatius of Loyola for the Society of Jesus (Jesuits) and spent his life ministering to Catholics and converting pagans in the Portuguese Indies. He was beatified in 1619 and canonized in 1622; he is the patron saint of India and the East Indies.

The new congregation lost no time erecting a small church with a single aisle nave at the corner of Biddle and Twenty-Fifth Streets, which over subsequent years was expanded by the addition of transepts and a handsome dome—perhaps influenced by the recently completed Cathedral of Saints Peter and Paul by Napoleon LeBrun (see pages 152–157). These additions date to 1866 and show in the surviving photographs of that building. However, the Baltimore and Ohio Railroad began blasting for a railroad tunnel and changed the grade of Twenty-Fifth Street. These disruptions forced abandonment of the original church and its replacement by a new structure at Twenty-Fourth and Green Streets. The cornerstone was laid on October 6, 1894, and the completed church was dedicated on December 18, 1898.

As architect the parish engaged Edwin Forrest Durang (1825–1911), one of the most successful Philadelphia architects specializing in Catholic buildings, with more than seventy-five churches and numerous schools, convents, rectories, and hospitals included in his impressive job list. A native of New York City, Durang's family relocated to Philadelphia, where he entered the office of John Carver (1803–1859) and continued the Carver practice after 1859. Fortunately for the young hopeful, Napoleon LeBrun (whose work is discussed on pages 86–91, 98–101, 152–157), the leading Catholic architect of Philadelphia, moved his practice to New York City, leaving Durang the dominant Catholic architect in the city. Saint Charles Borromeo (1868–1876) in southwestern Philadelphia and the Church of the Gesu in north Philadelphia (1879–1888; see pages 238–243) are among his most important commissions.

☞ *Saint Francis Xavier Church overlooks the Benjamin Franklin Parkway in the Fairmount area of Philadelphia. It was designed by Edwin F. Durang and erected over several years in the 1890s. After a fire in 1906 the handsome Romanesque Revival style building was extended to its present size.*

The resulting Romanesque Revival style church for the Catholics of Fairmount, so long in realization, proved to be ill-fated. On March 31, 1906, in a terrible echo of a similar tragedy at Saint John's seven years before, a fire in a nearby hat factory spread to the church, destroying the north wall and roof. Architect Durang, now in his eighties, returned to supervise repairs, and the church reopened in 1908 with a slightly extended sanctuary to the north, a rebuilt main altar, and the addition of two side altars. Over the main altar reredos is a large Crucifixion window dating from the 1906–1908 extension, possibly by Philadelphia stained-glass artist Martin Callanan.

Following the Second Vatican Council in 1962, Saint Francis Xavier adopted the new form of Mass, which replaced Latin with the vernacular, and began receiving communion in the hand. Fortunately the parish did not vandalize its high altar, adopting instead the simple expedient of constructing a new wooden altar to allow the priest to face the congregation while saying Mass, a solution that might have preserved the altars of many historic churches of several denominations during the revolutionary—some might say radical—days of the 1960s.

The interior of Saint Francis Xavier is a cruciform plan with a wide barrel-vaulted central nave and narrow side aisles. The Corinthian columns are cast iron covered in plaster and painted to resemble marble. The three altars are by Charles Hall and Company of Cambridge, Massachusetts, and date from the post-fire renovations of 1906–1908. The statue in front of the side altar to Jesus is Saint Francis Xavier, while on top of the Blessed Virgin's altar is a statue of Mary with head bowed and hands in prayer. The current paint scheme is modern and gives the interior a light feel, even though the windows contain a remarkable collection of stained glass.

RODEPH SHALOM SYNAGOGUE

615 North Broad Street
Philadelphia, PA 19123-2495

Edward P. Simon, of Simon and
Simon, architects, 1927–1928

Telephone for visitor information:
215.627.6747

www.rodephshalom.org

The Philadelphia Ashkenazic Congregation Rodeph Shalom is second only to the Sephardic Congregation Mikveh Israel in terms of age (see pages 19–22). Its roots trace to the growing numbers of newly immigrated Jews who wished to pray "according to the German and Dutch Rules." By 1795 this group had begun to gather for their own minyan. In 1801, land was acquired for use as a cemetery "for the Hebrew Tribe or Nation of and belonging to the synagogue to which they, the said guarantors, now belong." The following year (1802) they formally "dedicated our new German Shul," and named it Rodeph Shalom.

For the first half century of its existence, Congregation Rodeph Shalom wandered from rented space to rented space until 1847, when it could purchase a former Unitarian church on Juliana (now Randolph) Street between Fifth and Sixth Streets The congregation fitted this building out on Orthodox lines, with a *bimah* in the center of the sanctuary. Each move had been prompted by increasing attendance, and soon the Juliana Street building also proved inadequate, causing the congregation to purchase two lots on the southeast corner of Broad and Mount Vernon Streets on which to build a proper synagogue. This high visibility commission was awarded to Fraser, Furness, and Hewitt (1868–1869; demolished), who produced a polychromatic Saracenic confection, the loss of which remains a sorry chapter in the history of Philadelphia architecture.

The strongly Romanesque synagogue with its asymmetrical tower was suggestive of Stephen Decatur Button's First Baptist Church, also on Broad Street (1856; demolished, page 184). But here the Fraser, Furness, and Hewitt tower featured a bulbous dome and the polychrome horseshoe arches gave the entire composition an exotic air. For half a century this building served the congregation. By the 1920s, however, a new rabbi with expansionist plans began lobbying for a new building. "We have always been wanderers," he told the board. "Israel's spirit, always restless, eternally unsatisfied and discontented, marches on with the progress of the suns." Additional land on Mount Vernon Street was purchased, an architect hired, and the old synagogue razed in 1927.

To design the new synagogue, the board selected native Philadelphian Edward Paul Simon (1878–1949), who had received his diploma in architectural drawing from Drexel Institute's day school (1900) and a certificate in building construction from Drexel's night school the same year. He immediately opened his own office in partnership with a series of other architects until joined by his brother, Grant Miles Simon, who left the firm just before the Rodeph Shalom project was begun—although Edward P. Simon continued to use the Simon and Simon name for the firm. Known for monumental projects, Simon designed the Philadelphia Municipal Stadium, the Fidelity Trust Building on South Broad Street, and the Strawbridge and Clothier store on Market Street.

Simon's building looks back to the exotic Byzantine style favored by so many nineteenth-century synagogues and forward to the sleek lines of the early twentieth-century Moderne style. A massive block of Indiana limestone, the Broad Street façade is intended to be seen head on. The three entrances are deeply set and defined by columns with Byzantine capitals from which spring half-round arches. Above the doors are polychromatic mosaics by the studio of Philadelphia artist Nicola D'Ascenzo (1871–1954). This tripartite composition is flanked by unadorned vestigial towers with absolutely plain pilasters. While the exterior hints at what is to come, the main sanctuary with its massive pendentive dome overwhelms the viewer. Every surface is bejeweled with stencils or highlighted with mosaics. The work of D'Ascenzo is found in many sacred places of Philadelphia, but the Rodeph Shalom decoration is his best surviving example—and it may be the best that ever was. The subtle shading of the decoration and the gradual narrowing of the perspective focus the viewers' eyes on the

Edward P. Simon's Byzantine-Moderne synagogue for the Congregation Rodeph Shalom is one of the principal architectural embellishments of North Broad Street. It occupies the same site as the Fraser, Furness, and Hewitt synagogue that was demolished in 1926.

pink marble columns of the tabernacle that frame and surround the massive bronze doors of the ark holding the Torah scrolls (see pages 228–229).

One of the 613 commandments contained in the Torah admonishes Jews to beautify their ritual observance. The result has been the creation of extraordinary ceremonial objects that delight the senses and add to the aesthetic appreciation of ceremonies as well as daily events in Jewish life—including Torah ornaments (eternal light, pointer, finials) and objects associated with Rosh Hashanah, Yom Kippur, Hanukkah, Passover, Shabbat, Havdalah, and birth, bar mitzvah, marriage, and death. For most of their adult lives, Leon J. and Julia S. Obermayer collected these precious objects and in 1985 presented approximately 500 to Rodeph Shalom. Permanent exhibition cases have been erected in the vestibule for representative examples from the collection.

Congregation Rodeph Shalom commissioned this picturesque synagogue with an asymmetrical façade and stack of gables facing Broad Street, polychrome stone work, and bulbous dome from the architects Fraser, Furness, and Hewitt (1868–1869; demolished). Congregation Rodeph Shalom.

In the vestibule are several cases exhibiting the Obermayer Collection of Jewish Ceremonial Art. This photograph also provides details of the mosaic floors and stenciled decoration of the interior by the studio of Philadelphia artist Nicola D'Ascenzo (1871–1954).

CHURCH OF THE GESU

(Saint Joseph's Preparatory School)

*Eighteenth and Stiles Streets
Philadelphia, PA 19130*

*Edwin Forrest Durang, architect,
1879–1888; John Blatteau Associates,
restoration architects, 1990*

*Telephone for visitor information:
215.978.1950*

The powerful Baroque style Church of the Gesu towers over the surrounding row houses of its North Philadelphia neighborhood. Imposing as the exterior is, the visitor is not prepared for the vast scale and grandeur of the interior which nearly rivals Napoleon LeBrun's Cathedral Basilica of Saints Peter and Paul (pages 152–157). The Church of the Gesu evolved from a decision by the Society of Jesus to move its educational programs from Saint Joseph's Church on Willings Alley (pages 50–53) and develop a new college complex. For this purpose land was purchased in 1866 and a small chapel erected. As the North Philadelphia population rapidly expanded—fueled by the influx of Irish and German Catholic immigrants—the need for a new parish church of substantial size became obvious.

The Jesuits selected Edwin Forrest Durang (1825–1911) as their architect. Throughout a practice spanning six decades, Durang specialized in ecclesiastical

*⇐⤙ Portrait of Edwin Forrest
Durang (1825–1911) by Catholic church
artist and decorator Lorenzo C. Scat-
taglia, circa 1874. The Athenæum of
Philadelphia, gift of Edwina Hare.*

*⇐⤙⇐ The red brick and white-
painted cast-iron and sheet metal trim
of the main façade has recently been
restored to its 1880s appearance.*

This print illustrates Durang's original design for the Church of the Gesu, including the final stages of the twin towers that were omitted to save on construction costs. American Catholic Historical Society.

The barrel-vaulted nave is the most impressive feature of the Church of the Gesu. The nave terminates in a semidome over the main altar, which rises 70 feet above the sanctuary. This grand space is now used by Saint Joseph's Preparatory School for a variety of purposes.

design, especially for Catholics; his projects include scores of churches, schools, convents, rectories, and hospitals. Born in New York City, Durang moved as a youth to Philadelphia where his first recorded effort as an architect is a drawing submitted in the Academy of Music competition of 1854 that survives in The Athenæum of Philadelphia collection. That this early design is a theater should not be surprising; acting was a family birthright. His grandfather, John Durang, is often called the first native-born American actor, while his father and uncle, Charles and Richard Durang, are said to be the first persons to perform the "Star Spangled Banner." At the time Durang entered the Academy of Music competition his father was director of the Chestnut Street Theater.

By 1855 young Durang had entered the office of another unsuccessful Academy competitor, John Carver (1803–1859, pages 248–253), and he continued the practice after the older architect's death. When Napoleon LeBrun, favorite architect of

Philadelphia Catholics, departed to establish an office in New York City, Durang succeeded to that patronage, enjoying a highly successful career specializing in Catholic church architecture in Philadelphia, including such projects as Saint Charles Borromeo (1868–1876), Saint Francis Xavier (pages 230–233), and, what is probably his most important commission, the Church of the Gesu.

Construction on the church moved slowly after the cornerstone was laid in 1879; the unfinished church was not dedicated until 1888. Based loosely on Il Gesù in Rome—mother church of the Society of Jesus—the main façade consists of a symmetrical central block defined by two towers tied together by horizontal entablatures of contrasting color. Durang specified granite for the body and limestone trim, but to reduce costs red brick and white-painted iron and sheet metal trim were substituted. These gave the church a lively polychromatic effect, albeit different from that originally intended. Less successful was the decision to truncate the upper stages of the towers, again as a cost savings.

However disappointing the exterior, the visitor is compensated by the interior composed of a vast barrel vault without columns spanning the 76-foot-wide nave. According to a *Public Ledger* account of the dedication, "The interior, which is not finished yet, is a large open space, without pillars to obstruct the view. The ceiling is 105 feet from the ground, and is considered by many the finest piece of stucco work in this country. The main altar is 72 feet high, and in keeping with the surroundings." In plan the church is essentially a single space consisting of the nave without side aisles and only vestigial transepts holding altars, much in the manner of the Roman prototype. The high altar and its flanking altars were constructed of marbled wood when the church opened. Eventually there would also be five chapels down each side of the nave, again following the Il Gesù plan. The interior would not be embellished with marble altars and wainscot, decorative painting, and murals until the early decades of the twentieth century.

At its high point the Gesu Parish numbered 20,000 communicants, serving a densely populated, largely Irish neighborhood with strong social, political, and religious ties. But during the Depression of the 1930s, factories closed and banks failed. Further economic deterioration in the 1950s rent the social fabric; by 1980 half the population had fled the area and 40 percent of the housing stock had been abandoned. As the author of one report on these conditions remarked, North Philadelphia had become "a region of the very young, the very old and the very poor." By 1987 the parish congregation had dwindled to fewer than 200 souls. Reluctantly, it was decided to close the sanctuary and pass title to Saint Joseph's Preparatory School. In 1993 the Archdiocese of Philadelphia reorganized and consolidated fifteen North Philadelphia parishes—including Gesu. In several cases architecturally significant sacred places were closed. The Church of the Gesu, however, has been more fortunate. St. Joseph's Prep engaged the firm of John Blatteau Associates to prepare a master plan for the school that included restoration of the church for sympathetic use by the school. In 1990 the school received substantial funding to restore the exterior and to repaint and relight the interior.

This detail of two side chapels and the eighth station of the cross shows Durang's use of classical orders and heavy sculptural ornament. Most of the ten side altars date from the early twentieth century.

CHURCH OF THE ADVOCATE

(George W. South Memorial Protestant Episcopal Church of the Advocate)

Eighteenth and Diamond Streets Philadelphia, PA 19121

Charles M. Burns, architect, 1890–1897

Telephone for visitor information: 215.765.3650

www.churchoftheadvocate.org

☞ *Based on high Gothic French cathedrals, the Church of the Advocate demonstrates the rich visual effects created by pinnacles, flying buttresses, moldings, and window tracery. Typical of the rayonnant style is the circular rose window whose radial patterns of tracery suggest the term*

The Philadelphia architect Charles M. Burns (1838–1922) has already been introduced by one of his most important commissions, the Romanesque style Church of the Saviour in West Philadelphia (1889, 1902, pages 216–221). While the Church of the Saviour (and the Church of the Redeemer in Bryn Mawr, 1881) are significant commissions, one prominent architectural historian argues, "had Charles M. Burns designed but one church in the late nineteenth century, the George W. South Memorial Protestant Episcopal Church of the Advocate would sustain his reputation." Called "a cathedral in little" by artist and former Burns student Joseph Pennell, the Church of the Advocate is nothing less than a quadripartite, stone-vaulted French medieval Gothic church dropped into a north Philadelphia neighborhood that is now physically and economically devastated.

The Church of the Advocate originated as the Diamond Street Mission housed in Woodstock, a late Georgian villa erected circa 1798 for Philadelphia merchant Peter Kuhn. Rachel A. South purchased the Woodstock property in 1887, intending to create a church complex in memory of her husband, George W. South (1799–1884), a Philadelphia merchant of great wealth. That same year a parish house was constructed, followed by a chapel (1888), both designed by Burns. The demolition of Woodstock then provided space for the church itself (1890–1897). South, his wife, daughter, and other family members are interred in the vault below the nave.

The resulting church is one of the architectural treasures of Philadelphia. It is loosely based on thirteenth-century French sacred places, particularly the smaller rayonnant Gothic cathedrals—so called for the radiating tracery in the enormous rose windows characteristic of the period. Gradually the term came to be applied to an entire style of Gothic buildings with light and soaring structural skeletons and increasingly elaborate decoration. By reducing the size and weight of the masonry required to support the walls and roof, medieval master builders could enlarge the windows and illuminate the interior. In the late nineteenth century, the Church of the Advocate was often compared to the cathedral at Amiens (1220–1269) and the Abbey Saint-Denis (1140–1144) near Paris, although Burns wasn't inspired by a single prototype. He certainly would have been familiar with Charles Locke Eastlake's *History of the Gothic Revival* (London, 1872), wherein the author illustrated French cathedrals and admitted—no doubt reluctantly—that the French attained greater excellence in that art than the English. Nonetheless, the use of French rather than English prototypes for an Episcopal church is surprising. Burns's introduction of French Gothic at the Church of the Advocate must surely be one of the earliest Philadelphia examples in that style. Subsequently, it would rapidly grow in local popularity.

Built of smooth-cut Port Deposit granite, the church is cruciform with nave, transept, and apse. Entrance is gained through a low narthex joined on the south by an octagonal baptistery. The nave is triple height with load-bearing masonry walls.

Tracery rises from the columns and wall piers to support the ceiling vault ribs. A single-height ambulatory traces the semi-octagonal apse behind the high altar; off this is access to the organ room and sacristy.

The twentieth-century history of this handsome church is a metaphor for the challenges of post-industrial life in North Broad Street neighborhoods. After World War II, Philadelphia began to lose the industrial base on which the residents of North Philadelphia had always relied. Factory owners and workers alike—if they could—followed industry out of the city, leaving behind those without the opportunity or means to flee. What was originally a wealthy white congregation gradually integrated as the neighborhood changed to an African American majority. As the civil rights movement swept over Philadelphia, the Episcopal Diocese of Pennsylvania appointed the Rev. Paul M. Washington as rector in 1962 and began providing supplemental funding to keep the parish economically viable.

During the ministry of Father Washington, spanning a quarter-century, the Church of the Advocate became a center of social activism among the people of North Philadelphia, who were invited to use the church for community meetings on such controversial issues as adequate housing and police brutality. In the racially charged year 1968, the Third Annual National Conference on Black Power was held at the church. The next year Father Washington led African Americans out of the General Convention of the Episcopal Church, and in 1974 the Church of the Advocate hosted the unauthorized ordination of eleven women as Episcopal priests. Prior to the ceremony the parish approved the following statement: "The goals of the Advocate have always been to move towards one world, one people, and one love concept; we are not afraid to take any step or measure that will make that concept a reality." Within two years the Episcopal Church officially authorized the ordination of women.

Also in the 1970s, two Philadelphia artists—Walter Edmonds and Richard Watson—executed fourteen large-scale paintings on panels to be mounted around the nave in an effort to "correct the [white] cultural bias of the church." These paintings depict scenes of the historic black experience in America and are arranged in a traditional biblical cycle, coming up to the "I have a dream" speech of Martin Luther King, Jr.

Maintenance of such an architectural treasure has not been easy. Failure of the roof system made serious water damage inevitable until a new roof was installed in 1986. As this is written, water damage to the nave prevents it being used for services or photographed. Plans are underway to restore the church to its former glory and perhaps in future editions of this book it can be fully illustrated.

⇒ *Charles M. Burns, "Proposed Interior of the Memorial Church of the Advocate," ink and watercolor on paper, 1890. The completed church closely follows this drawing. The Athenæum of Philadelphia.*

CHURCH OF SAINT JAMES THE LESS

*3222 West Clearfield Street
Philadelphia, PA 19132-1822*

*John E. Carver, architect, after
drawings by George Gordon Place,
1846–1850*

*Telephone for visitor information:
215.229.5767*

*www.orthodoxanglican.org/
SaintJames*

Few American churches have both a distinguished architectural pedigree and the physical appeal of Saint James the Less. Its charms are intimacy, simplicity, and dignity rather than grandeur; the structure itself is diminutive by Victorian city church standards. Upon approaching the church through paths lined with monuments to the long-departed faithful, one cannot avoid that palpable sense of antiquity experienced at medieval English parish churches—if they survived the Reformation and enjoyed the uninterrupted care of a wealthy and thoughtful vestry. In fact, Saint James the Less was built in the mid-nineteenth century from measured drawings taken by George Gordon Place at Saint Michael's, Longstanton, Cambridgeshire—a thirteenth-century early English Gothic parish church—commissioned by the Cambridge Camden Society (pages 162–167). So successful did this transplant prove to be that Saint James the Less became a prototype for countless Episcopal churches erected across the United States in subsequent decades. In the words of the Historic American Buildings Survey, it is "the first pure example of a Medieval parish church in America."

How Saint James the Less came into being deserves mention. By the 1840s the China trade merchant Robert Ralston, who lived at nearby Mount Peace, proposed a church for Philadelphians who were moving to suburban villas along Ridge Road above the Schuylkill River. The new parish acquired a wedge-shaped acre of land donated by the recently established Laurel Hill Cemetery Company and began planning the new church. Ralston, who had been impressed by and in contact with the Cambridge Camden Society, became the chief patron and most persistent advocate for close adherence to the plans provided by the society, which was dedicated to reviving medieval ritual and church design. To supervise construction the vestry hired the Philadelphia builder/architect John E. Carver (1803–1859), who is generally thought to have followed the Place drawings except for lengthening the nave by one bay and adding the vestry, which was subsequently replaced by the present sacristy (1929). Throughout construction, Ralston was in constant correspondence with William Butterfield (1814–1900), official designer for the Camden Society, who supplied detail drawings, recommended the use of Minton tile floors, and ordered the Communion plate to be made in London to his designs. Butterfield, a follower of Augustus Welby Northmore Pugin (1812–1852), also supplied a copy of his *Instrumenta Ecclesiastica: A Series of Working Designs for the Furniture, Fittings, and Decorations of Churches and Their Precincts* (London, 1847), to which the Saint James the Less rectors, vestry, and their architects would regularly return for preapproved inspiration. By the May 1848 issue, the Society's journal could report with no little pride that it was

⌫ Built between 1846 and 1848 of the local metamorphic rock known as Wissahickon schist, St. James the Less is based on measured drawings of an early English chapel, Saint Michael's, Longstanton, Cambridgeshire, which dates from circa 1230. This is the first church in the United States directly supervised by the English Ecclesiologists. It immediately became a popular prototype for rural and suburban Episcopal churches across America.

glad to hear from a correspondent in the United States that the Church of St. James the Less, Schuylkill, is progressing well, and that the chancel has been more correctly arranged in consequence of a communication from our Society. The

The intimate interior is starkly simple, dignified, almost primitive: a nave with aisles and chancel, unpainted stone walls, simple arcades formed by alternating circular and octagonal piers, tile floors, and the exposed roof framing.

One of the most pleasing aspects of the Saint James the Less complex is the richness of subsequent additions to the grounds, most of which were inspired by the William Butterfield drawings in the Instrumenta Ecclesiastica *(London, 1847). In the distance is the Wanamaker Tower, designed by Philadelphia architect John Torrey Windrim (1866–1934) for Rodman Wanamaker in 1908. The lych gate dates to 1885 and the churchyard walls to 1898.*

internal walls of the cancel are to be ashlar; those of the nave are to be ranged but undressed stone. All the splays and moulded parts are to be of well cut stone. There is to be a well-intentioned though unsuccessful rood screen; but the error will, we trust be rectified.

Camden Society leaders thought the Gothic style of medieval parish churches particularly appropriate for sacramental liturgical worship. Consequently, Saint James the Less consists of two distinct parts: the nave to accommodate the laity, and the chancel reserved for the clergy, the two separated by a rood screen. The *Ecclesiologist* stated flatly, "every church of whatever kind, size, or shape, should have a distinct Chancel at least one-third of the length of the Nave, and separated from the latter, internally at least, if not externally, by a well-defined mark, a chancel-arch if possible, or at least by a screen and raised floor." At the eastern end of the chancel is the sanctuary—raised one step from the floor of the chancel—housing the stone high altar backed by a reredos. The western end of the chancel contained seats for the clergy and choir. The reintroduction of this high-church plan from pre-Reformation Roman Catholic parish churches constituted a rejection of the Protestant "priesthood of all believers," which had brought worship out into the nave.

Characteristic of medieval churches of this type, Saint James the Less has widely sloping roofs unbroken by a clerestory. Heavy buttresses support the west front; there are diagonal buttresses at the corners and a two-tiered bell cote. The cornerstone was laid on October 28, 1846, and two years later, on October 31, 1848, the Building Committee reported the building completed, declaring, "if not a model of economy is certainly one of beauty and durability." The church was consecrated on May 26, 1850.

Saint James the Less became an influential prototype in American suburban church design. Architects such as Richard Upjohn and Frank Willis spread its popularity across North America in the decades following the Civil War. In the Delaware Valley there are numerous examples erected on the medieval parish church plan—most notably Saint Timothy's, Roxborough (pages 288–291) and Saint Martin-in-the Fields, Chestnut Hill (pages 282–287). Other regional examples that might be mentioned include Saint Thomas's, Glassboro, New Jersey; Saint John's Chapel, Cornersville, Maryland; Saint Michael's Chapel, Reisterstown, Maryland; Trinity Church, Matawan, New Jersey; and Christ Church, Elizabeth, New Jersey. For the final word on this subject there is no better authority than Phoebe B. Stanton, author of *The Gothic Revival and American Church Architecture* (1968) who argues that Saint James the Less "demonstrated the aesthetic possibilities of building materials handled directly and without disguise and the potential power and beauty of unornamented structure." In Philadelphia we are fortunate to have the American prototype to enjoy.

The original rood screen between the nave and the chancel was replaced in 1878 with the one shown here made of copper, brass, and iron, donated by Moro Phillips, who also provided the pre-Raphaelite ceiling decorations in the chancel. The stained-glass window over the altar is an enrichment designed by Henry Gerente of Paris, whose work A. W. Pugin greatly admired. The Gerente shop continued after the founder's death, ultimately providing glass for the west lancet windows, executed by Alfred Gerente.

NORTHWEST PHILADELPHIA

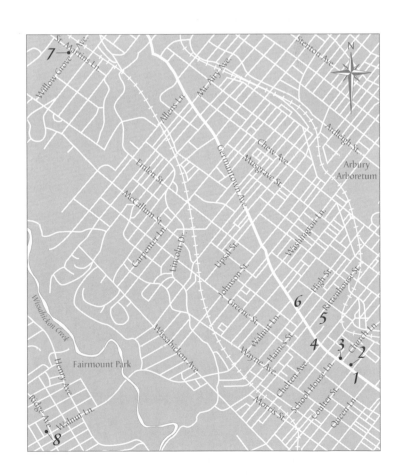

⊷⊨ Saint Luke's Episcopal Church: The handsome rood screen is the work of Cope and Stewardson and was dedicated in 1894. The French Gothic stone altar and reredos were designed by George T. Pearson and dedicated in 1903. See pages 260–263.

TRINITY LUTHERAN CHURCH

5300 Germantown Avenue
Philadelphia, PA 19144

Jacob and George A. Binder, builders,
1856–1857

Telephone for visitor information:
215.848.8150

Directly across Germantown Avenue from John Wister's Grumblethorpe is the colonial house formerly occupied by the publisher Christopher Sower, Jr. (1721–1784). Here, on the eve of the American Revolution, Sower operated the first American type foundry; and here would later be organized the Lutheran Publication Society. In 1836 the newly organized English Evangelical Lutheran Congregation in Germantown purchased the house (now used as offices) with its deep lot of ground on which to construct a church. The new congregation had split off from Saint Michael's Lutheran Church, a rift brought on by disagreements between the vestry and the congregation over the language to be used in services (German or English) and whether pew rents should be introduced as a prerequisite of church membership to provide a steady stream of income—and, ultimately, who had the power to make these decisions.

The present church is the second to occupy the site and dates from 1856–1857. To design and build this second church the congregation selected the local contractors Jacob and George A. Binder. For $11,500 the Binders provided a suitably modest two-story stuccoed stone structure (55' x 85') in the then popular Italianate style with round-headed windows, pilasters, and a gable roof. It is set well back from Germantown Avenue and is intended to be approached by a path leading through the graveyard (see pages viii–ix). (Entrance is now through a gate on Queen Lane.) The most interesting feature of this otherwise unremarkable structure, which differs little from dozens of Italianate preaching boxes erected throughout the region at the time, is the tower supporting an impressive octagonal steeple and hexagonal spire rising 181 feet. To this is applied a pedimented porch giving entrance to the ground floor Sunday School and meeting rooms and a double stair rising to the narthex and hence to the sanctuary on the second floor.

The sanctuary, with a seating capacity of 500, was originally an unembellished meeting house space focused on a high central pulpit with modest communion table in front. From this lofty station the pastor looked out across his flock seated in box pews with doors. The organ and choir were located at the rear in the balcony. In 1886 the box pews were replaced and the present recessed chancel was provided to contain a raised altar. This greater emphasis on the sacraments required the pulpit to be relocated to the side. The present marble altar and floor date from 1911, the same year the choir and organ were moved to the front. The communion rail dates from renovations in 1962–1964; at the same time the altar was moved away from the chancel wall to allow the officiating minister to face the congregation. Most of the stained-glass windows are by the Italian-born Philadelphia master Nicola D'Ascenzo (1871–1954), who received his formal artistic training at the Pennsylvania Academy of Fine Arts and the Pennsylvania Museum and School of Industrial Art. He

✏ *The steeple of Trinity Lutheran Church has been a notable Germantown landmark for 150 years. A clock by the Norristown, Pennsylvania, manufacturer Jacob D. Custer (1805–1872) was installed in 1858.*

opened his studio in 1896, and in the first decades of the twentieth century—a period when many of Philadelphia's sacred places were under construction or being embellished for the first time—the studio supplied murals and stained glass. The ten D'Ascenzo windows at Trinity Lutheran Church follow a plan developed in 1926 and recount the life of Christ.

⚬⚬ *The main sanctuary reflects several construction periods ranging from 1857 through the 1970s. The stained-glass window behind the altar dates to 1978 and illustrates the Holy Trinity. It is the work of Connick Associates of Boston. Charles J. Connick (1875–1945) established his studio in 1912, and after his death members of his staff continued in business until 1986.*

SAINT LUKE'S EPISCOPAL CHURCH

5411–5421 Germantown Avenue
Philadelphia, PA 19144

Henry M. Congdon, architect, 1875

Telephone for visitor information:
215.844.8544

www.stlukesger.org

✎← *Sited two hundred feet back from the hustle and bustle of Germantown Avenue traffic and surrounded by its own campus, Saint Luke's Church is an architectural essay in the polychromatic effects of different colored stone trimmings. The main building dates from 1875, and the tower, also designed by Henry M. Congdon, was completed in 1892.*

Saint Luke's is the first Episcopal congregation organized in Germantown (1811). By 1818 a small stuccoed stone church building with modest Gothic detailing had been erected; it would be enlarged several times during subsequent decades as the English-speaking population of Germantown expanded. Architecturally the interior differed little from the nearby churches of the Lutherans, Methodists, and Presbyterians. By the 1870s, however, the vestry recognized this modest preaching box no longer met their needs and called for an entirely new church on the site. Following an open competition they awarded the commission to New York architect Henry Martyn Congdon (1834–1922). Congdon specialized in Episcopal churches, and several of his commissions are sprinkled throughout New England and the Middle Atlantic region. According to his biographer, "bold surface detail, large, dominant towers, and a picturesque grouping of elements" characterize his designs.

Congdon's architecture also exemplified the latest Anglo-Catholic taste. Congdon was a reader of John Ruskin, influenced by William Burges and William Butterfield, and his architectural vocabulary clearly resonated with the vestry. The congregation already had a reputation in Germantown for greater emphasis on and more frequent celebration of the Holy Eucharist, and Congdon's design of a raised chancel certainly reflects a tendency to favor a return to pre-Reformation ritual. Congdon also provided a suitable backdrop for the High Church embellishments to come. Particularly noteworthy in his Saint Luke's design are the polychromatic effects of the stone. Here Congdon reflects the influence of Butterfield's "constructional polychromy," which he maintained could be achieved by using materials of varying colors and texture. This "honest" expression also echoes the views of the Cambridge Camden movement, which had influenced the American Episcopal Church for several decades and had found expression at Saint James the Less (pages 248–253) and Notman's Saint Mark's (pages 162–167).

During the tenure of the Rev. Dr. Samuel Upjohn (1883–1923), the parish, in the words of one of his successors, "embraced whole heartedly the Anglo-Catholic practices of the Anglican church. It was also during Dr. Upjohn's time that much of the beauty of the interior of the present church came to fruition." The most visible of these embellishments is the handsome French Gothic rood screen, designed by Philadelphia architects Walter Cope (1860–1902) and John Stewardson (1858–1896) as a memorial to Edward Ingersoll (1817–1893) and his wife Anna Chester Warren (1828–1891), dedicated in 1894 (see pages 254–255). Both Cope and Stewardson had studied abroad and are credited with introducing a taste for collegiate Gothic architecture to Philadelphia in the late nineteenth century.

Other significant embellishments are the oak organ screen and the French Gothic stone altar and reredos designed by George T. Pearson (1847–1920). The altar is Caen stone carved by the J. H. Whitman Company and completed in 1903 as

a memorial to William Penn Troth, Jr. By 1901 the south transept had become a Lady Chapel.

Saint Luke's sits back from Germantown Avenue at the end of a lane lined with a campus of other Gothic Revival buildings: Saint Margaret's House (1895), formerly the mother house of the Sisters of Saint Margaret and now used as a retreat house for abused and homeless women, the rectory (1896), and George T. Pearson's parish house (1909–1910). The entire composition is visually focused on Congdon's 88-foot tower, which had not been erected in the 1870s due to cost and was finally completed in 1892.

Throughout the early decades of the twentieth century, Saint Luke's was one of the leading Episcopal congregations in Germantown, supported by socially prominent and mostly white parishioners and financially well endowed. After World War II, however, the congregation began to dwindle as parishioners died and their children and grandchildren elected to desert Philadelphia for the suburbs. The future looked bleak. In 1904 Saint Luke's had founded the Saint Barnabas parish as a mission for neighborhood African Americans, and close ties between the two congregations remained. By the 1960s the Saint Barnabas parish had grown in numbers and programs to the point of outgrowing their facilities on Rittenhouse Street. In the words of the Rev. Canon Charles L. L. Poindexter of Saint Barnabas, "St. Luke's parish had the buildings and financial assets while St. Barnabas had the people and the guilds and organizations." In 1967, the Rev. Robert W. Hill, rector of Saint Luke's, approached Canon Poindexter with a remarkable proposal, that the two parishes join. While not entirely without stresses, given the racial tensions of the late 1960s, the resulting united congregation has maintained an important complex of historic buildings that serves the Germantown community as intended by the founders.

✎← *Congdon's carefully selected interior stonework sets off the stone doorway surround, carved details, and richly colored stained-glass windows. This rose window is similar to a pattern commonly used by high Victorian architect William Burges (1827–1881), whose work is believed to have influenced Congdon.*

IMPACTING YOUR WORLD CHRISTIAN CENTER

(formerly Market Square Presbyterian Church)

5507–5517 Germantown Avenue Philadelphia, PA 19144

George T. Pearson, architect, 1887

Telephone for visitor information: 215.438.7838

www.iywcc.org

Market Square is the heart of Germantown. From colonial times a church has stood on this land, which had been acquired in 1732 "by the direction and appointment of the inhabitants of Germantown belonging to the High Dutch Reformed Congregation for a place to erect a meeting house of the said congregation." The first church building to occupy the lot was erected in 1733 by the Dutch Reformed congregation and doubled in size in 1762. This church survived the Battle of Germantown in 1777, and George Washington could walk from the Deshler-Morris house to attend services there while living in Germantown during the terrible yellow fever epidemics in 1793 and 1794. In 1838 a simple Greek Revival building replaced the colonial church. By the 1850s the congregation, objecting to the "Romanizing tendency" of the Reformed Church in the United States, voted to transfer "our ecclesiastical relation to some other denomination," ultimately settling on the Presbyterians and becoming the Market Square Presbyterian Church of Germantown.

Expansion of the congregation after the Civil War dictated a new church building. As architect they selected George T. Pearson (1847–1920). A native of Trenton, New Jersey, and educated there, Pearson apprenticed with the Elizabeth, New Jersey, architect Charles Graham and appeared in Philadelphia circa 1870 working for Addison Hutton as a draftsman at about the time the Quaker architect was completing the Arch Street Methodist Church (pages 140–143). He later worked in the office of John McArthur, Jr., and established his own practice in 1880. Most of Pearson's work was residential, and he enjoyed the profitable patronage of hatmaker John B. Stetson, for whom he designed both a residence and a factory in Germantown as well as Stetson University in De Land, Florida. For many years Pearson also appears to have had a virtual lock on commissions in Germantown and Mount Airy for the Presbyterians. His ecclesiastical commissions included a chapel for Mount Airy Presbyterian Church, East Mount Pleasant Avenue, and Wakefield Presbyterian Church, the New Redeemer Church of Jesus Christ, and the Second Presbyterian Church of Germantown, all on Germantown Avenue.

For their new church the Market Square Presbyterians approved a Romanesque Revival design with a street-facing gable and a substantial bell tower, the entire church to be constructed of quarry-faced Indiana limestone and set flush to the street, as are the earlier structures on either side — on the north the parsonage, on the south the building now occupied by the Germantown Historical Society. An open walkway to the north gives access to the parsonage (1882) and a stone chapel (1884), the latter set to the back of the lot. The cornerstone was laid on September 25, 1887, and the completed church was dedicated on June 17, 1888.

The Romanesque as a style has already been mentioned in the context of John Notman's Saint Clement's Church and Holy Trinity Church erected before the Civil War (pages 168–177). Market Square Presbyterian owes more to the influence of the

☞ George T. Pearson's Romanesque Revival Market Square Presbyterian Church (1887) is directly opposite the Germantown Civil War memorial. Abandoned by a dissolved Presbyterian congregation, the church was purchased in 2000 and renamed Impacting Your World Christian Center.

Brookline, Massachusetts, architect Henry Hobson Richardson (1838–1886), who developed his own Romanesque idiom inspired by a rich vein of central French medieval churches—especially those in Auvergne—rather than English Norman prototypes. Especially after Trinity Church, Boston (1872–1877) was widely published, the Richardsonian mode of Romanesque Revival began more or less successfully to appear in the work of Philadelphia architects. For example, Isaac Pursell's Saint Paul's Reformed Episcopal Church (pages 206–209), dating from 1879–1880, Hazelhurst and Huckel's use of this grave and substantial style for Mother Bethel (pages 112–115) in 1889–1890, and Edgar V. Seeler's First Baptist Church (pages 184–187) in 1899–1900.

The Market Square Presbyterians eschewed the showy Gothic style used on the exterior of the two earlier churches, the First Presbyterian Church in Germantown (pages 267–271) and the First (Second) Presbyterian Church in Philadelphia (pages 194–199). It may be a stretch to declare the Market Square Presbyterians more aggressively Low Church than the congregations of the First churches, regardless of their sniffing out "Romanizing" tendencies thirty years before. The Gothic Revival style had been accepted by Presbyterians for a decade, and the Romanesque as popularized by Richardson was the latest fashion. Also, the interiors of both First churches had not yet drifted liturgically toward a greater emphasis on the sacraments. Both First churches retained the pulpit as the central feature of the sanctuary; the altars would only move to the center in the twentieth century.

There can be no doubt that the Word remained central in the Market Square interior. Entrance is gained from a porch recessed into the façade on axis with the front gable and protected by intricate iron gates. From the porch, doors open into the narthex and hence into the auditorium. Pearson brilliantly used the narrow, deep lot, which might have dictated an equally narrow auditorium space. Instead of being arranged serially on either side of a central aisle on axis with the chancel, like thousands of other churches of the time, the pews at Market Square form a sweeping ramped semicircle that not only focuses attention on the minister standing on a raised chancel but nearly places the pulpit in the round. No member of the congregation seated on the main floor is more than a few rows from the speaker.

In the post-World War II decline of traditional Germantown congregations, Market Street Presbyterian suffered a similar fate. The congregation eventually dispersed to other Presbyterian churches in Germantown and the suburbs. The abandoned building was first rented to and then in 2000 sold to a largely African American congregation, which renamed the church the Impacting Your World Christian Center; it is headed by a charismatic pastor who has given the complex new life and energy.

The semicircular arrangement of pews in the auditorium is dramatic, practical, and unexpected. Designed for services focused on preaching from the pulpit, the sweep of curved pews and ramped floor focuses on the minister, who is never more than a few rows from everyone seated on the main floor. Pearson's brilliant solution to a long narrow building site gives the large auditorium an intimacy that could not be realized in a traditional design with a central aisle on axis with the pulpit.

FIRST PRESBYTERIAN CHURCH IN GERMANTOWN

35 West Chelten Avenue
Philadelphia, PA 19144

James H. Windrim, architect, 1870–
1872; Frank R. Watson, architect of
transepts, 1888–1892

Telephone for visitor information:
215.843.8811

www.fpcgermantown.org

The English-speaking congregation that became the First Presbyterian Church in Germantown celebrates the year 1809 as its founding date, but not until 1811 was it possible to erect a church "for the use of a Christian society, formed on the principles and rules of the Presbyterian Church, under the superintendency of the General Assembly of said Church in the United States." This simple structure on the east side of Germantown Avenue, between Haines and Rittenhouse Streets, perhaps designed by the Philadelphia-born, London-trained civil engineer Isaac Roberdeau (1763–1829), who worked with Pierre Charles L'Enfant in laying out Washington, D.C., underwent extensive enlargement in 1854. Early surviving photographs of this building show it after these additions, which included a second floor.

An expanding congregation in the post-Civil War era encouraged the trustees to consider a new church building to be erected on the north side of Chelten Avenue a few paces west of Germantown Avenue. When it came to selecting an architect, the Presbyterians were particularly fortunate. They hired James Hamilton Windrim (1840–1919), who shortly after graduating from Girard College entered the office of John Notman, architect of Saint Mark's, Saint Clement's, Holy Trinity, and Calvary Presbyterian, among other area churches (pages 158–177). During this period

First Presbyterian Church was designed by James H. Windrim (1870–1872). Unlike many Germantown Gothic style churches, it sits squarely on the lot line in the manner of Center City churches.

The Annunciation mural in the Jennings Room is one of ten in the series "Great Women of the Bible" by the famous Philadelphia artist Violet Oakley. These murals are among the greatest artistic treasures of the First Presbyterian Church in Germantown.

✝ In the late nineteenth century, the east and west transepts were added from designs by Frank R. Watson. The present ceilings date from those renovations, and the organ and choir seating arrangement date to 1919. In the original 1872 design, the organ and choir had been positioned at the back of the sanctuary.

Windrim served as draftsman for the stonemason of Holy Trinity on Rittenhouse Square. His First Presbyterian design was under construction when he secured the Masonic Temple and Academy of Natural Sciences Building commissions. The first services were held in the new church on May 19, 1872.

What influence, if any, Windrim's Notmanesque Gothic design had on First (Second) Presbyterian Church in Philadelphia (pages 194–199) is not a matter of record. But it is noteworthy that both congregations declared their coming of age and social prominence by adopting the then fashionable Gothic style for their new buildings. In plan, of course, first Presbyterian in Germantown is more like the now demolished Calvary Presbyterian by Notman in Center City, a simple rectangle 137' x 88' with a plain plastered ceiling. There was no apse beyond a small rectangular recess. The pulpit remained the focal point of the chancel area; the organ and choir were opposite the pulpit at the rear of the sanctuary on a raised platform.

Within fifteen years the congregation had outgrown Windrim's church. The west and east transepts (in 1888 and 1892 respectively) were erected to designs by Frank R. Watson, one of the leading Philadelphia architects of the time specializing in church buildings. Watson (1859–1940) had apprenticed with the Catholic church architect Edwin F. Durang for five years; he established an independent practice in 1882 and, like his master, specialized in church buildings. To join the new transepts to the Windrim sanctuary required removing the original plaster ceiling and reframing with the open timber and beaded board ceilings seen today. At the same time an organ gallery was created above the pulpit. In 1919, to accommodate a new organ, the chancel and choir loft were rebuilt, retaining the pulpit in the central position it occupies today.

Not to be missed are the Violet Oakley murals in the Jennings Room, commissioned by the Pastoral Aid Society and completed in 1949. Mrs. W. Beatty Jennings, widow of the former pastor, knew Oakley's work, and she convinced the society— the women's organization of the church—to commission the murals. They commemorate great women of the Bible and were given by members of the society to honor women of the church. Only one of the ten panels is illustrated here: the Annunciation above the west wall fireplace, proclaiming: "Behold the Handmaid of the Lord; be it unto me according to Thy Word." In the early twentieth century, Oakley (1874–1961) was widely esteemed as one of the most successful artists of the American Renaissance mural movement. Appreciation of her prodigious output waned after World War II as modernism captured the artistic center stage. Fortunately her work is once again admired, and the survival of the murals at First Presbyterian Church in Germantown contribute to the growing reappraisal of her work in the twenty-first century. The "Great Women of the Bible" murals were Oakley's last major commission.

SAINT VINCENT DE PAUL CHURCH

*109 East Price Street
Philadelphia, PA 19144*

*Joseph D. Koecker, architect,
1849–1851; dome and transepts
added, 1857–1859*

*Telephone for visitor information:
215.438.2925*

www.saint-vincent-church.org

In the mid-nineteenth century there were few Catholics in Germantown, and those who lived there had to travel to Nicetown or Manayunk to attend Mass. Consequently, a new parish was authorized. Despite the Germantown reputation for religious tolerance, the anti-Catholic "nativist" riots in 1844 that culminated in the burning of Saint Augustine's Church (see pages 86–91) remained an open wound. The construction of a new Catholic church stirred deep-seated prejudice, and the cornerstone ceremony in 1849 drew a rock-throwing mob. Nonetheless, construction went ahead.

Saint Vincent de Paul, the mother parish of Germantown, is named for the early

⊶☞ *Page 272: The first section of Saint Vincent de Paul Church (1849–1851) consisted of the pedimented façade and three bays of the flank elevation. In 1857–1859 the transepts and dome were added, effectively doubling the size of the church. The present main doors and classical frontispiece with its low relief sculpture of Saint Vincent date from 1900–1901.*

⊶☞ *Page 273: Upon entering from Price Street through the vestibule installed in 1900–1901, worshipers and visitors pass under the organ balcony into the barrel-vaulted nave that dates to the first phase of construction.*

☞⊶ *The most recent repainting of Saint Vincent de Paul has simplified and lightened the decoration of the transepts, dome, and apse that architecturally date from 1857–1859. It is nonetheless a dramatic and robust composition. Most of the paintings are believed to have been executed by the Brooklyn decorators Arnold and Locke in 1900–1901.*

seventeenth-century French cleric who organized associations to assist the poor and established seminaries to train priests. In addition to its historic church, this Germantown complex includes a rectory (1875) and an extraordinary parish hall (1884–1885).

As architect the Vincentians selected Joseph D. Koecker (fl. 1840s; d. 1889). Like Napoleon LeBrun, he served an apprenticeship in the office of Thomas Ustick Walter, architect of Girard College who would soon design the dome of the United States Capitol. Koecker is a little-known figure today. He first appears in Philadelphia directories in 1846. A plan for a church dated 1842 in the Walter Archives at The Athenæum of Philadelphia, however, suggests that he was professionally at work in the city prior to the establishment of his own office. Saint Vincent de Paul Church is his best-known commission.

Initially Saint Vincent's consisted of a modest stuccoed Italianate box with clusters of engaged pilasters, a pedimented façade on Price Street, and a three-bay nave along Lena Street. In short, it was little different from other parish churches being produced to serve the first ring of Catholic immigrants pushing out from the city core traditionally served by Saint Joseph's, Saint Mary's, and Saint Augustine's. This pattern must have been common among Philadelphia Catholic parishes: begin with a modest Italianate building, then add transepts and dome once the parish achieves a degree of financial stability. Saint Vincent de Paul dramatically expanded in this fashion in 1857–1859, and a similar expansion would occur a few years later in Fairmount at Saint Francis Xavier Church (see pages 230–233).

These additions created a cruciform plan with shallow transepts and arches springing from a Corinthian entablature to support the central dome. The interior decoration is the product of several campaigns. The first redecoration—to upgrade the painting—occurred in 1880. In 1894 new pews were added, the flooring replaced, and marble wainscoting installed. Then, in 1900, the firm of Arnold and Locke from Brooklyn, New York , made extensive internal and external alterations. The present frontispiece and doors on Price Street replaced the 1849 entrance, and new windows, a new vestibule of oak and glass, and a new communion table and altar rail were installed. In 1978–1979, the altar rail was removed as part of the alterations relating to liturgical changes following Vatican II.

FIRST UNITED METHODIST CHURCH OF GERMANTOWN

6023 Germantown Avenue
Philadelphia, PA 19144

Rankin and Kellogg, architects,
1896–1898; Sundt and Wenner,
architects, 1931

Telephone for visitor information:
215.438.3677

www.fumcog.org

The extensive campus of first United Methodist Church is directly across Germantown Avenue from Wyck on land owned originally by Francis Daniel Pastorius, founder of Germantown and author of the earliest ecclesiastical protest in America against African slavery (1688). The first Fellowship Class of Germantown Methodists organized in 1796 and by 1804 had erected a modest stone meeting house on the south side of Pickius Lane (Haines Street). As the congregation expanded, it periodically enlarged or entirely replaced the preceding structure, first in 1818, then in 1823, and again in 1858. The need for a yet larger church in the 1880s led to the purchase of land at the corner of Germantown Avenue and High Street. The cornerstone of the present church was set on June 4, 1896; the completed church was dedicated on April 10, 1898. After three "meeting house plain" churches, the First United Methodist trustees and congregation, advised by Professor Warren P. Laird (1861–1948), director of the architecture program at the University of Pennsylvania, were ready for something more architecturally demonstrative.

Thirty years previously, Arch Street Methodist Church had proclaimed its break with Methodism's architectural conservatism by erecting a white marble Gothic confection in Center City (pages 140–143). For the Germantown church seventeen proposals from architects in different parts of the country had been received. Ultimately a Perpendicular Gothic Revival design by the young and about to be highly successful Philadelphia Beaux-Arts firm of John Hall Rankin (1868–1952) and Thomas Moore Kellogg (1862–1935), who established their office in 1891, would be accepted. Both partners had studied at the Massachusetts Institute of Technology; Kellogg apprenticed in the New York City office of McKim, Mead and White, while Rankin worked in the offices of James H. Windrim and Frank Miles Day in Philadelphia.

Constructed of Holmesburg granite with Indiana limestone trimmings, the new church can seat 1,000 worshipers in the sanctuary and 800 in the Sunday school. The tower at the southwest corner provides entrance to the sanctuary, and the gable facing Germantown Avenue is embellished by a Tiffany Studios stained-glass window set in stone tracery with the theme "The Resurrection Morn." The rose window on the east wall of the sanctuary is a design by John La Farge; the clerestory windows are by the Willet Studio. The Shelmerdine Memorial Carillon was added to the tower in 1927. Its bells were cast by the John Taylor Company, Loughborough, England.

As the nation slipped into the Great Depression, First Methodist launched one of its most ambitious expansions, resulting in the construction of the William Lewis Turner Memorial Chapel and Education Building. To make way for the chapel, the Pastorius Green Tree Tavern (erected in the 1740s) was moved a few feet north

The tower of the First United Methodist Church of Germantown holds the 63 bells of the Shelmerdine Memorial Carillon cast by the John Taylor Company of Loughborough, England, and installed in 1927. Carillon recitals have been a regular feature of Germantown life for many years.

The sanctuary windows are by the Tiffany Studios and the Willet Studio; the rose window in the chancel was designed by John La Farge. In 1923 the original chancel was reconfigured to accommodate a new organ and choir seating, resulting in the present split chancel rail.

The finely detailed wood carving of the baptismal font in the Turner Chapel is in stark contrast to the rustic exposed stone walls.

along Germantown Avenue in 1931; it now houses clerical offices. The Turner Memorial Chapel is the product of a fruitful collaboration of two University of Pennsylvania graduates, Thoralf M. Sundt (1896–1967) and Bruce C. Wenner (1893–c. 1947), whom the Methodist Episcopal Board of Home Missions and Church Extension declared in 1926 to be among their leading architects. As "house architects" it is perhaps not surprising that Sundt and Wenner would be selected over Rankin and Kellogg to design the extension. In describing the proposed chapel, the church fathers wrote, "the simple but beautiful chapel" would meet the need "our hearts demand [for] quiet, the stately, the beautiful, the symbolic, as aides to the mystical experience in worship when we are especially conscious of the Divine Presence."

The Turner Chapel is indeed a jewel, one of the last such structures in Philadelphia to take advantage of the rich artistic and craft talents available to church builders in the early decades of the twentieth century. The stained-glass windows are by Nicola D'Ascenzo, the carved wood elements came from Ellwood DeLong, and the dossal cloth behind the altar was designed and woven by Frances K. Talbot.

⟜➾ The Gothic William Lewis Turner Chapel—"simple but beautiful"—was added to the church in 1931 with stained-glass windows by Nicola D'Ascenzo. The burgundy silk and gold dossal cloth behind the altar was designed and woven by Frances K. Talbot.

CHURCH OF SAINT MARTIN-IN-THE-FIELDS

8000 Saint Martin's Lane
Philadelphia, PA 19118

George W. and William D. Hewitt,
architects, 1888–1889; Theophilus
Parsons Chandler, Jr., baptistry, 1899;
Kise, Straw and Kolodner, architects,
interior restoration/renovation, 2000

Telephone for visitor information:
215.247.7466

www.stmartinec.org

The Pennsylvania Railroad official and real-estate investor Henry Howard Houston (1820–1895) and his family deserve credit for establishing the Episcopal parish church of Saint Martin-in-the-Fields in Chestnut Hill. Houston speculated in Philadelphia real estate in the years following the American Civil War, ultimately acquiring 3,000-plus acres in Chestnut Hill, Upper Roxborough, and nearby Montgomery County. Realizing that easy railroad transportation would be critical to the creation of a successful new suburb, and being well known to the Pennsylvania Railroad board, Houston encouraged the establishment of a Chestnut Hill line. As track was laid, he developed Wissahickon Heights.

Houston erected the Wissahickon Inn—now Chestnut Hill Academy—and donated land for the Philadelphia Cricket Club. He also commissioned and moved into a castellated mansion called Druim Moir. To design both the inn and his own home, Houston turned to the versatile architectural firm of George W. Hewitt (1841–1916) and William D. Hewitt (1847–1924), who had demonstrated a flair for designing in the English Gothic mode. George Hewitt had already worked for Houston in 1873, at Saint Peter's Church at the corner of Wayne and Harvey Streets. At the time, Hewitt was a member of Frank Furness's office, for which he supervised several important church commissions, although church records attribute the Saint Peter's commission to Hewitt rather than the Furness office. (This Gothic Revival parish church complex still stands, unfortunately much decayed and overgrown.)

That the elder Hewitt would become one of Philadelphia's leading ecclesiastic architects comes as no surprise. His career began in the office of Joseph C. Hoxie, who excelled in church design (pages 149–150), and in 1859 he entered the office of John Notman, the most influential Philadelphia architect of mid-nineteenth-century Episcopal churches (pages 158–161). During his six years with Notman, Hewitt worked on Saint Clement's and Holy Trinity. Following Notman's death in 1865, Hewitt worked with John Fraser and completed the tower for Notman's Saint Mark's.

Saint Martin-in-the-Fields was to serve the new Wissahickon Heights community, and, as architects, Henry H. Houston not surprisingly turned to George and William Hewitt. The cornerstone of Saint Martin-in-the-Fields was laid on June 5, 1888, and the first service was held on February 2, 1889. The resulting church is a single-story cruciform plan in the English Gothic style with clerestory nave, side aisles, and elevated chancel not unlike Saint James the Less (pages 248–253) or Saint Timothy's (pages 288–290), both erected decades earlier to serve the needs of other suburbanites moving away from the industrial city. The Hewitts departed from the simple medieval English parish church format, however, by adding a dominating four-story bell tower that now boasts two sets of bells, including a change of eight installed in 1980.

☞ The exterior of Saint Martin-in-the-Fields reflects several building campaigns. The main church—including the bell tower—dates from 1889. The gray stone is Wissahickon schist. The chancel extension to the east (right in the photograph) dates from 1901.

⚑ The delicate, highly finished baptistry designed by Theophilus Parsons Chandler, Jr., is an 1899 addition to the south transept. A large stone shaft with spire buttresses each corner and holds a carved angel. Over each Gothic-arch window are stone gargoyles and a carved balustrade.

⚒ The gray stone chancel extension reflects a high church Anglo-Catholic period in Saint Martin's history at the beginning of the last century. Here are provided a sedilia (a seat for the clergy set into the south wall) and a piscina (sink to wash sacred vessels). This high altar is no longer used to celebrate the Holy Eucharist.

Upon entering the nave, the visitor is immediately struck by the polychromatic decoration: highlights of red and black against the buff brick interior handsomely set off the local gray stone trimmed with Indiana limestone. This original decorative scheme was only reexposed in 2001, having been painted over in 1956 in a misguided belief that white paint would brighten the interior and attract parishioners. A carefully conceived and installed lighting system now brightens the interior and allows the original polychromatic effects to be appreciated.

Within a few years of its construction, the original church received several embellishments. The baptistry was added to the south transept in 1899 as a memorial to Edith Houston, wife of Samuel F. Houston; it was designed by Theophilus Parsons Chandler, Jr. (1845–1928). Chandler had studied at the Atelier Vaudremer in Paris and evolved a polished style specializing in ecclesiastic projects (pages 188–193); eventually he would become the head of the Department of Architecture at the University of Pennsylvania. The Mexican onyx baptismal font—in use since 1889—was housed in the baptistry until relocated in 2001 to a position opposite the entrance porch on axis with the nave. This move reflects the more public role of baptism as the first Christian sacrament.

In 1901 the chancel was lengthened eastward to create a gray stone sanctuary, with funds donated by Mrs. Henry Howard Houston and children in memory of their husband and father. A few years later the choir stalls with their carved misericords were donated by Dr. and Mrs. George Woodward. In reaction to the Anglo-Catholic high church implications of an altar so distant from the congregation, a new altar has been positioned at the crossing and made the focal point of the church, as explained in the rededication literature in 2001, "just as the Holy Eucharist is central to the life of each Christian."

☞ *Looking down the nave from the chancel, one can appreciate the recent restoration of the original polychromatic decorative scheme. Here, too, is the modern holy table (altar), brought forward to the crossing of the transepts and nave. In the distance can be seen the relocated baptismal font. Both these liturgical changes reflect the twenty-first-century desire to engage the congregation in the celebration of both Holy Eucharist and baptism.*

SAINT TIMOTHY'S CHURCH, ROXBOROUGH

*5720 Ridge Avenue
Philadelphia, PA 19128-1734*

*Emlen T. Littell, architect, 1862–1863,
1885–1886; Charles M. Burns,
architect for interior decoration,
tower, and lych gate*

*Telephone for visitor information:
215.483.1529*

www.geocities.com/sttimothys1859

Philadelphia and its environs are sprinkled with appealing Victorian Gothic churches erected for small, prosperous Episcopal parishes established to serve the needs of Philadelphians moving to the country. Saint James the Less (pages 248–253) and Saint Martin-in-the-Fields (pages 282–287) are notable examples of this type already discussed. Saint Timothy's, Roxborough, surrounded by its stone-walled graveyard, is yet another of these churches originally in a near rural setting around which communities have now developed.

The architect of Saint Timothy's was Philadelphia-born Emlen T. Littell (1838–1891), who graduated from the University of Pennsylvania and eventually established an independent practice in New York City, specializing in churches. Exactly how the twenty-three-year-old Littell secured what may be his first important commission is not a matter of record, but it was probably through family association with J. Vaughan Merrick and D. Rodney King, who selected him to prepare plans in 1861. The cornerstone was laid on July 18, 1862, and the completed edifice was consecrated on February 14, 1863. During construction, Littell engaged his contemporary and Penn classmate Charles M. Burns (1838–1922) to supervise the interior decoration. (The Civil War was raging. Both Littell and Burns were serving in the military, and they dispatched detailed instructions for the construction and decoration when they were unable to be present on the site. Fortunately this correspondence and its accompanying drawings have survived to document the building history.)

What we see at Saint Timothy's today is the result of three major construction campaigns. The original church with buttressed walls of local stone was a typical medieval English plan, with entry through a porch surmounted by a bell cot, a nave with a patterned slate gable roof, an elevated chancel, and a sanctuary separated by a wooden rood screen. In 1869 Burns further embellished the chancel walls with polychromatic decoration, which, according to the *Evening Bulletin*, "had its origin in the middle ages, when the gorgeous colors and quaint devices of heraldry were gradually transferred from the painted monuments and tapestry on the walls of churches to the walls themselves." In 1871 Burns, following Littell's original design, added the tower at the northeast corner of the church, and in 1874 the baptistry was constructed on the north. At the same time the nave was extended by 23 feet, which allowed 140 additional places for the expanding congregation. Burns again directed the interior decoration and, in 1882, designed the lych gate and wall around the churchyard. This early work by Burns is particularly interesting because his later career would include such masterworks as the Church of the Redeemer, Bryn Mawr, the Church of the Advocate in North Philadelphia (pages 244–247), and the Church of the Saviour in West Philadelphia (pages 216–221).

  The handsome Gothic style Saint Timothy's Church, Roxborough, is the product of three major building campaigns spanning two decades from the 1860s through the 1880s, directed by architects Emlen T. Littell and Charles M. Burns. The nave was twice extended to the west (right in the photograph) and the tower and baptistry (center of photograph) were added to the north.

By 1885 the church required yet another extension. For this commission Emlen T. Littell returned to design the Lantern Tower and extend the choir—work that has incorrectly been attributed to Frank Furness but for which Littell's drawings survive. At this point the church had essentially acquired its present form. In 1914 electric lighting was introduced, although the operational gas fixtures survive; the Lady Chapel was created; and a single-color paint scheme was applied to eradicate most of Burns's handsome polychrome decoration in the nave, chancel, and sanctuary.

☞ *The baptistry was added to the north side of the church in 1874; this font was given in memory of Willie Fitch Merrick, who died May 5, 1868. Saint Timothy's has a notable collection of 46 stained-glass windows, five of which are in the baptistry.*

aisle — The area of a church flanking the *nave* and separated from it by columns or *piers*.

altar — A table formerly used as a place for offering sacrifices, now typically the center of worship. The High Altar is the centerpiece of the church or cathedral. It is set on steps so as to be visible to all and backed by a *reredos*; it is usually covered with a frontal, a colorful piece of fabric whose color varies according to the season of the church year.

altar canopy — A decorated ceiling directly above the altar to call attention to the altar below. See *baldachin*.

altar rail — A railing in front of the *altar* usually across the *chancel*.

ambo — A *pulpit* or reading desk in early Christian churches.

ambulatory — A corridor or gallery behind an *altar*, permitting passage from one side to the other.

apse — Semicircular end of a church, usually vaulted with a half dome.

architrave — The bottom horizontal element of a classical *entablature*; it rests directly on the capital and supports the frieze.

aron chodosh — The ark in a synagogue holding the Torah scrolls.

baldachin — Canopy over an *altar* (also baldachino).

baptistry — A building or part of a church designated for baptism; a tank for baptism by immersion.

bas-relief — Sculpture with figures projecting slightly from the background.

bell cot — Shelter for protecting a bell.

belt course — Horizontal bands of stone, brick, or wood, usually in a color contrasting with the background, intended to delincate floor levels of a building; see *string course*.

bimah — An elevated platform, the traditional center of a synagogue from which the Torah is read.

bosses — Carved and decorated pieces of stone set where ribs join the *vault*.

buttress — A structure erected against a wall to strengthen it by opposing its outward thrust.

cathedra — Bishop's chair or throne, usually in a *cathedral*.

cathedral — Principal church for a diocese.

chancel — The part of the church near the *altar*, often enclosed by the *screen*, where the *choir* and clergy sit.

⇌ *Church of the New Jerusalem. See pages 183–193.*

chantry	Endowment for the saying of prayers, commonly for the souls of the founder and family; a chapel so endowed.
choir	Group of singers, especially those organized in church services; the part of the church occupied by the choir or clergy; also, the part of the church where services are performed.
clerestory	Upper level of the *nave*, *transepts*, and *chancel*, containing windows (also clearstory).
cloister	A sheltered walkway, usually in a religious institution, often of rectangular shape, with one side walled and the other opening onto a courtyard.
coffer	Recessed panel in a ceiling.
colonnade	Series of regularly spaced columns with their *entablature*.
corbel	A stone projecting from a wall to support a roof *truss* or *cornice*.
cornice	The horizontal molded projection at the top of a structure; the uppermost member of the classical *entablature*.
credence	Receptacle for sacramental elements near the *altar*.
crenelation	Notches or indentations often appearing on Gothic Revival buildings (Old French *cre* = notch). Originally on battlements, they were intended to allow defenders of a fortified building to return fire without exposing themselves.
crossing	The intersection of the *nave* and *transepts* in a cruciform church.
crozier	A ceremonial staff in the style of a shepherd's crook carried by the bishop as a symbol of pastoral authority (also crosier).
cruciform	Cross-shaped; churches are laid out this way recalling the crucifixion of Jesus Christ (Latin *cruci figere* = to fasten to a cross).
ecclesiology	The art of designing, decorating, and furnishing churches.
entablature	Horizontal element of classical architecture that is supported by the columns; includes the *cornice*, frieze, and *architrave*.
episcopacy	Church government by bishops, as distinguished from *presbytery*.
Eucharist	Sacrament of Holy Communion, Mass, or Lord's Supper, central act of Christian worship. In it consecrated or blessed bread and wine are consumed as memorials of Christ's death or as the body and blood of Christ, symbolizing the spiritual union of communicant with Christ (from Greek for "thanksgiving").
fan vault	A *vault* constructed with curving ribs that spring from a slender shaft or *corbel* and radiated upward like the ribs of a fan.

fenestella	Wall niche near the altar for the *piscina* and often the *credence* (from Latin for "little window").
gargoyle	Grotesque sculptural projection used in Gothic architecture to direct rainwater away from a building.
grille	A decorative openwork screen, usually of wrought metal.
groin vault	An arched roof formed by the intersection of two or more curved *vaults*, suggested by the juncture in anatomy of the thighs and the abdomen.
Guastavino	A construction technique using rectangular tiles to form the inner shell of a dome, named after Rafael Guastavino, who introduced the technique to the United States.
hammer beam	A roof system of horizontal beams from opposite walls supporting the roof of a Gothic church without tie rods spanning the space between the walls.
hexastyle	A portico with six columns across the front or rear (from Greek for "six").
iconostasis	A screen or partition on which icons are placed, separating the *nave* and *sanctuary* in Orthodox churches.
Lady Chapel	A place of worship dedicated to the Virgin Mary.
lancet	A tall, narrow, pointed window.
lavabo	The washing of the celebrant's hands after the offertory in the sacrament of the *Eucharist*; the bowl or basin used.
lectern	Reading desk used in ecclesiastical services.
lych (lich) gate	Roofed gateway originally used as a resting place for a bier.
minyan	The quorum required by Jewish law for communal worship, consisting of ten adult males in Orthodox Judaism, or ten adults of either sex in other congregations.
misericord	A small ledge fixed to the underside of a hinged seat, which when turned up offers support for one standing (from Latin for "mercy"). Misericords are sometimes decoratively carved.
miter	Official headdress worn by a bishop as one of the symbols of office; its outline resembles a pointed arch (also mitre).
narthex	Vestibule often at the rear of the *nave*.
nave	The main interior area of a church or cathedral, not including *transepts*, generally used by the congregation.
niches	Recessed openings in a wall. Their function may vary, from holding vessels for services to housing a statue.

pediment	A broad triangular element over a portico or door.
pendentive	One of four corners of a square space that permit the area to be covered by a dome.
pier	A vertical support of an arch; a heavy column.
pilaster	A column or pillar with capital and base attached ("engaged") to a wall.
pinnacle	Tapered terminal ornament used as the high point of a roof or *buttress*.
piscina	Basin of stone used for draining water used in liturgical ablutions.
presbytery	In early Christianity, an elder of the church was called a presbyter (from Greek *presbyteros* = elder). In the Presbyterian church, a presbytery is a court composed of the clergy and one or more lay presbyters from each church in the district; the district itself (analogous to diocese). Also, government of a church by presbyters, as distinguished from *episcopacy*.
procathedral	A church used temporarily as a *cathedral*.
pulpit	Raised platform used by the preacher as a podium from which to deliver sermons.
quatrefoil	A stylized floral motif with four leaves or lobes.
rayonnant	French description of Gothic tracery emphasizing radial lines.
rectory	Residence of the rector, clergyperson in charge of a parish.
refectory	The dining hall of a religious order.
Reformation	A sixteenth-century European religious movement to reform the Roman Catholic Church, marked by emphasis on the people's participation in worship, removal of clerical power, more emphasis on the Bible at the expense of the Mass, and greater simplicity in worship and approach to God. Led to the establishment of Protestant denominations.
reredos	A decorative panel, such as a curtain, wall, or screen, behind an *altar*.
retable	Decorative structure above and behind an *altar*, sometimes including a shelf, as for ornaments.
retrochoir	The area in a church behind the high *altar* and *choir*.
Romanesque	Architectural style of the eleventh to thirteenth centuries characterized by the use of solid masses, round arches, and geometric decoration.
rood	A crucifix, especially one at the entrance to the *chancel*.
rood beam	A beam or *truss* near the front of the *chancel*, on which the *rood* is supported.

rood screen	A screen between the *chancel* and the *nave*, supporting the *rood*.
sacristy	A room in a church in which sacred vessels and vestments are stored and where the clergy and sometimes the choir robe.
sanctuary	In the Anglo-Catholic tradition, the part of the *chancel* in which the *altar* is set. In low church Protestant usage the term has gradually come to be used more broadly to include the entire area occupied by the congregation when worshiping.
screen	A partition of wood, metal, or stone, such as that which divides the *nave* from the *chancel* or *narthex*.
sedilia	Seats near the altar used by the clergy.
stations of the cross	Fourteen shrines marking scenes in the passion of Christ.
string course	A horizontal molding usually projecting along the face of a building; see *belt course*.
three-decker pulpit	A pulpit accommodating (from bottom to top) clerk, reader, and minister, made necessary by the high-sided box pews commonly found in colonial churches.
tracery	Branching ornamental stonework, especially in windows in Gothic architecture.
transepts	Lateral arms intersecting the *nave* of a *cruciform* church.
trefoil	A stylized floral motif with three leaves or lobes.
triforium	A gallery forming an upper story to a church, often between the *nave* arches and the *clerestory*.
truss	A braced framework of timber supporting a roof.
tympanum	The recessed space between the horizontal and sloping cornices of a *pediment*.
undercroft	*Vault* under a church.
vault	An arched structure of masonry, forming a ceiling or roof; the part of a church roofed by arched masonry.
vestibule	Small room between an outside and an inside door, in a church, usually opening into the *nave*.
vestry	A room in or attached to a church for storing ecclesiastical vestments; *sacristy*; a room for church meetings and classes. In an Episcopal church, the elective body that administers the temporal matters of the parish.

Old Pine Street Presbyterian Church: Some of the original Victorian stenciling that inspired the 1980s redecoration has been exposed by removing the later overpainting. See pages 66–69.

This bibliography is divided into two sections. The first section—which is by no means exhaustive—lists published sources I have found useful for the study of Philadelphia historic sacred places. The second section is arranged alphabetically by sacred place and lists in lieu of notes the sources specific to each site. Most of these sources are congregation histories, many of which are known in only a few copies, especially those published in the nineteenth century. In many cases photocopies of these ephemeral publications are available at The Athenæum of Philadelphia, either cataloged in the book collections—which may be confirmed by consulting the online catalog at www.PhilaAthenaeum.org—or filed with the research notes for this book, deposited at the Athenæum and arranged by the name of the sacred place. The research files for *Historic Houses of Philadelphia* (Philadelphia: University of Pennsylvania Press, 1998) have also been deposited with the Athenæum, as will be the notes for the forthcoming third and final volume in this series, *Historic Landmarks of Philadelphia*.

Philadelphia's built environment is the best documented in the nation. In the early 1980s the Athenæum conceived—and the National Endowment for the Humanities funded—a compilation of information on the architects and builders of Philadelphia, based largely on the rich collection of architectural drawings and photographs in the care of that library on Washington Square. The results of my research and that of my co-author, Sandra L. Tatman, then curator of architecture at the Athenæum, were published as the *Biographical Dictionary of Philadelphia Architects and Builders, 1700–1930* (Boston: G.K. Hall, 1985). From the beginning, Dr. Tatman and I knew the 900-page *Biographical Dictionary* was a preliminary step to what would ultimately be a larger project. Shortly after the publication of *Historic Houses of Philadelphia*, the William Penn Foundation agreed to fund a project jointly undertaken by the Athenæum, the University of Pennsylvania Architectural Archives, the Philadelphia Historical Commission, and the Pennsylvania Historical and Museum Commission to establish a free online database called the Philadelphia Architects and Buildings Project (PAB), available at www.philadelphiabuildings.org and managed by the Athenæum's department of architecture headed by Bruce Laverty, Gladys Brooks Curator. As *Historic Sacred Places* goes to press, PAB provides biographical sketches of 4,000 architects and builders known to have worked in Philadelphia, detailed descriptions of 225,000 buildings, and digital images of 40,000 structures. Perhaps most important, each architect, building, and image is supported by meticulously detailed sources and locations in regional institutions that have been surveyed by the PAB staff. *As a consequence, every sacred place and architect mentioned in this book may be researched on the PAB website.* So complete and extensive is this resource that every individual site bibliography in the second section could begin with an electronic citation to the Philadelphia Architects and Buildings website.

GENERAL SOURCES

Ahlstrom, Sydney E. *A Religious History of the American People.* New Haven, Conn.: Yale University Press, 1972.

Alexander, William. *Observations on the Construction and Fitting Up of Meeting Houses.* York, England, 1820.

Andrews, Dee E. *The Methodists and Revolutionary America, 1760–1800.* Princeton, N.J.: Princeton University Press, 2000.

Anson, Peter F. *Fashions in Church Furnishings, 1840–1940.* London: Faith Press, 1960.

Atterbury, Paul and Clive Wainwright, eds. *Pugin: A Gothic Passion.* New Haven, Conn: Yale University Press, 1994.

Baigell, Matthew E. "John Haviland." Ph.D. dissertation, University of Pennsylvania, 1965.

Bantel, Linda et al. *William Rush: American Sculptor.* Philadelphia: Pennsylvania Academy of the Fine Arts, 1982.

Beer, Jennifer, Sandi Adams, Chel Avery, Eileen Stief, and Charles Walker, eds. *Silent Witness: Quaker Meetinghouses in the Delaware Valley, 1695 to the Present.* Philadelphia: Philadelphia Yearly Meeting, 2002.

Boonin, Harry D. *The Jewish Quarter of Philadelphia, 1881–1930: A History and Guide.* Philadelphia: Jewish Walking Tours of Philadelphia, 1999.

Burke, Bobbye, Otto Sperr, Hugh J. McCauley, and Trina Vaux. *Historic Rittenhouse, a Philadelphia Neighborhood.* Philadelphia: University of Pennsylvania Press, 1985.

Clark, James L. *". . .To Set Them in Order": Some Influences of the Philadelphia Baptist Association upon Baptists of America to 1814.* Springfield, Mo.: Particular Baptist Press, 2001.

Commager, Henry Steele, ed. *Documents of American History.* New York: Appleton-Century-Crofts, 1958.

Cook, George Henry. *The English Mediaeval Parish Church.* London: Phoenix House, 1954.

D'Ascenzo: The Art of Stained Glass from the Collection of Stanley Switlik. Trenton, N.J.: Rider College, 1973.

Ennis, Arthur J. *No Easy Road: The Early Years of the Augustinians in the United States, 1796–1874.* New York: Peter Lang, 1993.

Fairbanks, Jonathan. "John Notman, Church Architect." M.A. thesis, University of Delaware, 1961.

Faris, John T. *Old Churches and Meeting Houses in and Around Philadelphia.* Philadelphia: Lippincott, 1926.

Farnsworth, Jean, Carmen R. Croce, and Joseph F. Chorpenning. *Stained Glass in Catholic Philadelphia.* Philadelphia: Saint Joseph's University Press, 2002.

Fogleman, Aaron S. *Hopeful Journeys: German Immigration, Settlement, and Political Culture in the Middle Colonies.* Philadelphia: University of Pennsylvania Press, 1996.

Friedman, Murray, ed. *Jewish Life in Philadelphia, 1830–1940.* Philadelphia: Institute for the Study of Human Issues, 1983.

Garvan, Beatrice B. *Philadelphia: Three Centuries of American Art.* Philadelphia: Philadelphia Museum of Art, 1976.

Gaustad, Edwin Scott. *A Religious History of America.* Revised edition. New York: HarperCollins, 1990.

Geffen, Elizabeth May. *Philadelphia Unitarianism, 1796–1861.* Philadelphia: University of Pennsylvania Press, 1961.

George, Carol V. R. *Segregated Sabbaths: Richard Allen and the Emergence of Independent Black Churches, 1760–1840.* New York: Oxford University Press, 1973.

Gilchrist, Agnes A. *William Strickland: Architect and Engineer.* Philadelphia: University of Pennsylvania Press, 1950.

Giles, Richard S. *Re-Pitching the Tent: Reordering the Church Building for Worship and Mission.* Collegeville, Minn.: Liturgical Press, 1999.

Glatfelter, Charles H. *Pastors and People: German Lutheran and Reformed Churches in the Pennsylvania Field, 1717–1793.* 2 vols. Breinigsville, Pa.: Pennsylvania German Society, 1980.

"Grant Ban Ends: Religious Properties Approved for Federal Funding." *Preservation* 55 (September/October 2003): 34.

Greiff, Constance M. *John Notman, Architect, 1810–1865.* Philadelphia: The Athenæum of Philadelphia, 1979.

Hammonds, Kenneth A. *Historical Directory of Presbyterian Churches and Presbyteries of Greater Philadelphia.* Philadelphia: Presbyterian Historical Society, 1933.

Handy, Robert T. *A History of the Churches in the United States and Canada.* New York: Oxford University Press, 1977.

Hitchcock, Henry Russell. *Early Victorian Architecture in Britain.* 1954. Reprint New York: Da Capo Press, 1972.

Hotchkin, Samuel Fitch. *Ancient and Modern Germantown, Mount Airy, and Chestnut Hill.* Philadelphia: P.W. Ziegler, 1892.

Jackson, Joseph. *Encyclopedia of Philadelphia.* Harrisburg, Pa.: National Historical Association, 1931.

Kalm, Peter. *Travels into North America.* Trans. John Reinhold Forster. Barre, Mass.: Imprint Society, 1972.

Kinghorn, Kenneth Cain. *The Heritage of American Methodism.* Nashville, Tenn.: Abingdon Press, 1999.

Klett, Guy S. *Presbyterians in Colonial Pennsylvania.* Philadelphia: University of Pennsylvania Press, 1937.

Klingensmith, Samuel. "The Architecture of Napoleon LeBrun: The Philadelphia Churches, 1840–1865." M.A. thesis, University of Virginia, 1975.

Lewis, Michael J. "Edwin Forrest Durang and Catholic Church Architecture." *Inspired* 6, 4; 7, 1.

Leyburn, James G. *The Scotch-Irish: A Social History.* Chapel Hill: University of North Carolina Press, 1962.

Lloyd, Mark Frazier. "Germantown, 1683–1983." *Antiques* (August 1983): 254–58.

——. "Presbyterian and Episcopal Churches in Germantown." *Inspired* (Summer 1987).

Mackie, Alexander. "The Presbyterian Churches of Old Philadelphia." In *Historic Philadelphia, from the Founding Until the Early Nineteenth Century: Papers Dealing with Its People and Buildings.* Transactions of the American Philosophical Society 43, Part 1. Philadelphia: American Philosophical Society, 1953. 226–29.

Mahony, Daniel H. *Historical Sketches of the Catholic Churches and Institutions of Philadelphia: A Parish Register and Book of Reference.* Philadelphia: Daniel H. Mahony, 1895.

Maslin, Simeon J., Phyllis A. Grode, and Leon Clemmer. *One God, Sixteen Houses: An Illustrated Introduction to the Churches and Synagogues of the Old York Road Corridor.* Elkins Park, Pa.: Keneseth Israel Press, 1990.

Meier, Richard. *Recent American Synagogue Architecture.* New York: Jewish Museum, 1963.

Miles, Joseph Starne. *An Historical Sketch of Roxborough, Manayunk, Wissahickon.* Philadelphia: G. Fein, 1940.

Miller, Randall M. and William Pencak, eds. *Pennsylvania: A History of the Commonwealth.* University Park: Pennsylvania State University Press, 2002.

Minutes of the Provincial Council of Pennsylvania, from the Organization to the Termination of the Proprietary Government. Philadelphia: J. Severns, 1852.

Moreau de St. Méry, M. L. E. *American Journey.* Ed. and trans. Kenneth Roberts and Anna M. Roberts. Garden City, N.Y.: Doubleday, 1947.

Moss, Roger W. *Philadelphia Victorian: The Building of the Athenæum.* Philadelphia: The Athenæum of Philadelphia, 1998.

Myers, Alfred Cook, ed. *Narratives of Early*

Pennsylvania, West New Jersey, and Delaware, 1630–1707. New York: Scribner's, 1912.

Nevin, Alfred. History of the Presbytery of Philadelphia, and of the Philadelphia Central. Philadelphia: W.S. Fortescue, 1888.

O'Gorman, James F. The Architecture of Frank Furness. Philadelphia: Philadelphia Museum of Art, 1973.

O'Gorman, James F., Jeffrey A. Cohen, George E. Thomas, and G. Holmes Perkins. Drawing Toward Building: Philadelphia Architectural Graphics, 1732–1986. Philadelphia: University of Pennsylvania Press, 1986.

Penn, William. The Papers of William Penn, 1680–1684. Ed. Mary Maples Dunn and Richard S. Dunn. Philadelphia: University of Pennsylvania Press, 1982–1986.

Pennell, Joseph. Charles M. Burns, Artist and Teacher. Philadelphia: Privately published, 1922.

Peterson, Charles E., Constance M. Greiff, and Maria M. Thompson. Robert Smith: Architect, Builder, Patriot, 1722–1777. Philadelphia: The Athenæum of Philadelphia, 2000.

Placzek, Adolph K., ed. Macmillan Encyclopedia of Architects. New York: Free Press, 1982.

Rose, Harold W. The Colonial Houses of Worship in America. New York: Hastings House, 1963.

Scharf, John Thomas and Thompson Westcott. History of Philadelphia, 1609–1884. Philadelphia: L.H. Everts, 1884.

Shoemaker, Mary M. "Thomas Somerville Stewart, Architect and Engineer." M.A. thesis, University of Virginia, 1975.

Smith, R. A. Philadelphia as It Is in 1852. Philadelphia: Lindsay and Blakiston, 1852.

Stanton, Phoebe B. The Gothic Revival and American Church Architecture. Baltimore: Johns Hopkins University Press, 1968.

Synnestvedt, Sig. The Essential Swedenborg. New York: Swedenborg Foundation, 1977.

Tatman, Sandra L. and Roger W. Moss. The Biographical Dictionary of Philadelphia Arch-itects, 1700–1930. Boston: G.K. Hall, 1985.

Thomas, Abel C. A Century of Universalism in Philadelphia and New York, with Sketches of Its History in Reading, Hightstown, Brooklyn, and Elsewhere. Philadelphia: Collins, 1872.

Thomas, George E., Michael J. Lewis, and Jeffrey A. Cohen. Frank Furness: The Complete Works. New York: Princeton Architectural Press, 1991.

Thomas, Robert. A Century of Methodism in Germantown. Philadelphia: Germantown Independent, 1895.

Thompson, Paul Richard. William Butterfield. London: Routledge and Kegan Paul, 1971.

Thompson, William D. Philadelphia's First Baptists: A Brief History of the First Baptist Church of Philadelphia, Founded 1698. Philadelphia: First Philadelphia Baptist Church, 1989.

Tinkcom, Harry M., Margaret B. Tinkcom, and Grant Miles Simon. Historic Germantown, from the Founding to the Early Part of the Nineteenth Century. Philadelphia: American Philosophical Society, 1955.

Trotter, Joe William and Eric Ledell Smith, eds. African Americans in Pennsylvania. University Park: Pennsylvania State University Press, 1997.

Twelves, J. Wesley. A History of the Diocese of Pennsylvania. Philadelphia: Episcopal Diocese of Pennsylvania, 1969.

Van Trump, James D. "The Gothic Fane: the Medieval Vision and Some Philadelphia Churches, 1860–1900." Charette (September 1963): 20–27.

Warner, Sam Bass, Jr. The Private City: Philadelphia in Three Periods of Its Growth. Second edition. Philadelphia: University of Pennsylvania Press, 1987.

Watson, John Fanning. Annals of Philadelphia and Pennsylvania in the Olden Time. Vols 1, 2. Philadelphia: Carey and Hart, 1830, 1850. Vol. 3 added by Willis P. Hazard. Philadelphia, 1877.

Webster, Richard J. Philadelphia Preserved: Catalog of the Historic American Buildings Survey. Philadelphia: Temple University Press, 1976.

——. "Stephen D. Button: Italianate Stylist." M.A. thesis, University of Delaware, 1963.

Weigley, Russell, ed. Philadelphia: A 300-Year History. New York: Norton, 1982.

Westcott, Thompson. The Historic Mansions and Buildings of Philadelphia: With Some Notice of Their Owners and Occupants. Philadelphia: Porter and Coates, 1877.

White, James F. The Cambridge Movement: The Ecclesiologists and the Gothic Revival. Cambridge: Cambridge University Press, 1962.

White, William P. and William H. Scott. The Presbyterian Church in Philadelphia: A Camera and Pen Sketch of Each Presbyterian Church and Institution in the City. Philadelphia: Allen, Lane, and Scott, 1895.

Williams, Kim-Eric. The Eight Old Swedes' Churches of New Sweden. Wilmington, Del.: New Sweden Center, 1999.

Williams, Peter W. Houses of God: Region, Religion, and Architecture in the United States. Urbana: University of Illinois Press, 1997.

Wilson, Thomas. Picture of Philadelphia for 1824 Containing the "Picture of Philadelphia, for 1811, by James Mease, M.D." with All Its Improvements Since That Period. Philadelphia: T. Town, 1823.

Wischnitzer, Rachel. Synagogue Architecture in the United States. Philadelphia: Jewish Publication Society, 1955.

Withey, Henry F. and Elsie Rathburn Withey. Biographical Dictionary of American Architects. New York: New Age, 1956.

Wolf, Edwin, II and Maxwell Whiteman. The History of the Jews of Philadelphia from Colonial Times to the Age of Jackson. Philadelphia: Jewish Publication Society, 1957.

Yarnall, Elizabeth Biddle. Addison Hutton, Quaker Architect, 1834–1916. Philadelphia: Art Alliance Press, 1974.

SOURCES SPECIFIC TO INDIVIDUAL HISTORIC SACRED PLACES

ARCH STREET MEETING

Alexander, William. Observations on the Construction and Fitting Up of Meeting Houses. York, England, 1820.

Biddle, Owen. The Young Carpenters' Assistant; or, A System of Architecture Adapted to the Style of Building in the United States. Philadelphia: Johnson and Weaver, 1805.

Bronner, Edwin B. "Quaker Landmarks in Early Philadelphia." In Historic Philadelphia, from the Founding Until the Early Nineteenth Century: Papers Dealing with Its People and Buildings. Transactions of the American Philosophical Society 43, Part 1. Philadelphia: American Philosophical Society, 1953. 210–16.

Nelson, Lee H. and Penelope Hartshorne Batcheler. An Architectural Study of Arch Street Meeting House. Philadelphia: Philadelphia Yearly Meeting of the Religious Society of Friends, 1968. This is the most complete analysis of the structure, published in a limited edition of thirteen copies, one of which is deposited at The Athenæum of Philadelphia. It contains photocopies of the key construction documents from Philadelphia Monthly Meeting Archives.

Peterson, Charles E. "Notes on the Free Quaker Meeting House." Compiled for Harbeson, Hough, Livingston, and Larson, 1966. Copy on deposit at The Athenæum of Philadelphia.

Tatman and Moss, 68, 216.

ARCH STREET PRESBYTERIAN CHURCH

Hammonds, Kenneth A. *Historical Directory of Presbyterian Churches and Presbyteries of Greater Philadelphia*. Philadelphia: Presbyterian Historical Society, 1993.

Magee, James F. "The Arch Street Church Building." *Journal of the Presbyterian Historical Society* (Philadelphia) 2 (1904): 229–42.

Nevin, Alfred. *History of the Presbytery of Philadelphia, and of the Philadelphia Central*. Philadelphia: W.S. Fortescue, 1888.

The Presbyterian (New York and Philadelphia), May 28, 1853.

Tatman and Moss, 396–97.

Westcott, Thompson. *The Official Guide Book to Philadelphia*. Philadelphia: Porter and Coates, 1875. 176–277.

White, William P. and William H. Scott. *The Presbyterian Church in Philadelphia: A Camera and Pen Sketch of Each Presbyterian Church and Institution in the City*. Philadelphia: Allen, Lane, and Scott, 1895.

ARCH STREET UNITED METHODIST CHURCH

Arch Street United Methodist Church: 125th Anniversary, 1862–1987. Philadelphia, 1987.

"Church—Dedicatory Services." *Philadelphia Public Ledger*, November 18, 1870.

Kling, Vincent. "Architectural Description: Arch Street United Methodist Church." Report prepared for the congregation, c. 1956. Copy in church archives and at The Athenæum of Philadelphia.

Maser, Frederick E. *Facing the Challenge of Change: The Story of a City's Central Church*. Philadelphia: Arch Street United Methodist Church, 1982.

Van Trump, James D. "The Gothic Fane: The Medieval Vision and Some Philadelphia Churches, 1860–1900." *Charette* (September 1963): 20–27.

Yarnall, Elizabeth Biddle. *Addison Hutton, Quaker Architect, 1834–1916*. Philadelphia: Art Alliance Press, 1974.

CATHEDRAL BASILICA OF SAINTS PETER AND PAUL

American Catholic Historical Society. *A Cathedral Is Built: Cathedral of Saints Peter and Paul*. Philadelphia: American Catholic Historical Society, 1964.

Dugan, Virginia. *A History of the Cathedral Basilica of Saints Peter and Paul*. Philadelphia, 1979.

Greiff, Constance M. *John Notman, Architect, 1810–1865*. Philadelphia: The Athenæum of Philadelphia, 1979.

Kenrick, Francis Patrick and Marc Antony Frenaye. *The Kenrick-Frenaye Correspondence, 1830–1862*. Philadelphia, 1920.

LeBrun, Napoleon. Seven original drawings for the Cathedral of Saints Peter and Paul, 1846–1862. The Athenæum of Philadelphia Collection.

Prendergast, E. F. *Brief History and Description of the Cathedral of SS. Peter and Paul*. Philadelphia, 1917.

CENTER CITY LUTHERAN CHURCH OF THE HOLY COMMUNION

Centennial History, "100 Years." Philadelphia, 2002. Copy on file at The Athenæum of Philadelphia.

Tatman and Moss, 636–38.

Thomas, George E., Michael J. Lewis, and Jeffrey A. Cohen. *Frank Furness: The Complete Works*. New York: Princeton Architectural Press, 1991.

CHRIST CHURCH

Gough, Deborah Mathias. *Christ Church Philadelphia: The Nation's Church in a Changing City*. Philadelphia: University of Pennsylvania Press, 1995.

Peterson, Charles E., Nicholas L. Gianopulos, and Bruce Gill. *The Building and Furnishing of Christ Church Philadelphia*. Philadelphia: Old Christ Church Preservation Trust, 2001.

Peterson, Charles E., Constance M. Greiff, and Maria M. Thompson. *Robert Smith: Architect, Builder, Patriot, 1722–1777*. Philadelphia: The Athenæum of Philadelphia, 2000.

CHURCH OF SAINT JAMES THE LESS

"Accounting Wardens Book, 1846–1867" and "Vestry Minutes, 1846–1918." Saint James the Less.

Atterbury, Paul and Clive Wainwright, eds. *Pugin: A Gothic Passion*. New Haven, Conn.: Yale University Press in conjunction with the Victoria and Albert Museum, 1994.

Berghaus, Millicent E. Norcross. *The Church of St. James the Less, 1847–1971*. Philadelphia, 1971.

"The Church of Saint James the Less." Historic Building Survey, Historical and Descriptive Data, Measured Drawings and Photographs, HABS No. PA-1725. Copies deposited at The Athenæum of Philadelphia and the Library of Congress, Washington, D.C.

Cook, George Henry. *The English Mediaeval Parish Church*. London: Phoenix House, 1954.

Placzek, Adolf K., ed. *Macmillan Encyclopedia of Architects*. New York: Free Press, 1982. 1: 359–60.

"Report of the Thirty-Ninth Meeting of the Cambridge Camden Society on Thursday, November 7." *Ecclesiologist* 5 (January 1845): 23.

Stanton, Phoebe B. *The Gothic Revival and American Church Architecture: An Episode in Taste, 1840–1856*. Baltimore: Johns Hopkins University Press, 1968.

Tatman and Moss, 133.

Thompson, Paul Richard. *William Butterfield*. London: Routledge and Kegan Paul, 1971.

Wagner, Samuel T. *A Brief History of the Church of St. James the Less*. Philadelphia: Saint James the Less, 1923.

White, James F. *The Cambridge Movement: The Ecclesiologists and the Gothic Revival*. Cambridge: Cambridge University Press, 1962.

CHURCH OF SAINT LUKE AND THE EPIPHANY

Broadley, Rodger C. *Parish History: The Church of St. Luke and the Epiphany*. Philadelphia, n.d. Copy on file at The Athenæum of Philadelphia.

Shoemaker, Mary M. "Thomas Somerville Stewart, Architect and Engineer." M.A. thesis, University of Virginia, 1975. Copy on file at The Athenæum of Philadelphia.

Stewart, Thomas Somerville. Original drawings for Saint Luke's Church, 1839. The Athenæum of Philadelphia.

Thomas, George E., Michael J. Lewis, and Jeffrey A. Cohen. *Frank Furness: The Complete Works*. New York: Princeton Architectural Press, 1991.

Walter, Thomas Ustick. Original drawings for the Church of the Epiphany, 1833–1835. The Athenæum of Philadelphia.

CHURCH OF SAINT MARTIN-IN-THE-FIELDS

Contosta, David R. *A Philadelphia Family: The Houstons and Woodwards of Chestnut Hill*. Philadelphia: University of Pennsylvania Press, 1988.

———. *A Venture in Faith: The Church of Saint-Martin-in-the-Fields, 1889–1999, Chestnut Hill, Pennsylvania*. Philadelphia: Church of Saint Martin-in-the-Fields, 1988.

Hotchkin, Samuel Fitch. *Ancient and Modern Germantown, Mount Airy, and Chestnut Hill*. Philadelphia: P.W. Zeigler, 1892. 424–26.

Philadelphia Inquirer, June 6, 1888. Dedication description.

Rumney, Theodore. *History of St. Peter's Church, Germantown: In the City of Philadelphia, Pa*. Philadelphia: Saint Peter's Church, 1897.

Woodward, George. *The Memoirs of a Mediocre Man*. Philadelphia: Harris and Partridge, 1935.

CHURCH OF THE ADVOCATE

"Art and Architecture of the Church of the Advocate." Philadelphia: Church of the Advocate, n.d. Copy on file at

The Athenæum of Philadelphia.

"An Assessment of the Church of the Advocate." Report by John Milner Associates, 1992. Copy on file at The Athenæum of Philadelphia.

Mikelberg, Sheryl. "A Study of Woodstock, a Late Colonial Country Mansion." Report, Historic Preservation Program, University of Pennsylvania, 1990. Copy on file at The Athenæum of Philadelphia.

Thomas, George E. "George W. South Memorial Protestant Episcopal Church of the Advocate." In James F. O'Gorman, Jeffrey A. Cohen, George E. Thomas, and G. Holmes Perkins, *Drawing Toward Building: Philadelphia Architectural Graphics, 1732–1986.* Philadelphia: University of Pennsylvania Press, 1986. 157–59.

CHURCH OF THE GESU

Gesu Parish Centennial. Philadelphia, 1969.

Golden Jubilee, 1888–1938 Church of the Gesu. Philadelphia, 1938.

"An Historical and Architectural Analysis of the Church of the Gesu." Report by John Milner Associates, 1987. Copy on file at The Athenæum of Philadelphia.

Lewis, Michael J. "Edwin Forrest Durang and Catholic Church Architecture." *Inspired* 6, 4; 7, 1.

"Long Range Apostolic Plan: Teaching People to Dream." Report, 1987. Copy on file at The Athenæum of Philadelphia.

Mahony, Daniel H. *Historical Sketches of the Catholic Churches and Institutions of Philadelphia: A Parish Register and Book of Reference.* Philadelphia: Daniel H. Mahony, 1895.

Tatman and Moss, 229–34.

CHURCH OF THE NEW JERUSALEM

Chandler, Theophilus Parsons, Jr. Collection. The Athenæum of Philadelphia.

Gilchrist, Agnes A. *William Strickland: Architect and Engineer, 1788–1954.* Philadelphia: University of Pennsylvania Press, 1950. Reproduces the George and Twelfth Streets temple by Strickland.

O'Gorman, James F., Jeffrey A. Cohen, George E. Thomas, and G. Holmes Perkins. *Drawing Toward Building: Philadelphia Architectural Graphics, 1732–1986.* Philadelphia: University of Pennsylvania Press, 1986. Reproduces the Collins and Autenrieth drawing from The Athenæum of Philadelphia Collection.

Tafel, Leonard I. "Background and Origin of the Church of the New Jerusalem." *New Christianity* (Spring 1949): 3–11.

Tatman and Moss, 139–43.

FIRST BAPTIST CHURCH

Keen, William W. *The Bi-Centennial Celebration of the Founding of the First Baptist Church of the City of Philadelphia: 1698–1898.* Philadelphia: American Baptist Publication Society, 1898.

Rose, Ivan Murray. *The First Baptist Church of Philadelphia: A Brief History and Interpretation.* Philadelphia: First Baptist Church, 1963.

Thompson, William D. *Philadelphia's First Baptists: A Brief History of the First Baptist Church of Philadelphia, Founded 1698.* Philadelphia: First Philadelphia Baptist Church, 1989.

FIRST PRESBYTERIAN CHURCH

Beadle, E. R. *The Old and the New, 1743–1876: The Second Presbyterian Church of Philadelphia: Its Beginning and Increase.* Philadelphia: J.B. Chandler, 1876.

Decker, John P. *The Art and Architecture of First Presbyterian Church in Philadelphia.* Philadelphia: J.P. Decker, 2001.

Kocher, Donald Roth. *The Mother of Us All: The First Presbyterian Church in Philadelphia, 1688–1998.* Philadelphia: First Presbyterian Church in Philadelphia, 1998.

Mackie, Alexander. "The Presbyterian Churches of Old Philadelphia." In *Historic Philadelphia, from the Founding Until the Early Nineteenth Century: Papers Dealing with Its People and Buildings.* Transactions of the American Philosophical Society 43, Part 1. Philadelphia: American Philosophical Society, 1953. 226–29.

Nevin, Alfred. *History of the Presbytery of Philadelphia, and of the Philadelphia Central.* Philadelphia: W.S. Fortescue, 1888.

Peterson, Charles E., Constance M. Greiff, and Maria M. Thompson. *Robert Smith: Architect, Builder, Patriot, 1722–1777.* Philadelphia: The Athenæum of Philadelphia, 2000.

Thomas, George E., Michael J. Lewis, and Jeffrey A. Cohen. *Frank Furness: The Complete Works.* New York: Princeton Architectural Press, 1991.

Watson, John Fanning. *Annals of Philadelphia and Pennsylvania in the Olden Time.* Vols. 1, 2. Philadelphia: Carey and Hart, 1830, 1850. Vol. 3 added by Willis P. Hazard. Philadelphia, 1877.

FIRST PRESBYTERIAN CHURCH IN GERMANTOWN

Dripps, J. Frederick. *History of the First Presbyterian Church in Germantown.* Germantown, 1909.

"First Presbyterian Begins Observance of 150th Birthday." *Germantown Courier,* October 8, 1959.

Oakley, Violet. *Great Women of the Bible.* Philadelphia: Eldon Press, 1949.

"Violet Oakley." *Philadelphia Museum of Art Bulletin* (June 1979).

FIRST UNITARIAN CHURCH

Collier, W. Edwin. *First Unitarian Church of Philadelphia: Biography of a Downtown Church.* Philadelphia, 1981.

Frey, Richard. *First Unitarian Church of Philadelphia.* Philadelphia, 1986.

Geffen, Elizabeth May. *Philadelphia Unitarianism, 1796–1861.* Philadelphia: University of Pennsylvania Press, 1961.

Laying the Cornerstone of the Third Church Edifice of the First Unitarian Society of Philadelphia. Philadelphia, 1885.

O'Gorman, James F. *The Architecture of Frank Furness.* Philadelphia: Philadelphia Museum of Art, 1973.

———. *Living Architecture: A Biography of H. H. Richardson.* New York: Simon and Schuster, 1997.

Thomas, George E., Michael J. Lewis, and Jeffrey A. Cohen. *Frank Furness: The Complete Works.* New York: Princeton Architectural Press, 1991.

FIRST UNITED METHODIST CHURCH OF GERMANTOWN

Blackwell, Edward and Gordon Smyth. *History of the First Methodist Church.* Germantown, 1946.

Centennial Souvenir of the First Methodist Episcopal Church. Germantown, 1896.

Eddy, Paul D. *"Therefore When We Build": The Proposed New Church House and Chapel of the First Methodist Episcopal Church, Germantown.* Germantown, 1929.

Parkin, Frank P. *Historical Sermon by the Rev. Frank P. Parkin, DD, on the One-Hundred-Twenty-Fifth Anniversary of the First Methodist Episcopal Church (May 29, 1921).*

Pictorial Representation of the First Methodist Episcopal Church / William Lewis Turner Memorial Chapel and The Church House. Germantown, 1935.

Thomas, Robert. *A Century of Methodism in Germantown.* Philadelphia: Germantown Independent, 1895.

GLORIA DEI (OLD SWEDES') CHURCH

Clay, Jehu Curtis. *Annals of the Swedes on the Delaware.* 4th edition. Chicago: John Ericsson Memorial Committee, 1938.

Moss, Roger W. "Two Seventeenth-Century Swedish Churches in the Delaware River Valley." *Journal of the Society of Architectural Historians* 34 (December 1975): 300–301.

Tatman and Moss, 339–40, 888.

Westcott, Thompson. *The Historic Mansions*

and Buildings of Philadelphia: With Some Notice of Their Owners and Occupants. Philadelphia: Porter and Coates, 1877. 56–67.

Williams, Kim-Eric. *The Eight Old Swedes' Churches of New Sweden*. Wilmington, Del.: New Sweden Center, 1999.

GREEK ORTHODOX CATHEDRAL OF SAINT GEORGE

Baigell, Matthew E. "John Haviland." Ph.D. dissertation, University of Pennsylvania, 1965.

———."John Haviland in Philadelphia." *Journal of the Society of Architectural Historians* 25 (1966): 197–208, 307–9.

Charter and By-Laws of the Rector, Church Wardens and Vestrymen of St. Andrew's Church. Philadelphia: Jesper Harding, 1823.

Dickey, John M. "The Greek Orthodox Cathedral of Saint George." Report prepared for Cooper and Pratt, architects, September, 1983. Copy on file at The Athenæum of Philadelphia.

Haviland, John. Papers. The University of Pennsylvania Rare Book Collection holds the most significant collection of 26 manuscript volumes of Haviland's papers. His drawings are scattered among several institutions, including The Athenæum of Philadelphia.

Philadelphia Gazette, May 31, 1823.

Smith, R. A. *Philadelphia as It Is in 1852*. Philadelphia: Lindsay and Blakiston, 1852. 284.

Wilson, Thomas. *Picture of Philadelphia for 1824 Containing the "Picture of Philadelphia, for 1811, by James Mease, M.D." with All Its Improvements Since That Period*. Philadelphia: Thomas Town, 1823. The description on pages 38–41 was probably written by Haviland.

HOLY TRINITY CHURCH

Jackson, Joseph. *Encyclopedia of Philadelphia*. Harrisburg, Pa.: National Historical Association, 1931.

Mahony, Daniel H. *Historical Sketches of the Catholic Churches and Institutions of Philadelphia: A Parish Register and Book of Reference*. Philadelphia: Daniel H. Mahony, 1895.

Minutes of the Trustees for Holy Trinity Church, 1788–1839.

Receipt Book of Holy Trinity Church, 1788–1813.

Tatman and Moss, 589–90.

IMPACTING YOUR WORLD CHRISTIAN CENTER

Lloyd, Mark Frazier. "Presbyterian and Episcopal Churches in Germantown." *Inspired* (Summer 1987).

Market Square Presbyterian Church. *A Church at Market Square*. Philadelphia, 1985. Photo-

copy at The Athenæum of Philadelphia. Tatman and Moss, 595–97.

Tinkcom, Harry M., Margaret B. Tinkcom, and Grant Miles Simon. *Historic Germantown, from the Founding to the Early Part of the Nineteenth Century*. Philadelphia: American Philosophical Society, 1955. 62–63.

Watson, John Fanning. *Annals of Philadelphia and Pennsylvania in the Olden Time*. Vols 1, 2. Philadelphia: Carey and Hart, 1830, 1850. Vol. 3 added by Willis P. Hazard. Philadelphia, 1877.

White, William P. and William H. Scott. *The Presbyterian Church in Philadelphia: A Camera and Pen Sketch of Each Presbyterian Church and Institution in the City*. Philadelphia: Allen, Lane, and Scott, 1895.

KESHER ISRAEL SYNAGOGUE

Boonin, Harry D. *The Jewish Quarter of Philadelphia, 1881–1930: A History and Guide*. Philadelphia: Jewish Walking Tours of Philadelphia, 1990.

First Independent Church of Christ Archives, 1810–1890. Historical Society of Pennsylvania. Church's name changed in 1842 to First Universalist Church.

First Independent Church of Christ/Universalist Church Minute Books, 1810–1890. Historical Society of Pennsylvania.

"Preservation Plan for Kesher Israel Synagogue." Report by Martin Jay Rosenblum, RA & Associates, Philadelphia, 1990. Photocopy on file at The Athenæum of Philadelphia, 1990.

Tatman and Moss, 773–76.

Thomas, Abel C. *A Century of Universalism in Philadelphia and New York, with Sketches of Its History in Reading, Hightstown, Brooklyn, and Elsewhere*. Philadelphia: Collins, 1872.

MOTHER BETHEL AFRICAN METHODIST EPISCOPAL CHURCH

Allen, Richard. *The Life Experience and Gospel Labors of the Rt. Rev. Richard Allen*. New York: Abingdon Press, 1960.

Kinghorn, Kenneth Cain. *The Heritage of American Methodism*. Nashville, Tenn.: Abingdon Press, 1999.

Payne, Daniel A. *History of the African Methodist Episcopal Church*. Nashville, Tenn., 1891. Reprint New York: Arno Press, 1969.

Tatman and Moss, 350–56, 397–98.

THE NOTMAN CHURCHES

Aspinwall, Marguerite. *A Hundred Years in His House: The Story of the Church of the Holy Trinity on Rittenhouse Square, Philadelphia, 1857–1957*. Philadelphia: Church of the Holy Trinity, 1957.

Fairbanks, Jonathan. "John Notman, Church Architect." M.A. thesis, University of Delaware, 1961.

Greiff, Constance M. *John Notman, Architect, 1810–1865*. Philadelphia: The Athenæum of Philadelphia, 1979.

Hitchcock, Henry Russell. *Early Victorian Architecture in Britain*. 1954. Reprint New York: Da Capo Press, 1972.

Lilly, May. *The Story of St. Clement's Church, Philadelphia: Written in Commemoration of the 100th Anniversary of the Consecration, April 12, 1864–April 12, 1964*. Philadelphia, 1964.

Memorial on the Moving of St. Clement's Church Philadelphia. Philadelphia: Saint Clement's Church, c. 1930.

Mortimer, Alfred. *S. Mark's Church, Philadelphia, and Its Lady Chapel, with an Account of Its History and Treasures*. New York: DeVinne Press, 1909.

Ninde, Edward S. *The Story of the American Hymn*. New York: Abingdon Press, 1921.

Notman, John. Archives. The Athenæum of Philadelphia. Includes original drawings for Holy Trinity, Saint Clement's, and Saint Mark's.

Stanton, Phoebe B. *The Gothic Revival and American Church Architecture*. Baltimore: Johns Hopkins University Press, 1968.

OLD FIRST REFORMED CHURCH

Fogleman, Aaron S. *Hopeful Journeys: German Immigration, Settlement, and Political Culture in Colonial America*. Philadelphia: University of Pennsylvania Press, 1996.

Klein, H. M. J. *The History of the Eastern Synod of the Reformed Church in the United States*. Lancaster, Pa.: Eastern Synod, 1943.

Lucas Paint Company. *Diamond Anniversary, 1849–1924*. Philadelphia, 1924. Copy at The Athenæum of Philadelphia. Contains interior and exterior photographs of Old First Reformed Church building during its use as a warehouse.

Peterson, Charles E., Constance M. Greiff, and Maria M. Thompson. *Robert Smith: Architect, Builder, Patriot, 1722–1777*. Philadelphia: The Athenæum of Philadelphia, 2000.

OLD PINE STREET PRESBYTERIAN CHURCH

Allen, Richard Howe. *Leaves from a Century Plant: Report on the Centennial Celebration of Old Pine Street Church, (Third Presbyterian), Philadelphia, Pa. May 29, 1868*. Philadelphia: H.B. Ashmead, 1870.

Gibbons, Hughes O. *A History of Old Pine Street, Being the Record of an Hundred and Forty Years in the Life of a Colonial Church*. Philadelphia: J. C. Winston, 1905.

Mackie, Alexander. "The Presbyterian Churches of Old Philadelphia." In *Historic Philadelphia, from the Founding Until the Early Nineteenth Century: Papers Dealing with Its People and Buildings*. Transactions of the American Philosophical Society 43, Part I. Philadelphia: American Philosophical Society, 1953. 226–29.

Nevin, Alfred. *History of the Presbytery of Philadelphia, and of the Philadelphia Central*. Philadelphia: W.S. Fortescue, 1888.

Peterson, Charles E., Constance M. Greiff, and Maria M. Thompson. *Robert Smith: Architect, Builder, Patriot, 1722–1777*. Philadelphia: The Athenæum of Philadelphia, 2000.

Scott, John Welwood. *An Historical Sketch of the Pine Street, or Third Presbyterian Church*. Philadelphia: n.p, 1837.

OLD SAINT GEORGE'S CHURCH

Andrews, Dee E. *The Methodists and Revolutionary America, 1760–1800*. Princeton, N.J.: Princeton University Press, 2000.

Corson, Fred P. "St. George's Church: The Cradle of American Methodism." In *Historic Philadelphia, from the Founding Until the Early Nineteenth Century: Papers Dealing with Its People and Buildings*. Transactions of the American Philosophical Society 43, Part I. Philadelphia: American Philosophical Society, 1953. 230–36.

Glatfelter, Charles H. *Pastors and People: German Lutheran and Reformed Churches in the Pennsylvania Field, 1717–1793*. 2 vols. Breinigsville, Pa.: Pennsylvania German Society, 1980.

Kinghorn, Kenneth Cain. *The Heritage of American Methodism*. Nashville, Tenn.: Abingdon Press, 1999.

Peterson, Charles E., Constance M. Greiff, and Maria M. Thompson. *Robert Smith: Architect, Builder, Patriot, 1722–1777*. Philadelphia: The Athenæum of Philadelphia, 2000.

OLD SAINT JOSEPH'S CHURCH

Burke, Bobbye. *A Brief Archival Report, 2001–2002*. Philadelphia, 2002.

Kurjack, Dennis C. "St. Joseph's and St. Mary's Churches." In *Historic Philadelphia, from the Founding Until the Early Nineteenth Century: Papers Dealing with Its People and Buildings*. Transactions of the American Philosophical Society 43, Part I. Philadelphia: American Philosophical Society, 1953. 199–203.

Minutes of the Provincial Council of Pennsylvania, from the Organization to the Termination of the Proprietary Government. Philadelphia: J. Severns, 1852. 3: 546–47, 563–64.

Walton, M. Maury. *Old Saint Joseph's Philadelphia, 1733–1933*. Philadelphia, 1933.

Wolanin, Barbara A. *Constantino Brumidi:*

Artist of the Capitol. Washington, D.C.: U.S. Government Printing Office, 1998.

OLD SAINT MARY'S CHURCH

Eckert, John C. "The History of Old St. Mary's." Student paper, 1970. Copy on file at The Athenæum of Philadelphia and the Catholic Archives.

Kurjack, Dennis C. "St. Joseph's and St. Mary's Churches." In *Historic Philadelphia, from the Founding Until the Early Nineteenth Century: Papers Dealing with Its People and Buildings*. Transactions of the American Philosophical Society 43, Part I. Philadelphia: American Philosophical Society, 1953. 199–203.

Moreau de St. Méry, M. L. E. *American Journey*. Ed. and trans. Kenneth Roberts and Anna M. Roberts. Garden City, N.Y.: Doubleday, 1947.

"St. Mary's Graveyard." *Records of the American Catholic Historical Society of Philadelphia* 3 (1888–91): 253–61.

Tourscher, Francis E. *The Hogan Schism and Trustee Troubles in St. Mary's Church Philadelphia, 1820–1829*. Philadelphia: Peter Reilly, 1930.

Zuccarini, Sister William Catharine. "History of St. Mary's Church, Philadelphia." Student paper, 1969. Copy on file at The Athenæum of Philadelphia and the Catholic Archives.

PHILADELPHIA CATHEDRAL

Burns, Charles M. *North American*, July 25, 1922.

Farnsworth, Jean M. *The Census of Stained Glass Windows in America: A Surveyor's Guide*. Philadelphia: Philadelphia Historic Preservation Corporation. Copy on file at The Athenæum of Philadelphia.

Giles, Richard S. *Re-Pitching the Tent: Reordering the Church Building for Worship and Mission*. Collegeville, Minn.: Liturgical Press, 1999.

Gregory, John. "About the Cathedral Church of the Saviour." Philadelphia, c. 1995.

"Our Cathedral: Its Form." Philadelphia, Cathedral Church of the Saviour, 2002. Flyer describing renovations.

Parish Messenger of the Church of the Saviour. Philadelphia, 1902–1925.

Pennell, Joseph. *Charles M. Burns, Artist and Teacher*. Philadelphia: Privately published, 1922.

Tatman and Moss, 119–21.

RODEPH SHALOM SYNAGOGUE

Congregation Rodeph Shalom. *200 Years of Living Young*. Philadelphia: Jewish Exponent, 1994.

D'Ascenzo, Nicola. Studio Archives. The Athenæum of Philadelphia.

Friedman, Murray, ed. *Jewish Life in Philadel-*

phia, 1830–1940. Philadelphia: Institute for the Study of Human Issues, 1983.

Hochman, Anndee. *Rodeph Shalom: Two Centuries of Seeking Peace*. Philadelphia, 1995.

Kleeblatt, Norman L. *The Leon J. and Julia S. Obermayer Collection*. Philadelphia: Congregation Rodeph Shalom, 1988.

Tatman and Moss, 721–24.

Thomas, George E., Michael J. Lewis, and Jeffrey A. Cohen. *Frank Furness: The Complete Works*. New York: Princeton Architectural Press, 1991.

Wischnitzer, Rachel. *Synagogue Architecture in the United States*. Philadelphia: Jewish Publication Society, 1955.

Wolf, Edwin, II and Maxwell Whiteman. *The History of the Jews of Philadelphia from Colonial Times to the Age of Jackson*. Philadelphia: Jewish Publication Society, 1957.

SAINT AUGUSTINE'S CHURCH

Ennis, Arthur J. *No Easy Road: The Early Years of the Augustinians in the United States, 1796–1874*. New York: Peter Lang, 1993.

Ennis, Arthur J. *Old St. Augustine's Catholic Church in Philadelphia*. Philadelphia, 1965.

McGowan, Francis X. *Historical Sketch of St. Augustine's Church*. Philadelphia, 1896.

Tourscher, Francis E. *Old Saint Augustine's in Philadelphia*. Philadelphia: Peter Reilly, 1937.

Warner, Sam Bass, Jr. *The Private City: Philadelphia in Three Periods of Its Growth*. Second edition. Philadelphia: University of Pennsylvania Press, 1987.

SAINT FRANCIS DE SALES CHURCH

Currant, Frances F., ed. *The First Hundred Years*. Philadelphia: St. Francis de Sales Parish, 1989.

Dagit, Henry D. Archives, The Athenæum of Philadelphia. Contains original drawings for design and construction of Saint Francis de Sales Church.

Guastavino Company Archives. Catalan Archive of Art and Architecture, Columbia University. Contains extensive documentation on the Saint Francis de Sales Church project.

"Historical and Architectural Analysis of St. Francis de Sales Roman Catholic Church." Report by John Milner Associates, July 1988. Copy on file at The Athenæum of Philadelphia

Jaeger, A. Robert. "Exploring the Layers of Old Worship Places." *Inspired* (January–February 1989).

Official Jubilee Volume. Philadelphia: St. Francis de Sales Parish, 1940.

"Saint Francis de Sales Church," *Liturgical Arts* 38 (August 1970): 125–26.

"Saint Francis de Sales Church." Structural survey. Report by Keast and Hood, June 30, 1987. Copy on file at The Athenæum of Philadelphia.

SAINT FRANCIS XAVIER CHURCH

Historical Sketch of Saint Francis Xavier's Parish. Philadelphia: Saint Francis Xavier Parish, 1939. Photocopy at The Athenæum of Philadelphia.

Lewis, Michael J. "Edwin Forrest Durang and Catholic Church Architecture." *Inspired* 6, 4; 7, 1.

Saint Francis Xavier, 1839–1989. Philadelphia: St. Francis Xavier Parish, 1989. Photocopy at The Athenæum of Philadelphia.

Tatman and Moss, 229–34.

"Technical Report to St. Francis Xavier Roman Catholic Church." Report by Kieran, Timberlake, and Harris, 1988. Photocopy at The Athenæum of Philadelphia.

SAINT JOHN THE EVANGELIST CHURCH

A Century and a Quarter, 1830–1955. Philadelphia, 1955.

Huckel, William Samuel, Jr. Obituary. *Philadelphia Evening Ledger*, April 18, 1917.

Mahony, Daniel H. *Historical Sketches of the Catholic Churches and Institutions of Philadelphia: A Parish Register and Book of Reference.* Philadelphia: Daniel H. Mahony, 1895. 52–55.

"Re-Opening Brochure." Saint John the Evangelist Church, 1900. Copy on file at the Archdiocesan Research Center, Philadelphia.

"Sprucing Up a Landmark Church." *Philadelphia Inquirer*, August 3, 1990.

Watson, Frank Rushmore. Obituary. *Philadelphia Inquirer*, October 31, 1940.

SAINT LUKE'S EPISCOPAL CHURCH

Crook, J. Mordaunt. *William Burges and the High Victorian Dream.* Chicago: University of Chicago Press, 1981.

Hotchkin, Samuel Fitch. *Ancient and Modern Germantown, Mount Airy, and Chestnut Hill.* Philadelphia: P.W. Zeigler, 1892.

Landau, Sarah B. "Henry M. Congdon." In Adolf K. Placzek, ed., *Macmillan Encyclopedia of Architects.* New York: Free Press, 1982. 1: 446.

Poindexter, Charles L. L. *The History of St. Luke's Church, Germantown, Pennsylvania 1968 to the Present.* Philadelphia, 1991.

Yerkes, Royden K. *The History of Saint Luke's Church.* Philadelphia, 1912.

SAINT NICHOLAS CHURCH

Album of St. Nicholas' Russian Orthodox Ind. Church. Philadelphia, October 28, 1945.

St. Nicholas Eastern Orthodox Church: 60th Anniversary, 1917–1977. Philadelphia, 1977. Includes a brief history of the church by Michael Peleszak.

"St. Nicholas Orthodox Church: Structural Assessment of Choir Loft and Sanctuary Floor." Report by Keast and Hood Co., March 12, 1999.

Tatman and Moss, 122–25.

Tenth Anniversary of the Sunday Schools Attached to the Second Reformed Dutch Church. Philadelphia, April 13, 1862.

SAINT PETER'S CHURCH

Bantel, Linda et al. *William Rush: American Sculptor.* Philadelphia: Pennsylvania Academy of the Fine Arts, 1982.

Gilchrist, Agnes A. *William Strickland: Architect and Engineer.* Philadelphia: University of Pennsylvania Press, 1950.

Peterson, Charles E., Constance M. Greiff, and Maria M. Thompson. *Robert Smith: Architect, Builder, Patriot, 1722–1777.* Philadelphia: The Athenæum of Philadelphia, 2000.

Richards, Frederick L., Jr. National Historic Landmark Nomination, Saint Peter's Church, Philadelphia, 1994. Saint Peter's entered as an NHL, 1996.

Shoemaker, Robert W. "Christ Church, St. Peter's and St. Paul's." In *Historic Philadelphia, from the Founding Until the Early Nineteenth Century: Papers Dealing with Its People and Buildings.* Transactions of the American Philosophical Society 43, Part 1. Philadelphia: American Philosophical Society, 1953.

SAINT PHILIP NERI ROMAN CATHOLIC CHURCH

Diamond Jubilee: St. Philip Neri's Church. Philadelphia, 1916. Copy on file at The Athenæum of Philadelphia.

Historical Sketch of St. Philip Neri's Parish. Philadelphia, 1940. Copy on file at The Athenæum of Philadelphia.

Klingensmith, Samuel. "The Architecture of Napoleon LeBrun: The Philadelphia Churches, 1840–1865." M.A. thesis, University of Virginia, 1975. Copy on file at The Athenæum of Philadelphia.

Tatman and Moss, 469–71, 832–39.

SAINT STEPHEN'S CHURCH

Burd Family Papers, 1703–1937. Special Collections Department, University of Delaware Library, Newark. Contains an extensive correspondence with Steinhäuser concerning the Burd memorials.

Dryfhout, John H. *The Work of Augustus Saint-Gaudens.* Hanover, N.H.: University Press of New England, 1982.

Duffy, Henry J. and John H. Dryfhout. *Augustus Saint-Gaudens: American Sculptor of the Gilded Age.* Washington, D.C.: Trust for Museum Exhibitions, 2003.

Gilchrist, Agnes A. *William Strickland: Architect and Engineer, 1788–1854.* Philadelphia: University of Pennsylvania Press, 1950.

Kaiser-Strohmann, Dagmar. *Theodor Wilhelm Achtermann (1799–1884) und Carl Johann Steinhäuser (1813–1879): Ein Beitrag zu Problemen des Nazarenischen in der deutschen Skulptur des 19 Jahrhunderts.* Frankfurt am Main: Peter Lang, 1985.

Price, Alfred W. *The Rich Heritage of 125 Years of Christian Service: St. Stephen's Church in the City of Philadelphia.* Philadelphia, 1948.

Saint-Gaudens, Augustus. *The Reminiscences of Augustus Saint-Gaudens.* Ed. Homer Saint-Gaudens. New York: Century, 1913.

Stanton, Phoebe B. *The Gothic Revival and American Church Architecture: An Episode in Taste, 1840–1856.* Baltimore: Johns Hopkins University Press, 1968.

Tharp, Louis Hall. *Saint-Gaudens and the Gilded Era.* Boston: Little, Brown, 1969.

SAINT TIMOTHY'S CHURCH, ROXBOROUGH

Barrett, J. Elwood. *Ninety Years of Work and Worship, 1859–1949: The History of Saint Timothy's Church, Roxborough.* Philadelphia, 1949.

Manton, John Charles. *A Splendid Legacy: Saint Timothy's Roxborough, 1859–1984.* Philadelphia: Saint Timothy's, 1984.

Miles, Joseph Starn and William H. Cooper. *An Historical Sketch of Roxborough, Manayunk, Wissahickon.* Philadelphia: G. Fein, 1940.

Tatman and Moss, 119–21.

Vestry Minutes, St. Timothy's Church, 1861–present. The church archives also contain original architectural drawings and correspondence relating to the construction and decoration of the church.

Withey, Henry F. and Elsie Rathburn Withey. *Biographical Dictionary of American Architects.* New York: New Age, 1956.

SAINT VINCENT DE PAUL CHURCH

Golden Jubilee, 1851–1901. Philadelphia: St. Vincent De Paul, 1901.

Hotchkin, Samuel Fitch. *Ancient and Modern Germantown, Mount Airy, and Chestnut Hill.* Philadelphia: P.W. Zeigler, 1892.

Mahoney, Daniel A. *Historical Sketches of the Catholic Churches and Institutions of Philadelphia: A Parish Register and Book of Reference.* Philadelphia: Daniel H. Mahony, 1895.

Tatman and Moss, 458–59.

Taylor, Richard K. *God's Love Is Fire: A Parish*

Becomes a People. Philadelphia: Saint Vincent De Paul Church, 2001.

SAMUEL S. FLEISHER
ART MEMORIAL

Ricci, Patricia L. "Violet Oakley: American Renaissance Woman." *Pennsylvania Magazine of History and Biography* 127 (April 2002): 217–48.

Thomas, George E., Michael J. Lewis, and Jeffrey A. Cohen. *Frank Furness: The Complete Works*. New York: Princeton Architectural Press, 1991. Revised 1996. In the revised edition (344), the authors cite the obituary of Charles M. Burns, Jr. *Philadelphia Public Ledger* (July 25, 1922), wherein appears a list of his projects, including "the quaint edifice on Catharine street now used by the Graphic Sketch Club."

"Violet Oakley." *Philadelphia Museum of Art Bulletin* (June 1979).

Zieget, Irene N. *History of the Samuel S. Fleisher Art Memorial*. Philadelphia, 1963.

SHRINE OF SAINT RITA OF CASCIA

Saint Rita of Cascia Roman Catholic Church, Drawings and Photographs in the Ballinger Collection. The Athenæum of Philadelphia.

Tatman and Moss, 30–43, 489–92, 602–4.

SOCIETY HILL SYNAGOGUE

Boonin, Harry D. *The Jewish Quarter of Philadelphia, 1881–1930: A History and Guide*. Philadelphia: Jewish Walking Tours of Philadelphia, 1999.

Klein, Esther H. *A Guidebook to Jewish Philadelphia*. Philadelphia: Jewish Times Institute, 1965.

Walter, Thomas U. Papers. The Athenæum of Philadelphia.

Wolf, Edwin, II and Maxwell Whiteman. *The History of the Jews of Philadelphia from Colonial Times to the Age of Jackson*. Philadelphia: Jewish Publication Society, 1957.

TABERNACLE UNITED CHURCH

Chandler, Theophilus P. Archives. The Athenæum of Philadelphia. Includes drawings, manuscripts, and professional library.

Edmands, John. "Some Facts Pertaining to the Tabernacle Presbyterian Church of Philadelphia." *Journal of the Presbyterian Historical Society* 8 (1915–1916): 287–88, 348–50.

Hammonds, Kenneth A. *Historical Directory of Presbyterian Churches and Presbyteries of Greater Philadelphia*. Philadelphia: Presbyterian Historical Society, 1993.

Nevin, Alfred. *History of the Presbytery of Philadelphia, and of the Philadelphia Central*. Philadelphia: W.S. Fortescue, 1888.

"The Reverend Henry Christopher McCook." *Journal of the Presbyterian Historical Society* 6 (December 1911): 97ff.

Tatman and Moss, 139–43.

White, William P. and William H. Scott. *The Presbyterian Church in Philadelphia: A Camera and Pen Sketch of Each Presbyterian Church and Institution in the City*. Philadelphia: Allen, Lane, and Scott, 1895.

TENTH PRESBYTERIAN CHURCH

Boice, James Montgomery. *Foundations of the Christian Faith: A Comprehensive and Readable Theology*. Downers Grove, Ill.: InterVarsity Press, 1986.

———, ed. *Making God's Word Plain: One Hundred and Fifty Years in the History of Tenth Presbyterian Church of Philadelphia*. Philadelphia: Tenth Presbyterian Church, 1979. Photocopy on file at The Athenæum of Philadelphia.

Hammonds, Kenneth A. *Historical Directory of Presbyterian Churches and Presbyteries of Greater Philadelphia*. Philadelphia: Presbyterian Historical Society, 1993.

Tatman and Moss, 192–97, 510–12.

Tenth Presbyterian Church in Philadelphia, 1829–1929. Philadelphia: Tenth Presbyterian Church, 1929. Includes a transcription of a document placed in the cornerstone of the original 1828–1829 church, attributing the design to William Strickland.

White, William P. and William H. Scott. *The Presbyterian Church in Philadelphia: A Camera and Pen Sketch of Each Presbyterian Church and Institution in the City*. Philadelphia: Allen, Lane, and Scott, 1895.

TRINITY LUTHERAN CHURCH

Congregational Minutes and Treasurer's Records. At Lutheran Theological Seminary, Philadelphia.

D'Ascenzo: The Art of Stained Glass from the Collection of Stanley Switlik. Trenton, N.J.: Rider College, 1973. The D'Ascenzo Studio Archives are in the collections of The Athenæum of Philadelphia.

Hocker, Edward W. *History of Trinity Lutheran Church, Germantown, Philadelphia, 1836–1936*. Philadelphia: Trinity Lutheran Church, 1936.

Malone, Dumas, ed. *Dictionary of American Biography*. New York: Scribner's, 1935. 17: 4166–4417.

Silvernail, Jeff. *Portrait of a Breakup: The Events Leading Up to the Founding of Trinity Lutheran Church*. Philadelphia: Trinity Lutheran Church, 1996.

Tinkcom, Harry M., Margaret B. Tinkcom, and Grant Miles Simon. *Historic Germantown Germantown, from the Founding to the Early Part of the Nineteenth Century*. Philadelphia: American Philosophical Society, 1955. 62–63.

Page references in *italics* refer to photographs and the information in photograph captions.

⇌ *Church of Saint James the Less. See pages 248–253.*